Joe
&
Marilyn
★

SOME BOOKS BY ROGER KAHN

Good Enough to Dream, 1985
The Seventh Game, 1982
But Not to Keep, 1978
A Season in the Sun, 1977
How the Weather Was, 1973
The Boys of Summer, 1972
The Battle for Morningside Heights, 1970
The Passionate People, 1968

Joe and Marilyn on their wedding day

Joe & Marilyn

A Memory of Love

Roger Kahn

WILLIAM MORROW AND COMPANY, INC.
NEW YORK

Library of Congress Cataloging-in-Publication Data

Kahn, Roger.
  Joe & Marilyn.

  1. DiMaggio, Joe, 1914– . 2. Baseball
players—United States—Biography.   3. Monroe,
Marilyn, 1926–1962.   I. Title.   II. Title: Joe and
Marilyn.
GV865.D5K34   1986   796.357′092′4 [B]   86-17990
ISBN 0-688-02517-X

Printed in the United States of America

First Edition

1 2 3 4 5 6 7 8 9 10

BOOK DESIGN BY PATRICE FODERO

This book is dedicated to my son,
Roger Laurence Kahn, who has learned
through courage and with pain,
what a tough love story life is—

Contents

Chapter ★ 1

The Almost-Perfect Knight

Still formidable in his eighth decade, he is patient with a public that does not want him to grow old. His manner is practiced, courteous, even smooth. Certainly he will sign an autograph. He is flattered that you asked. Yes, the pennant race this season looks exciting and no, he certainly wouldn't count out the New York Yankees. How is his golf? Well, it's not as good as he'd like it to be, but he has some fun.

The geniality—it is the solemn geniality of a solemn figure—appears innate, but it is something Joe DiMaggio has cultivated, nurtured, worked for half a century. It surrounds him, pleasing his idolators and concealing by its large expanse the complex, sometimes brooding man within. DiMaggio is comfortable with these circumstances. He wants his admiring public. He *enjoys* being fussed over, and who can blame him for that? But he wants a distance from the public, a deep greenbelt of privacy, and who can blame him for that either? His has been a thrilling life, but it also has been lonely and jolted by tragedy.

When someone approaches to ask about Marilyn Monroe, the geniality dissolves. He rises and says in measured, icy tones, "Stop right there." The words fall like a black curtain in front of him.

They were exquisite lovers, wonderful friends, but perfectly wretched as husband and wife. And, of course, their love, affection, play, their shouted bickerings and private lusts were foreclosed beyond redemption when she took her life one August night in 1962.

After that he wept and said, "I love you," and kissed her corpse as it lay in an open coffin.

What really can he, can anyone, say about *that*? He had tried to love her well.

Somehow he failed.

He has been a public figure for fifty years, seizing the American consciousness first as a young ballplayer of glorious gifts and grace. He could run and he could throw and he could hit and his special quality was the apparent ease with which he played the game. "Ease, my foot," he says today. "I had to work like hell." But through a kind of sporting alchemy the hard work fused with grace and became his art.

Fans, who like Joe himself are getting on in years, remember stylish plays from long ago. A catch among the monuments in the deepest reach of Yankee Stadium, flagging one of Hank Greenberg's mighty drives. A critical series in Boston where he outslugged the great Ted Williams. Another catch in a World Series game at the Polo Grounds that won the approbation of Franklin Roosevelt. (It was, to be sure, an election year.) Without much effort, you can make a very long list.

But it is not simply that so many summer memories of DiMaggio endure. It is the quality of the memories themselves. The old fans speak of him with reverence. They exult in sunlit afternoons when they beheld a hero. Their fervor still glistens as they describe a game, now medieval history in baseball terms. Then they say, in one way or another, "There'll never be another one like Joe."

There was a song for him in his glory days, a bit of doggerel fluff that blared out of a million table radios:

He'll live in baseball's Hall of Fame,
He's got there blow-by-blow.
Our kids will tell their kids his name,
Joltin' Joe DiMaggio.
Joe . . . Joe . . . DiMaggio . . . We want you on our
  side.

When he retired from the Yankees in 1951, he did not lose his hold on the public, nor did he even vanish from song. Long after he receded from the ball fields (but a bit too soon for our kids to be telling *their* kids his name), he reappeared in Paul Simon's forlorn, déjà vu lyric from a stylish, 1968 movie called *The Graduate*. Bemoaning the passage of time, in the accepted manner of bittersweet balladists, Simon wrote:

Where have you gone, Joe DiMaggio?
A nation turns its lonely eyes to you
(Ooo ooo ooo).
What's that you say, Mrs. Robinson?
"Joltin' Joe" has left and gone away
(Hey hey hey, hey hey hey).

These lines touched throngs who had never seen him play. DiMaggio himself, who is made uncomfortable by certain public displays of sentiment, insists, "I've never been able to figure out what that song means."

In truth, long after baseball, Joe DiMaggio goes anywhere he wants.

*   *   *

Old ballplayers often become citizens of a twilight land, with their high deeds, their youthful sunbursts left far behind in other eras on baseball diamonds that no longer exist. To the young, they become curios, relics. Who remembers the summer of '37 in Sportsman's Park, St. Louis? Who really cares? To the intolerant, they become merely tiresome, their stories ever more vague, ever more threadbare, ever more diffused in inconsequential details. The old ballplayers sense this. Their approach becomes tentative and apologetic. You greet them a bit too enthusiastically, offer a drink and a smile, and move on feeling faintly saddened.

But DiMaggio is not simply an old baseball player. He is captain of that particular team, the man the other old ball-players call "The Big Guy." He times his public appearances skillfully so that he never quite recedes nor is he ever overexposed. He grants interviews infrequently, but when he does he tells a story or two vividly, playing down his great skills with careful modesty. The skills, he understands, speak for themselves.

When they began to fade, he stepped out of baseball. No one had to shove him off the stage. He weighed an offer of $100,000 to play for the Yankees in 1952 against his profound professional pride. He was time-weary and suffering from arthritis. He reduced this to a simple issue: Money vs. Dignity. Ever the prideful man, he walked away from the Yankee contract and the fields of praise where he had played major league baseball for thirteen years. Sportswriters composed columns that read like hymns. They praised his talent, his manner, his long-boned grace, and his sure sense of who he was.

Three years later, in 1954, he married Marilyn Monroe, that phenomenon of innocence and lust, blond hair and parted lips, the squirming nude on the calendar who aspired to play a Dostoevsky heroine. He had always liked show girls—his first wife was a minor starlet—but now he was moving out of the clubby sporting scene into the harsher, driving world of Hollywood. He doesn't like Hollywood. It is too public, too shrill, too naked for him. But he had chosen a Hollywood star who was newly famous, seductive, witty, exhibitionistic, and coy, and who wanted, or believed she wanted, a merry family, a golden career, culture and motherhood all at once. He wanted, as far as anyone knows, the most beautiful housewife in the world. They split within nine months, with gossip columnists swarming over their lawn on a day of locusts.

The press, which traffics in triumphs and misery, snickered in its headlines: JOE DIMAGGIO STRIKES OUT. The publicity confused and wounded him. He said he didn't invade anyone else's privacy and he didn't like people invading his. He did not understand, or at least would not accept, the reality that he had ventured beyond the protective nets New York sportswriters had rigged for him when he married a reigning, willful, impulsive Hollywood princess. She added to his legend, as in a lesser way he added to hers, but not in ways he cared for. He enjoyed fame but despised notoriety. Now he was a notorious failed lover.

When he married her, he was able to make a small joke involving a Yankee pitcher who had been his buddy. "It's got to be better," he said, "than rooming with Joe Page." But once they parted, he fought to protect his dignity with the only weapon he had—silence. The silence has lasted as long as his grief.

What, then, gives DiMaggio his enduring and solitary place among old athletes? Surely it is the memories created by his talent. The Yankee teams he led won the pennant in ten of thirteen seasons at the Stadium. Just as surely it is his own developed sense of public relations. Although he was a reticent and almost backward adolescent, he grew to manage his own image with a high degree of skill.

But beyond that there is the woman. After the last line drive, after the last long-legged running catch, he bedded and married and in the end had to entomb a most fantastic blonde.

*   *   *

Although it is arguable, I think that only two other men in
DiMaggio's time captured the American consciousness with
comparable enduring virile symbolism. One would be Frank
Sinatra, the other John F. Kennedy. Curiously, both men's
lives interweave with Joe DiMaggio's, and not in entirely
pleasant ways.

Sinatra crooned his sad-voiced songs to a generation of
aroused young women, moved on to Hollywood, burned
brightly, briefly, then declined. For all his macho manner, he
also found a hopeless love, the stately, dark-haired beauty
Ava Gardner. He married Gardner, who had been mistress to
a Spanish bullfighter and a beauteous pet to an aging Ernest
Hemingway. Sinatra lost her (as DiMaggio lost Marilyn) just
when he seemed to be losing his career. But Sinatra has a
core as hard as marble. He rallied and began again. He is still
a working entertainer, still projecting sex and pop-music
credos on many millions of phonograph records. He has kept
his voice, although it has grown a bit more hoarse since the
days of the big bands. Properly respectful of time's kindness,
he sometimes speaks a favorite toast. "May you live to be one
hundred," Sinatra says across a glass of Jack Daniel's, "and
may the last voice you hear be mine."

For a period in the 1950s, Sinatra and DiMaggio were
close friends. No longer. Convinced that Sinatra had care-
lessly helped Marilyn along the way to destruction, DiMaggio
barred him from her funeral. He also barred almost everyone
else in Hollywood, including Sinatra's cronies, Dean Martin
and the late Peter Lawford.

Lawford led Marilyn into the Kennedy circle where, Di-
Maggio believes, she had a short affair with the president and
a longer, rougher episode with Robert F. Kennedy, the attorney general. The Kennedy brothers are said to have used
Marilyn badly in her last days, when Joe was doing all he
could to keep her sober and sane, and even to refire their
romance. People in DiMaggio's close circle say that when
Marilyn died she had recently learned that she was pregnant

with Bobby Kennedy's child. There is a persistent report that the last telephone call she lived to make was to Bobby. She was, of course, distraught and desperate. She couldn't go on, she said, without his help.

Tough-eyed Bobby Kennedy listened impatiently. "I can't help you," he said. "I'm a married man."

According to one attractive, dark-haired New York lady who had dated Joe, "Before we went out, mutual friends gave me a little list of things I was never to bring up. Marilyn, of course. Sinatra. The Kennedys. Johnny Carson."

Carson? Why Johnny Carson?

"Because Joe believed that Marilyn's heavy drinking really began when she had to do some talk shows. She'd be nervous and she'd drink for a release. Joe didn't see her drinking coming out of her childhood or anything else. Just the talk shows. And when Joe is convinced of something, you learn pretty quickly not to argue. He has a temper."

(Actually, I can find no record that Marilyn ever appeared with Carson. She was interviewed by Edward R. Murrow for his fluffy celebrity series called *Person to Person*. It was on *that* show that she appeared nervous, overwhelmed and a bit tipsy.)

DiMaggio the ballplayer—"Joe the Slugger," Marilyn called him, with affection and perhaps as a bit of a put-down—was so tightly controlled that only three incidents of visible emotion emerge from his years on major league ball fields.

On August 2, 1939, in the ninth inning of a game against Detroit, DiMaggio raced to the deepest point in Yankee Stadium and caught a fly between the monuments and the dark bleacher wall, 461 feet distant from home plate. It was such an astonishing play that some newspapermen wrote more about the catch than about the game (which the Yankees lost). "I remember it clearly," Hank Greenberg says. "I hit the ball. An amazing catch, but don't let them tell you that DiMaggio never showed his feelings. He got so excited when he caught my drive that he started running toward the infield holding up his glove, and he forgot to double the runner [Pinkie Higgins] off first base.''

After a Brooklyn pitcher named Whitlow Wyatt threw several fastballs near his head during the 1941 World Series, DiMaggio stopped the game to curse out Wyatt. He did not, like some modern ballplayers, actually pummel the pitcher. He merely cursed and threatened and then the game resumed.

On another World Series occasion in 1947, a Brooklyn outfielder named Al Gionfriddo made a remarkable catch of a high drive DiMaggio had poled more than 400 feet into left field. DiMaggio was close to second base by the time the ball was caught, and he kicked dirt. His old teammates and opponents recall these incidents vividly. With more demonstrative baseball players, a Ted Williams, a Reggie Jackson, such reactions would not stand out nearly as sharply.

Major league baseball is a highly emotional game. You have a band of strong young men, with powerful egos, who play together, eat together, live together on the road with the common purpose of winning games. Their livelihood and the nature of their lives depend on their performance, which is observed by thousands of fans and studied in the media by millions more. A bad week, four or five lost games, agitates everybody. What's going wrong? Why can't we win? Why is the press ripping us? What the hell? Conversely, a good week, a winning streak, abruptly elevates the mood. It is a roller-coaster life that rubs the nerve ends raw.

"I didn't let myself get excited playing baseball," DiMaggio insists, and he never leaped in exultation when he hit a home run or raged at an umpire when he was called out on strikes. No umpire ever had to eject him from a game. But Joe is remembered as a heavy smoker and a drinker of great quantities of coffee. Before his baseball career was very old, he had ulcers.

To conduct yourself with such outward calm is a considerable accomplishment. The fire—and no one ever played the game as well as DiMaggio without competitive fire raging in his gut—burned in his bat. He did not, as he says, "mouth off." But hard as that was, the evidence argues that it was even more difficult to exercise self-control when married to so vexing, appealing, and conflicted a woman as Marilyn Monroe.

Joe and Marilyn were man and wife when she flew to New York City for location shooting on George Axelrod's teasing comedy *The Seven Year Itch.* Marilyn plays the upstairs neighbor, all sex and ingenuousness, to a bumbling summer bachelor (Tom Ewell). She tempts him in a maddening variety of ways but seems to be unaware that she is a temptress. Since this was filmed in the 1950s, when chastity ruled American movies with a cold hand, nothing happens beyond a little labored breathing. Watching, you ask yourself if Marilyn can really be that sexy and at the same time that naïve about her own sexiness? Of course not. In real life she came to understand the power that her dewy, wriggly beauty worked on men. But the conceit works well in George Axelrod's screenplay.

In the most famous scene, Marilyn, wearing white shoes and a billowing white skirt, stands over a subway grating. When a train passes, the updraft blows her skirt high, revealing fine legs and white underpants about a bottom that no less a connoisseur than Groucho Marx acclaimed as "the greatest ass in Hollywood."

The scene was shot over the grating at Lexington Avenue and Fifty-first Street, with a wind machine installed below. Although it was close to midnight, a few hundred New Yorkers stopped behind police barricades to see as much as they could see.

DiMaggio appeared with Walter Winchell, the Broadway columnist, and stood quietly to one side. "I remember it," says a photographer named Frank Morse, "because [Twentieth Century] Fox had hired me to take still shots for publicity and it was a damn good job. I figured I'd take the best angle I could find; we could always airbrush the stills later so that the newspapers could use them. I lay down on the side-walk in front of her."

While movie cameras were positioned at more discreet lo-cations, Morse settled onto the cement. A few onlookers fol-lowed suit. "Here comes the wind machine," Morse says, "up goes the skirt and damned if she isn't wearing something filmy. From back of me I hear a voice, pure New York, saying loud and clear, 'Chees, I thought she was a real blonde.'

"DiMaggio hears it too, and this is his *wife*. He walks on the set, sorer than hell, and Marilyn has to go into the trailer and change into some underpants you couldn't see through with a spotlight."

Later, still angry and upset, DiMaggio repaired to Toots Shor's restaurant, where Shor, a large, gruff, big-hearted character, tried to console him with drinks. Shor got nowhere. After a while, still trying to cheer his friend, Shor said, "Aw, Joe. What can you expect when you marry a whore?"

DiMaggio left the restaurant, for years his favorite hang-out in New York. He did not speak to Shor again for a long, long time.

Before Marilyn brightened and confused his life, DiMag-gio had amassed twenty years of experience as a public figure. He had learned the changing ways of the public and how to handle the demands of the baseball reporters and sports pho-tographers. But this incident—Mrs. Joe DiMaggio displaying her flesh and pubic hair to strangers—surpassed any experi-ence he had known. It would have tried a less possessive man.

DiMaggio's background was poor, Roman Catholic, puri-tan, and barely literate. His parents were Sicilian immigrants and there is some doubt that his father, Giuseppe, or his mother, Rosalie, ever learned to read English. He himself dropped out of high school early and joked to a friend, "I went to Galileo High for about one day."

Although fame arrived with a sudden tumultuous rush, he seems to have understood from the beginning that a profes-sional ballplayer is a public figure. When he was still a minor leaguer playing for the San Francisco Seals, he got himself out of windbreakers and imitated the more sophisticated dressing style of a veteran first baseman named Jack Fenton. Although this led him toward excessively loud sport jackets, he continued to work at his attire until he became, by baseball standards, a fashion plate.

His vocabulary was limited—his parents spoke Italian in the home—and here he turned to the Seals' trainer, a former lightweight boxer named Bobby Johnson, who seldom used a one-syllable word when he could find a four-syllable substitute.

"What have you been doing, Joe?" a San Francisco sportswriter asked one day in 1935.

"Oh," said Joe DiMaggio, high school dropout and public relations apprentice, "I've just been nonchalantly meandering down the pike." The words were Johnson's. The effort at goodwill toward the press derived from Fenton. The particularly incongruous manner was pure young DiMaggio, growing up.

The Yankee management of the 1930s had formed its own ideas on player deportment. The press was important in selling tickets; the Yankees, like the other two New York baseball teams, paid expenses for all the newspapermen who traveled with the club. "We were guests of the Yankees," an old newspaperman named Rud Rennie explained, "and one way or another, we weren't allowed to forget it." Writers were discouraged from digging into the conflicts that are part of every team. Their stories on personalities generally went no further than the puff that appeared on Wheaties boxes. All the players were nice, hardworking fellows who loved children, and some were even nicer than others. The term "investigative reporting" had not yet been invented.

Still, the Yankees insisted that their players be careful. They did not want another gargantuan character like Babe Ruth drinking and roistering through a baseball career. The model Yankee when DiMaggio broke in was their quiet and dignified first baseman, Lou Gehrig, who, according to one columnist, spent his spare time on trains reading Voltaire. Through a scout, Bill Essick, and two older players from the San Francisco area, Tony Lazzeri and Frank Crosetti, the Yankee management passed on rules of conduct for DiMaggio. Don't say too much. Don't go out of your way to be rude, but keep your distance from the press.

By the time he joined the Yankees in 1936, DiMaggio had taken the counsel to heart. A certain native friendliness was dampened by shyness. Trying to catch up on his life all at once, DiMaggio seemed aloof, which bothered some writers. Mostly, say his old friends, this was a symptom of uncertainty, not hostility. He had gone from an obscure adolescence to national fame within four years.

"Hey, Joe," one New York writer asked during DiMaggio's first major league spring training. "Can you get me a quote?"

"Sure," DiMaggio said. "Go over to that cooler there and help yourself." Learning on the job, he thought that a quote was a soft drink.

Early in his career, DiMaggio made a number of public relations mistakes centered around financial disputes with the Yankees. Although he would later say, "I thank the good Lord for making me a Yankee," he did not confuse his calling with a charity. He had been a poor boy. A trick knee reminded him of the transience of a baseball career. He thanked the Lord above but, meanwhile, on this earth he wanted to be paid every dollar that he, and several advisers, concluded he was worth.

This led to a series of disputes with the Yankees' tough management. The Depression still choked the land, and as these quarrels splashed across newspaper pages, not every fan, struggling for his hamburger and his rent, took DiMaggio's side. Joe heard hoots around the American League.

He even got himself accused of engaging a fight manager as his de facto business agent. The boxing man, an unctuous, rather sly sort named Joe Gould, affected a beret, chomped cigars, and managed a former heavyweight champion, Jimmy

Braddock. By 1940, DiMaggio's fifth season in New York, rumors of his connection to Gould reached such a crescendo that Kenesaw Mountain Landis, the first and most dominant commissioner of baseball, ordered an investigation. If the reports were true and DiMaggio actually was paying 12½ percent of his growing Yankee salary to Gould as a commission, the young star would find himself facing fines and a possible suspension. Ballplayers were not then permitted to employ agents or lawyers to refine their contract demands. No agent was allowed even to enter the room when an athlete sat down to talk contract with a general manager. Commissioner Landis leaked the news that he was alarmed and angered at DiMaggio's supposed challenge to one of organized baseball's accepted ways of doing business.

Landis ordered DiMaggio into his office and interrogated him at length. He then cleared DiMaggio of a high crime: paying for professional help before signing his Yankee contract. DiMaggio and Gould, Landis concluded, were acquaintances, but not business partners. Although the incident seems like arrant autocracy today, the press of the time depicted DiMaggio as something of a culprit, touched by hints of indiscretion and greed. Commissioner Landis emerged from the controversy as he always did: the white-maned, incorruptible Protector of The Game. Thanks to his efforts, baseball was safe from grasping agents and an invasion of body snatchers from the shadowy world of boxing. (For another three decades baseball was also safe from free enterprise.)

DiMaggio learned from these mistakes and grew more careful in his choice of confidants. He never lost his healthy passion for large salaries, but he kept his future negotiations private and stopped talking to the press about money, which anybody from a fight manager to a baseball commissioner will tell you is a good idea.

In 1941 DiMaggio carved a fresh, clean image. He hit safely in 56 consecutive games, an achievement widely regarded as the most remarkable of all baseball records and, as we shall see, a paradigm of talent, discipline, and concentration. Coincidentally, his timing was perfect. He had the fortune to flower in an increasingly barren world.

Generally, the summer of 1941 was an excruciating time. The year before Western Europe had fallen, with terrifying impotence, to Nazi armies. Denmark, Norway, the Netherlands, Belgium, France. Now looking east, Hitler turned on Russia, and German troops, cracking the Stalin Line, fanned out toward Kiev, Leningrad, and Moscow. Newspapers described "an unstoppable Nazi juggernaut." In Asia the Japanese militarists ominously collected their strength and Japanese soldiers trampled innocent peasants in China. A beast was abroad on earth. No one could cage it.

During such a summer, when reasonable people believed that civilization was doomed, you turned compulsively to the sports page for relief. And what did you read? DiMaggio gets *another* two hits. Forget Hitler, ultimately too horrible to contemplate within America's still tranquil shores. Hitler was more than three thousand miles away. The hell with the bloody Japanese. Up from depression. Root for the Yankees. *Attaway, Joe.*

DiMaggio moved through his batting streak with becoming modesty and dignity. He emerged in the nightmare summer of his streak not as a gifted though avaricious young ballplayer, but as an artist at the game of baseball. In the public eye, his record hitting lifted him beyond such mundane matters as money, contracts, agents. He became a young prince in the only world power still at peace.

You can look back on the summer of '41 in disparate ways. It was a period when mankind almost lost its future. It was a time when Joe DiMaggio hit safely every day.

DiMaggio has never been inclined toward introspection about social forces and balances. Abstractions seem to confuse him. He understands that he has a particular place in sporting legend and becomes angry when he is not treated as he feels he should be. But long ago he hardly saw himself as a sunlit hero in gathering darkness. He got his hits. The people cheered. He made his catches. The writers exulted. He was earning good money. It was a glorious life for a fisherman's kid from San Francisco. That was about the size of it. He didn't talk at length. His bat spoke volumes.

Without great effort, he befriended, or was befriended by, the most influential columnists of the time: Winchell, Jimmy Cannon, Grantland Rice, Bill Corum, Earl Wilson, and later, Red Smith. Acquiring a new sense of leadership, he also showed a decent respect for beat writers, less renowned journalists who wrote about the Yankees, and DiMaggio, each day.

Heywood Hale Broun, an observer with great wisdom and sensitivity, remembers being assigned to the Yankees by a struggling (and now late) newspaper called the *New York Star*. Broun was then a young reporter and in the context of sports, the *Star* was the least influential paper published in New York after *The Daily Worker*. But on the morning of Broun's first trip with the Yankees, DiMaggio invited him to breakfast and insisted on picking up both checks. It was Di-Maggio's way of saying welcome to the team.

To this day, it is a rare ballplayer who touches a tab in the presence of the press. The ballplayer is the talent, and talent doesn't tote a wallet. Woodie Broun observes, "The DiMaggio I knew didn't create an image. He was one." In the early 1980s, Broun threatened to leave a party when another guest remarked casually that he thought DiMaggio was an arrogant man.

Without cutting off his San Francisco roots, DiMaggio created a comfortable world for himself in Manhattan. He lived in hotels, except for the few years when his first marriage was going fairly well. His hangout, and his first wife, Dorothy Arnold, complained it was too often his hangout, was Toots Shor's, that cavernous, essentially masculine restaurant, where he liked to sit at Table One with the proprietor.

Entering the old Shor's in the West Fifties, you passed a

large, round bar, packed at appropriate hours by characters from sports, theater, advertising, and public relations, including those sportswriters who could afford the stiff price for drinks. Within, the dining room was huge, well lighted, and decorated with paintings of sport scenes hung on brick walls. It was not a romantic nook, like a score of candlelit French restaurants where hand-holding or clutching a thigh beneath a table was as much a part of the ambience as the waiters. Men generally liked Toots Shor's. Women generally did not. One called it "a gymnasium with room service."

Shor himself was a hulking, hard-drinking man, who delighted in calling pompous customers "crum bums." The customers, proud to be noticed, smiled at Shor's abuse. He was given to acts of great generosity. During one newspaper strike, he decreed that anyone with a press card automatically had a charge account at the bar. He also liked to make sweeping pronouncements, which found their way into columns, typically: "Anybody who can't get drunk by nine o'clock ain't tryin'." What Shor liked best of all was sitting at Table One with good fellows, talking man's talk and drinking the night away.

DiMaggio had an open invitation to join him. Shor did not, of course, call DiMaggio a crum bum. He preferred "Big Guy," or after some drinks, "Dago." Other regulars included Jimmy Cannon, Bob Considine, the late Hearst columnist, and Georgie Solotaire, a garrulous, chubby, ticket broker who could find not only a pair of third-row center for a hot new musical but also—*quietly*—the phone number of the lusty blonde, fourth from the end in the chorus line. You did not drop into a chair at Table One. You sat there only when you were invited.

This was a clubby company of men. Conversation was informal, ceaseless, anecdotal, and as the night wore on, increasingly boozy. (I once saw a nationally famous journalist carted away from Table One by two busboys. He had drunk himself into oblivion. Shor paid for a limousine to drive the man home to his colonial mansion in Connecticut.)

There were stories of Babe Ruth, Jack Dempsey, John McGraw, Damon Runyon, Ernest Hemingway, and a variety of Broadway characters. Sometimes amiable disputes erupted. Who was a more valuable ballplayer, Hank Greenberg of the Bronx or Columbia Lou Gehrig? That could take an hour to wind down with no one moving an inch from his original position.

An ethic of jock puritanism prevailed. You didn't sit in that particular club and recount sexual conquests. You didn't even tell dirty jokes. The company was male, doggedly male. Women, when they crept into the chatter, were referred to as "broads." But at Table One, you did not, so to speak, undress a pretty broad sitting across the room. Bad form. Under the house rules, you were not even allowed to send a waiter to her table with a drink. Indiscreet. "There's plenty of crummy East Side joints where you can diddle them broads all night," Shor said. "Not at my place."

I find it somewhat easier to remember the glow of the old Shor's than to describe it in stenographic detail, probably because there is no longer an equivalent place or an equivalent restaurateur to reinforce memory. But when the talk was good, and when the last regular had left, and one of Shor's lieutenants pulled the shades and you knew that conversation and the drinks would flow on for as long as you liked, you felt very close to the heart of a vanished New York.

DiMaggio was a patient listener in the Shor setting. Given their drinks, Solotaire and Shor became nonstop talkers. Cannon, who usually did not drink, was a nonstop talker under any conditions, day or night. So the fisherman's boy, now The Big Guy, sat out in public in a protected environment. If a stranger bothered him for an autograph at Table One, the stranger was told to leave the restaurant. Joe's interests were baseball, show girls, boxing, the flashy conversation around him, and *The Adventures of Batman and Robin*. Although DiMaggio put his name on two baseball books, his reading interest focused on sports pages and the comics.

Amid all the competitive talk, heady stuff, DiMaggio

slipped easily into the classic role of the strong man who was silent. Although Ted Williams was on the record a more skillful batsman and Hank Greenberg hit home runs more consistently, the consensus at Shor's and elsewhere held that DiMaggio was the finest all-around ballplayer of his time and perhaps of any time. Since his bat, his glove, his throwing arm, made stirring music, DiMaggio didn't *have* to talk. But when his opinions were solicited, he could contribute insightful observations. "A ballplayer's got to be hungry to become a big leaguer," he said. "That's why no boy from a rich family ever made the major leagues.

"It's just some writers who say that I play effortlessly. It's hard as hell to make the plays I do.

"Getting serious at the racetrack doesn't interest me. The only people who get rich on horses are guys who own them.

"It's almost a joke when some fan tells me I'm a great man. I'm just a ballplayer who works hard trying to get by."

Through such comments, innate candor, and a mysterious . . . *presence* is the only word . . . DiMaggio created an impression of profundity. As one of the Shor's crowd once complained, "If *I'm* standing in a corner saying nothing, the broads think it's because I got nothing to say. If DiMaggio stands in a corner saying nothing, the broads figure he must be thinking deep thoughts."

The spell of this presence not only excited "the broads." The tall, large-nosed, serious, graceful ballplayer drew idolatry from other men, cab drivers and bellhops and sophisticates. That idolatry has resisted even time.

In the very last column that he wrote, within days of his death from cancer, Red Smith explained to his readers that he was cutting back on his weekly schedule. "Three columns instead of four. We shall have to wait and see whether the quality improves." Smith then reflected a bit on his trade and athletes he had met and watched. Fans asked, he reported, which athlete was the best. "There was," he wrote, "a longish period when my rapport with some who were less than great made me nervous. Maybe I was stuck on bad ball players. I told myself not to worry. Some day there would be another Joe DiMaggio."

With that gracious little tribute, Smith bade ten million readers farewell.

The writers who so admired DiMaggio believed him to be a man of vigorous lust; many had a vigorous lust themselves. But in his baseball time one never wrote about such things, any more than one would write about a lady's navel. Until 1971, when Jim Bouton tore away Victorian veils with a spicy best-seller called *Ball Four,* sports heroes in the public prints did not have groins.

But quite beyond the sports pages, DiMaggio's sure hand with show girls added to his legend in the circle of the men he allowed to get close to him. They remarked to one another, "Joe's a helluva hitter in that league, too." He was, in a sense, the Zeus of the Toots Shor's set.

The late sports editor Stanley Woodward once warned Red Smith against the journalistic sin of "godding up" the athletes. "You've got to keep telling your readers and mostly yourself," Woodward said, "that these people are as human as anybody else." Woodward was an intellectual, fond of Milton's epics, who had studied "non-Shakespearean Elizabethan drama" at Amherst under Robert Frost. His reasoned counsel was followed by some in the Shor's set, most of whom had never read a non-Shakespearean Elizabethan drama. You gave DiMaggio, or any other superstar, total respect for what he did on the ball field. But off the field you expected him to behave like a regular guy. Pomposity, when it appeared at Table One, was promptly pricked, like an overblown balloon.

Louis Effrat, for many years a sportswriter at *The New York Times,* liked to recount an amusing erotic incident.

For reasons he forgets, Effrat was assigned to interview DiMaggio, and he arrived, late of an afternoon, at DiMaggio's room in the Edison hotel, a block away from Times

Square. (The neighborhood, crowded with theaters and restaurants, was a safe place to wander forty years ago.) "Can
we get this done in twenty minutes, Lou?" DiMaggio said.
"I've got somebody coming over."

Effrat said that he would try, but while asking a question
with an exuberant waving of arms, he suddenly winced and
slipped to the floor in pain. "Back," Effrat cried. "My back is
bad. Don't touch me, Joe. Let me lie here. I'll pop it back
myself."

The interview was suspended while DiMaggio paced and
Effrat, squirming and grimacing, administered ad-hoc chi-
ropractic to himself. "Lou," DiMaggio said. "You gotta go.
She'll be here any minute."

"Don't touch me. Just don't touch me. Hurts like hell."

The bell rang, and a girl both men recall as blond and
gorgeous entered. No one remembers her name. We might as
well call her Bubbles Larue.

"Hiya, Joe," Bubbles said. "What's with the guy on the
floor?"

"He's a friend of mine," DiMaggio said. The ballplayer
then formally introduced Effrat to Bubbles. The two shook
hands, Effrat supine and Bubbles bending far forward.

"Come on, Lou," DiMaggio said. "Out of here."

"I'm working on it," Effrat said, "but when my back's like
this I can't be moved."

"I don't have all night, Joe," Bubbles said. "I've got to get
to the club for the first show."

Now Bubbles joined DiMaggio in anxious and lubricious
pacing. Effrat continued to squirm, emitting small sounds of
pain. At length, the show girl said, "I'm sorry, Joe, but I can't
wait any longer. I can't be late for work."

She left to a mournful farewell from DiMaggio. A few
minutes later, Effrat grunted in triumph and sprang back to
his feet. "Got it," he said. "I can always work out my back
myself if I take a little time." He collected his notes and
thanked DiMaggio for the interview.

This story, which Effrat told with great animation and frequency, enjoyed wide currency for a time. Eventually, although not that night, DiMaggio was able to laugh at it. But it was not written about or even hinted at in the columns.

In essence, DiMaggio became open and direct with reporters whom he knew, and the reporters responded by protecting him. At the same time, he stayed close-mouthed with strangers, cold and aloof. The strangers had to work to win his trust. Many tried to do just that. Trust from Joe DiMaggio was a distinct badge of honor. Although a few of DiMaggio's difficulties with his first wife spilled out on news pages, the first major breach in the press's self-imposed protective code did not appear until 1951, DiMaggio's last season as a ballplayer. *Life* magazine gave DiMaggio his due as a ballplayer but approached him in a patronizing way. In a cover story printed in 1939, a *Life* reporter wrote, "Instead of olive oil, he [DiMaggio] keeps his hair slick with water. He never reeks of garlic." *Life* people regarded themselves as a higher order of journalists than mere newspapermen and as a higher breed of mortal than the offspring of Sicilian immigrants.

"Newspapermen," Sidney L. James, a former assistant managing editor of *Life,* once told me, "don't report the hard stuff. They'd rather be friends with the ballplayers." (True of many.) "Besides that, they don't polish their work. They think there's something sissy in going back and rewriting a line." (True of some.)

During the summer of 1951, Clay Felker, who later founded *New York* magazine, was working as a statistician for the Giants' broadcasting team, a humble job. He focused his gaze on loftier places, say a position at *Life.* His application led him into James's office.

After routine questions established Felker's baseball credentials, James said he would hire the young man with one proviso. "The Yankees are going to win the American League pennant," he said. "Get me a National League scouting report on them. Not newspaper stuff. The real thing."

Felker started digging and made his way into the front office of the Brooklyn Dodgers, who were the most approachable of the three New York teams. There he convinced E. J. (Buzzy) Bavasi, the Dodgers' vice-president, to "lend" him the scouting report prepared by Andy High, a former major league third baseman.

High, who had no suspicion his comments would appear in print, dismissed the veteran DiMaggio in a clinical, professional way. "His reflexes are very slow. He can't pull a good fast ball at all. He can't run and he won't bunt. . . ."

One of DiMaggio's old teammates, a highly educated man who requests anonymity, says, "Joe was a fine leader and he was capable of self-criticism, but his reaction to criticism from anyone else was paranoiac." Now, from beyond the flattering crowd at Shor's and the protective network of newspapermen, came a report that said DiMaggio's skills were fading and that his attitude was flawed. Great sluggers may not like to bunt, but a great team player *does* bunt whenever his manager asks him to. *Life* splashed the scouting report across six pages and newspapers across the country picked it up.

DiMaggio, then approaching the age of thirty-seven, had indeed lost many of the gifts of youth. But he was accustomed to being depicted as a gallant fighter against time. The *Life* report hurt, angered, humiliated him. A few months later he announced his retirement.

Life's enterprise (and Felker's brash reporting) marked the beginning of a tougher kind of sports journalism. The magazine would go on to report that Casey Stengel drank when the Yankees were beaten. The times, they were a-changing. Rather than live with a new, rougher journalism and suffer possible further humiliations, DiMaggio withdrew. He says he was getting ready to retire anyway, that he didn't want to continue at a level so far below his prime. At the very least, *Life* magazine forced the issue.

But obscurity and Joe DiMaggio would remain strangers. When he courted and won Marilyn Monroe in 1954, DiMaggio hurled himself back into public view. This time there was no protective web. A joke that accompanied reports of their courtship described Marilyn simply. She was "the ballplayer's ball player." Beyond such impudent humor lurked the Hollywood gossip press, a relentless beast, which feeds itself on scandal, and which, when there is no scandal, tries out its creativity by inventing some.

Unlike ballplayers, who have to meet the press by themselves while wearing only underwear in clubhouses, actors and actresses are forever hiring publicists to guard and launder their images. This helps the performers, but only in a limited way. Devout gossip readers today can frequently find out which entertainers are drinking too much, who is pregnant though unmarried, and, along those lines, who has been sleeping with whom and for how long. This kind of journalism is anathema to DiMaggio.

After he married Marilyn on January 14, 1954, before Judge Charles Peery at San Francisco City Hall, reporters were able to track the couple to a motel in Paso Robles, California, where they spent their wedding night. Although they had been lovers for many months and the reporters knew it, someone interviewed the room clerk who had checked them in, probably paying for information. Yes, the clerk said, DiMaggio had asked for a double bed.

Anything else?

He had also wanted to know if their room came with a television set. Another impudent joke. Who in the world, on his wedding night with Marilyn Monroe, wants to watch television? Joseph Paul DiMaggio, the almost-perfect knight. (She would later complain seriously and sometimes angrily that he spent much too much of their time together fixated before a television set, and not enough tending to her sexual needs.)

Neither party was getting an unsullied rose. To a degree, DiMaggio was foreshadowed in Marilyn's life by her first husband, James Dougherty, an athletic, physical sort, whom she'd wed when she was sixteen years old. Marilyn's predecessor as DiMaggio's wife, the late Dorothy Arnoldine Olsen, was also a blonde, also an actress (under the name of Dorothy

Arnold), although her career never got beyond second-rate pictures with titles like *Secrets of a Nurse.*

So she had experience with athletic men and he had experience with show-business blondes. But neither had experience with a fishbowl married life, in which the press first called them "Mr. and Mrs. America," and then, having invented a god and goddess, looked pantingly for mortal flaws.

The old Yankees remember Dorothy Arnold DiMaggio as a pleasant woman and a gracious hostess. Dorothy and Joe rented a penthouse apartment on West End Avenue for the season of 1940 and that winter gave some parties for Joe's teammates who lived in the New York area. "Nothing spectacular," says Buddy Hassett, a stylish first baseman who possessed a fine Irish tenor. "Just nice gatherings. I remember that Joe would make the drinks."

But this particular marriage was charged with troubles almost from the start. Joe loved Dorothy and he also loved his nights at Shor's. Dorothy complained about being left behind, and then, being left behind while pregnant. Later she told a reporter for the *Los Angeles Times* that even when Joe did spend time around the house, "he treated me like a stooge."

As with Marilyn, divorce proceedings, which Dorothy began in 1942, did not end the relationship. (She did not actually get the divorce until 1944.) For a time they flirted with reconciliation. Intimates say that it took Marilyn Monroe finally to get Dorothy out of Joe's system.

At times, during the stresses of his first marriage, DiMaggio talked openly with columnists he knew. He hoped that things could be patched up, he said. He couldn't guarantee that because "I'd really be sticking my neck out there." But he was trying. As the press and public came to understand him, Joe was a lonely, rather sympathetic figure, carrying a torch after the lights of his first marriage had gone out.

In 1946, when he batted below .300 for the first time, a friend said he had lost his concentration because he was "pining for Dorothy. All the time he's out there on the ball field, he misses her and he misses his son." But when Dorothy re-married—to a stockbroker named George C. Schubert—late in 1946, Joe's dream of reconciliation was destroyed. The next year his average improved by 25 points.

With Dorothy and Marilyn, DiMaggio fell into a difficult but classic pattern. He couldn't live with the women. They both left him. And he couldn't live happily without them. Although his life was busy, successful, crowded with acquaintances, ultimately it was rooted in solitude.

Dorothy, after telling friends that she was through with Joe forever, took a less-than-Olympian view of his love affair with Marilyn. In 1952, Joe took his son, Joe junior, on a swimming date with Marilyn under the palm trees that surround the pool of the Bel-Air hotel. This little story made the newspapers and prompted Dorothy to ask in court that DiMaggio's visitation rights be revoked and that his child-support payments be increased. Both motions were denied.

What led to such a hostile action? Dorothy may have been motivated by financial need or greed, or both. But beyond that, she was not happy to find her former husband dating a blonde more beautiful than she. And the charged implications of her suit, which not many missed, were plainly nasty. Marilyn was not a suitable companion for a boy entering adolescence. Marilyn was masquerading as an actress. She was, in short, a whore.

Stories that Marilyn worked as a prostitute persist to this day. Legends about the princess with the golden hair range from the exotic to the gamey. But this particular story rings somewhat off-key. Before she broke into movies, Marilyn made a living as a model. She had lean times but in the end she always found more work posing for photographers. She never actually *had* to sell her favors. In all probability, the real Marilyn never worked as a hooker any more than she said devotions as a nun.

DiMaggio went through three phases in his devouring relationship with her. He was first the swain, surprisingly courtly for someone from the rough-hewn world of baseball. After he first slept with her, he sent flowers. Then he was the husband, dominant, possessive, jealous, and demanding. This doomed the marriage. Marilyn wanted to be protected, not possessed. Finally, when passions no longer rocked him so fiercely, he became an attentive, loyal friend.

Her emotional deterioration spanned many years. She did not become suicidal overnight. Psychotherapy may have slowed the process, but by 1961 Marilyn was so distraught that she checked herself into Payne Whitney, the mental hospital connected to Cornell Medical School in New York. Once there, she discovered that it was easier to get into a mental hospital than to get out.

She was in such bad shape at Payne Whitney that she was put on the so-called suicide watch. That is, she was observed constantly by psychiatrists, nurses, and attendants, even when she had to use the toilet. This infuriated her. She tore off her little white hospital gown. Naked, she screamed, "If they're gonna watch, I'll give them something to look at."

Somewhat more calmly, she called DiMaggio in California and begged him to get her out. The hospital wasn't helping. It was only making her feel worse.

How could he get her out?

He was Joe DiMaggio. He'd find a way.

DiMaggio flew to New York, mixed diplomacy and bluster, and freed his former wife from the clinicians. A source at Payne Whitney says DiMaggio made two telling points. First, he personally would look after Marilyn. Second, if she was not released, he would tear down the hospital brick by brick. "Imagine," says the source, "the ghastly publicity we would have gotten, if DiMaggio had made a raging fuss."

Such personal horrors were a universe away from the sunlit afternoons when he loped in Yankee Stadium for an adoring press and public. Why is he adamantly, angrily unwilling to discuss Marilyn to this day? Apart from his sense of privacy, it hurts too much.

Indeed, he has confided to a few friends, if Marilyn had

not died, they might have married again. This sounds like nothing more than sorrowful fantasy. Before her death Marilyn was acutely disturbed, "beyond analysis," according to the late Dr. Ralph Greenson, a psychiatrist she was seeing on almost a daily basis in Los Angeles.

Her career seemed to be dead in the water. She had been fired from a movie called *Something's Got to Give.* She was so worried about money she resolved never to carry more than $20 with her when she left the house. She slept around. A Mexican actor. Probably Bobby Kennedy. But she was growing increasingly solitary and crotchety, incapable of an enduring commitment to anyone, even to her great friend Joe the Slugger.

After he ran her funeral with an iron hand, while a voracious press tried to break into the Westwood Village Mortuary, he entered a period of agony. The old protective web, the Toots Shor's crowd, was far away. His baseball days were gone. His wives had vanished. His youth had slipped away. Joe retreated into forbidding silence on serious things. He was embarked on what one writer called the silent season of a hero.

In death Marilyn has assumed a durability she never possessed in the thirty-six years of her life. You find her in a hundred paintings, a thousand photographs, in gaudy picture books and earnest biographies, beckoning, pulsing, sexual, and sometimes even real.

I remember meeting her in September of 1954 at a carefully produced little cocktail party in a New York hotel called the Savoy Plaza. The setting was a room with mirrored walls; when she entered, suddenly she was everywhere.

She wore a black sheath skirt and a low-cut diaphanous bodice over a filmy brassiere. The Broadway columnist Earl Wilson approached her, with his camera at the ready, and bluntly asked her to lean forward so he could take a picture. She obliged, smiling, and suddenly said, "But, Earl. My bosoms will show." She then tugged her bodice a bit higher, which also had the effect of making it more transparent. Conversation stopped as people stared at Marilyn or at the Marilyn in one of the wall mirrors. She seemed nude without being quite naked. She looked radiant.

At length, I found myself standing next to her and expected to make conversation. I knew, of course, that she was married to DiMaggio, without knowing that the marriage was dissembling, and I said, somewhat desperately, that I had spent time traveling with baseball teams.

She seemed puzzled. "I wouldn't know very much about that."

"It was a job," I said. "I was a newspaperman."

Her smile became metallic and she said, "Interesting." I was elbowed from her path and she was guided toward a second Broadway columnist. I turned to my companion, an older journalist named Dick Johnston, and asked why he hadn't helped out in my labored discourse with the goddess. "I wanted to talk to her," Johnston said, "but my tongue got stiff."

Sly laughter and intense drinking followed as Marilyn made her way about the room. She was, I later learned, no more confident at this sort of event than I had been in speaking to her. But small, demanding sexual parties with selected members of the press were part of the dues she was willing to pay in her vaulting ambition to be a star.

Hollywood, with its relentless demands, its shabby values, its hard-edged unrelenting focus on busts and bucks, destroyed her. That is a popular approach to the life and death of Marilyn, one with which DiMaggio himself generally agrees.

Nonsense, argue proponents of another, possibly deeper point of view. Her childhood without family, a childhood of foster homes and an orphanage, never created a base for stable adult life. Hollywood was only a locale. Life destroyed Marilyn Monroe. Or, put differently, she destroyed herself.

She had appeared in twenty-one films before she married DiMaggio, working her way from something called *Scudda*

Hoo! Scudda Hay!, featuring a pair of mules, to big expensive musicals like *How to Marry a Millionaire,* where she starred along with Betty Grable and Lauren Bacall. She flourished in an era when the big studios still ran Hollywood and developed talent under long-term contracts. She had great difficulty convincing executives at Twentieth Century-Fox to let her play anything other than a dumb blonde. Then, when she seemed about to break away from the cliché, she had great difficulty convincing herself that she was capable of acting departures. She wanted to have her acting taken seriously, as, say, the work of Bette Davis was taken seriously, but her discipline was execrable and, aside from that, her dumb-blonde performances were commercial successes. No one gets very far in Hollywood arguing against profits.

"I'm a joke," she would later complain. "An expensive joke, but still a joke." When she announced that she wanted to play Grushenka, the beguiling seductress in Dostoevsky's masterpiece *The Brothers Karamazov,* critics and intellectuals derided the idea. But she was serious and would spend painful years trying to become an actress of range and passion. Arthur Miller, her husband during that period, feels that she had outgrown DiMaggio even before she and Joe were married. She was cultivating tastes for Vivaldi and Bach, Whitman and Yeats, which would carry her beyond the tall, silent Toots Shor's clubman and comic-book enthusiast.

Joe married a diffuse, decorous, intelligent, restless, hungry blonde. Then, to his pain, he discovered that such women are complicated.

They can even be devouring.

DiMaggio's baseball admirers, themselves growing older, are appalled to hear that anyone thinks of him first as the failed husband of a sexy Hollywood doll. They shake their heads and fall back on reverential descriptions that suggest all by himself he defined the poetry and gliding beauty of baseball.

Beyond that, but also as a part of that, they talk about his poise, his style, his lordly reserve. "I made a trip with him to Vietnam to visit troops," says former commissioner of baseball Bowie Kuhn, "and at one point we were in a helicopter with the Viet Cong shooting up at us. I don't mind telling you I was sweating. I took a look at Joe. Talk about regal cool! It was something. I never saw such self-control."

After speaking to enough baseball people, you get a sense that you are discussing a deity. Good enough. Joe is a god of baseball. Not flawless. Ballplayer stories persist of overwhelming pride, approaching arrogance. But these do not make him notably less godlike. Most deities of human legend display elements of pride and wrath, like Joe DiMaggio.

Only when you move away from baseball into the world of show business does DiMaggio become human, vulnerable, and even, once in a while, the butt of a joke.

Marilyn told friends that DiMaggio had the finest male body she had seen and remarked that he reminded her of Michelangelo's statue of David. Joe is not immune to flattery, and years later told one Hollywood actress, whom he knew well, that he was aware that he had a great body. Then, so to speak, he focused his boasts on a particular organ.

The actress, a dark-haired, irreverent lady, heard him out on the topic several times. For DiMaggio's next birthday, she sent him two gifts. A mirror and a ruler.

DiMaggio's response is lost to contemporary history and the Baseball Hall of Fame.

Chapter ★ 2

Up from Sicily

After he retired from the fishing boat in 1932, the father, Giuseppe Paolo, walked about the house in shirtsleeves, wearing a fedora and looking for things to keep him busy. He was a compact, mustachioed man, known as Zio Pepe to his friends, who was neither expansive nor comfortable with strangers. He spoke with a heavy accent and what he did say was often reported in a phonetic and rather mocking way.

"You talka to me about Joe? He's-a justa one my boys. They alla the same-a to me."

The Italian immigrant was a stock comic character during the 1920s and 1930s, except for those who were not comic at all, like Little Caesar. They were funny little men, barbers and fruit peddlers crying, "Hey, banan-oh!" as they pushed their heavy carts, or they were cold-eyed killers from a myste-

rious criminal organization called *La Mano Nera,* The Black
Hand. That was the harsh, derisive image of Italian-Americans when Joe DiMaggio was growing up and moving toward
the rocky heights of fame. Italians were wops, guineas, dagos.
If they didn't shoot you on the sidewalk, their breath smelled
from all the spices at their most recent meal.

The racial stereotype was, of course, offensive, and ig-
nored the true marvels of an Italian heritage. Italy cradled the
Renaissance and nurtured poets (Dante), saints (Francis), sci-
entists (Galileo), painters (Giotto), playwrights (Pirandello),
musicians   (Verdi),   thinkers   (Croce),   and   statesmen
(Garibaldi). But the racial generalities swept away Italian tradition and history and fed patterns of paranoia among Italian-
Americans. (Why is everybody laughing at us?) In turn, this
bolstered a certain clannishness that is common to immigrant
groups. (If we stay with our own people, nobody will laugh.)

The author Gay Talese remarked early in the 1960s that
what he *really* wanted to write was a book of profiles, all composed about successful Americans from Italian backgrounds.
Having relieved himself of the idea, Talese managed to look
unhappy. There was DiMaggio, he said, and Frank Sinatra,
but who else?

I mentioned Pietro Di Donato, who wrote a powerful, nat-
uralistic novel called *Christ in Concrete.*

Talese continued to look unhappy, musing about his own
collective Italian-American heritage. There were so few Italian-American authors and intellectuals, he said, compared to
those from, say, the ranks of American Jews. Talese did go on
and write excellent profiles of DiMaggio and Sinatra for
Esquire, without much help from either subject, but ironically
the author who has been most successful with tales of Italian-
Americans is the novelist Mario Puzo. Puzo writes about vil-
lains, not heroes, in books about the leaders of the American
Mafia, which is a bastard descendant of the old despised
Black Hand. Italian-Americans worry about their achievements and their image and when finally a chronic best-selling

author rises from their ranks, he writes about Italian-Americans who are criminals.

Ralph Gambino agonizes over the "dilemma of Italian-Americans," in his study *Blood of My Blood.* He recalls that during his college days students called the television crime program *The Untouchables* "Cops and Wops." Gambino writes that he wanted to strike back with the argument that few Italian-Americans actually were criminals. But he did not. "I had seen the controlled supercilious smirks that answered this defense."

Joseph Paul DiMaggio, named for his immigrant father, Giuseppe Paolo, is capable of searing rages, but he does not directly address the punishing clichés thrown at his ethnic group. On the surface at least, he goes with the flow. As a boy he stayed exclusively within the Italian community of his San Francisco neighborhood and, inside that tight circle, he did not venture far beyond his own large family. As a ball-player, he accepted the caustic racial attitudes of clubhouse and dugout and simply adopted the prevailing vocabulary, even when it was self-derisive.

During the 1947 World Series, when he was playing against the Brooklyn Dodgers and Jackie Robinson, the first black admitted to the major leagues, DiMaggio had to make an awkward leap to avoid spiking Robinson at first base. He explained to a reporter later: "If it's a white guy playing first, maybe I don't jump. I just run over him and spike him. But if I spike Robinson, then it's gonna look like the guineas against the niggers. And I don't want that, the guineas against the niggers." You get the impression of a sensible, seemingly unselfconscious American who carries a decent strain of practical idealism buried beneath blustery baseball talk.

But DiMaggio is a second-generation American from a modest, although not impoverished, immigrant family, and he has been highly sensitive to misspellings and mispronunciations of his name. As a minor league rookie, he went to some lengths to correct the spelling. Some San Francisco newspapers had been calling him DeMaggio. Later, as a young major league star, he collaborated with a ghost on a brief auto-biography for the *New York World-Telegram*. He made a point in installment one that his name was to be pronounced Di-Mahg-io, not Di-Maag-io.

In those early Yankee Stadium years, before fans had begun carrying homemade banners into ballparks, some Italian-Americans cheered his home runs by waving aloft the green-and-white-and-red flag of Italy.

He was not permitted to forget that he was Italian. Other ballplayers referred to him as "The Big Dago," and some ad-dressed him genially enough, "Hey, Dago." While accepting and even being a part of the ambient ethnic ways, DiMaggio has shown subtle symptoms of being affected by them.

He is intensely concerned that outsiders are taking advan-tage of him. "Everybody who calls me," he says, "wants something." Recently he agreed to sign autographs at a base-ball-card show for a fee of $4,000 for one hour. When the hour was up, his check was not ready. DiMaggio rose, chill and remote, and stalked away, without a word or even a nod to the fans who were still waiting. The promoters, he sus-pected, were "playing me for a chump."

A television producer asked him to make an appearance on a syndicated sports show for a smaller fee. DiMaggio de-clined politely and when the producer followed up with a tele-phone call, DiMaggio stopped speaking to him. "I told him no once," DiMaggio said. "That ought to be enough."

The distrust and the irritability that follows have grown partly from all the demands made on a man of fame. You have to ration time and energies or none will be left. But DiMaggio is so passionate and unyielding on "not being taken" that his angers may well trace from earlier days when outsiders were forever making jokes about Italians and Di-Maggio found safety and security only with his family and their Italian neighbors. Significantly, he has described Marilyn as "a warm, big-hearted girl that *everybody took advantage of*" (emphasis added).

Neither his New York world nor his wives was Italian, but for all his adventurous traveling, he has stayed close to his Italian roots in San Francisco. For most of his life, more than forty-five years, he owned the same house on Beach Street in the Marina district.

The DiMaggios of San Francisco were descended from generations of hardworking Sicilian fishing stock. Giuseppe was raised on Isola del Femmine, a small island off Palermo on the northern coast, which is steep and cliff-bound and illuminated by glaring, white Mediterranean light. It is a region where farmers and fishermen alike share poverty.

Italians call the region of their country that stretches south of Rome the Mezzogiorno or the Meridionale. The late Luigi Barzini called the Mezzogiorno "by far the most miserably poor" section of Italy. The farther south you travel, down through the hills of Abruzzi and then toward the Bay of Naples, the more profoundly poverty and illiteracy extend their clutch on the land and people. Sicily, the southernmost region of Italy, is poor, rocky, provincial. Although the Mafia holds little sway in the eastern Sicilian cities of Syracuse and Messina, no one denies its deadly grip on the western part of the island, including the Palermo region from which the DiMaggios sprang.

When Sicily was incorporated into the Italian kingdom in 1860, fewer than 10 percent of the populace could read or write. The Italian government established free elementary schools and provided textbooks, but progress was slow. The families needed their children to work in the fields, pick oranges, or to mend fishing nets. As recently as 1930, roughly 40 percent of the Sicilians still were illiterate.

Many Italians in the northern industrial cities of Turin and Milan or the artistic centers of Venice and Florence regard Sicily as closer sociologically to North Africa than to Italy itself. The island is something of a national embarrassment, much as the old sharecropping South embarrassed liberal Americans in the North.

Separated from the boot of Italy by the Strait of Messina,

the site of Homer's twin perils, Scylla and Charybdis, Sicily
has remained cut off from most of the vital mainstreams that
stir Italian life. The natives, a dark-haired mixture of Italian,
Catalonian, and even Carthaginian strains, have developed a
defensive, insular personality. They tend to focus on close
family bonds and to view outsiders, including Italians from
the mainland, with suspicion. "Rome," one Italian journalist
reports, "has its fast life, its ruins, and its Vatican. Venice has
St. Mark's and the canals. Sicily has hot weather and paranoia."

Men rule Sicilian families and life. Women, accepting
household chores and childbearing as the lot handed to them
by God, may be forceful characters within familial confines,
but women's liberation as it is preached in the United States
and was practiced in her own incomplete and erratic way by
Marilyn Monroe, is unknown. You can find echoes of Sicilian
defensiveness, machismo, suspicion, and paranoia in the ma-
ture personality of Joe DiMaggio.

What hookworm was to the barefoot American South, the
Mafia is to Sicily: a plague that will not go away. The word
mafia itself derives not from Italian but from Arabic, in which
mahyah means boasting. Used generically in the Sicilian di-
alect, *mafia* means both lawlessness and boldness.

Although the origins of the Mafia are somewhat obscure—
no authorized history has yet been published—the most reliable accounts suggest that the organization began during the
eighteenth century, when Sicily fell under the domination of
Spain. Spaniards were brutal conquerors and the early Mafia
appears to have been a secret society whose members were
sworn to exact revenge on *conquistadores* who had murdered
farmers and fishermen for spoils, or who had raped the flower
or even the weeds of Sicilian maidenhood.

From this curious guerrillalike beginning—one can imagine early Mafioso referring to themselves as freedom fight-
ers—the Mafia evolved into an organization that inflicted a
bloody discipline on all the areas of Sicily where it held sway,
long after the Spaniards were gone. You have that sometimes

·with secret terrorist groups. When the old enemy departs, they find new ones.

Leaders assumed the title of "don," a corruption of the latin *dominus,* or, colloquially, lord. Disputes over, say, the proceeds of a citrus crop were settled not by discussion or even argument, but by gunfire. Where business in Milan was conducted in offices, business in western Sicily was often settled on a lonely road late at night.

Semicomic stories of Mafia ways persist. A friendly landloard from the Italian mainland, visiting his Sicilian fields, was distressed to discover that his wife's fur coat had been stolen. He complained to Mafia associates. Within hours a veritable warehouse of furs was brought before him. The Mafia was efficient enough to have rounded up almost every fur stolen in Palermo over a period of weeks. Unfortunately for the visitor, his wife's coat was not among them. A lone-wolf free lance had been at work. He went undiscovered and unpunished.

But the Mafia is far more frightening than funny and the violent greed of the dons has contributed mostly to misery in Sicily. No one has been able to root it out. In 1909, a New York City police lieutenant named Joseph Patrosino landed at Palermo on a supposedly secret mission. He was to investigate the connections between the Mafia in Sicily and the Black Hand, which was intimidating innocents in the Italian ghettos of New York. Since only the Sicilian police had been informed that he was coming, Patrosino felt safe enough to stroll the streets.

As he walked in the Piazza Marina, before the Palermo courthouse, Petrosino was shot to death in a rattle of gunfire. Don Vito Cascio Ferro, the most powerful mafioso of his time, took personal credit for the assassination. Petrosino, the intruding outsider, had not survived a single day in Palermo.

Neither Italian kings nor even Benito Mussolini, with all his clamorous blackshirts, was able to blunt the Mafia's power. To many ordinary, hardworking Sicilians, the Mafia is one more curse added to a weary, unrewarding life, brightened by the distant hope of heaven.

Aside from escaping into religion, another response to the conditions of life in Sicily was simply to leave. Emigration mounted during the late decades of the nineteenth century and reached a peak in 1906, when 127,000 Sicilians, more than 3 percent of the total population, departed from the island for good.

The DiMaggios of Isola del Femmine were fishermen for as far back as anyone remembers. (In an essentially illiterate community you cannot precisely trace genealogy back many generations.) It was a grinding, marginal life, with strains reaching to ancient times in the Mediterranean. Sicily was first inhabited by allied races, the Sicels and the Sicans, both originally seafarers from Iberia and Libya. The island was successively colonized or dominated by Greeks, Carthaginians, Romans, Saracens, Normans, and Spaniards before its eventual incorporation into modern Italy. Wars came with almost every change.

Although tourist posters depict the Mediterranean as a tranquil pond lined with pretty women taking the sun in a fraction of a bikini, the life of adventurous Sicilian fishermen was turbulent and dangerous. They ranged as far as the coast of Africa and storms were a constant peril to their small boats. Storms at sea. Wars and later the Mafia at home. Sicilian fishermen who survived, like the DiMaggios, were a rugged and courageous lot.

Giuseppe DiMaggio fished on the family boat, served a term in the Italian army and, like many Sicilians, heard stories of a more fruitful land, America. He was married and the father of an infant girl named Nellie when he put Sicily behind him in 1902. He had saved enough money for his passage; no one knows how. He would sail to New York and then proceed by train to California, where a number of his old neighbors had already settled and where, according to their letters, a man could find plenty of work. He would get situated, he told his wife, Rosalie, and then send for her and the baby.

This short, stocky, determined man, who comes down to

us as an almost mute figure in shirtsleeves and fedora, made the great sea voyage, crossed the expanse of America, and became a laborer on the Union Pacific Railroad. Living poor, he saved enough in a year to send for Rosalie and Nellie. In time he built himself a skiff and resumed the fisherman's life seven thousand miles from Sicily, in the waters of the Pacific Ocean. The family lived in Martinez, a small town north of San Francisco on the eastern shore of the bay. "I know about the house we had," Joe DiMaggio says. "It wasn't anything more than a cabin."

Children arrived with the regularity of the seasons. After Nellie, Rosalie DiMaggio gave birth to Mamie, Thomas, Marie, Michael, Frances, Vincent, Joseph, and Dominic. Three—Vince, Joe, and Dom—grew up to become major league center fielders, a truly astonishing phenomenon, not simply for baseball enthusiasts but for geneticists.

All the boys carried the middle name Paul. It was impossible in the cabin-household to forget that Paul was Giuseppe's favorite saint. Tom DiMaggio, who died in 1980 at the age of seventy-six, would become the businessman, a union official, a financial adviser to Joe during the contract arguments with the Yankees, and finally manager of the family restaurant on Fisherman's Wharf. Tom was cut from a tough fiber, but he wandered beyond his depth in urging Joe to take a hard-line approach against the Yankees and their rock-hard general manager, Ed Barrow. The holdouts that resulted cost Joe some popularity and the hoots he heard from the stands stayed with him for decades, right into a famous exchange of dialogue with Marilyn in 1954.

Michael, the sunniest of the boys, became a fisherman. He was popular, undriven by ambition. He drowned in 1953, at forty-four, when he fell overboard on a rough day at sea.

The last three, the DiMaggio center fielders, Center fielders, Inc., had markedly distinct careers and followed markedly different paths after baseball. Vince, who played for four National League teams, never batted .300. He was a wild swinger who set a record for most strikeouts in a season. He was less intense than Joe or Dom, less troubled by a bad game, a bad inning. When I found him a few years ago, he lived in North Hollywood and supplemented his Social Security income by selling Fuller brushes door to door. His baseball career ran down before the funding of the players' pension plan. Occasionally a newspaperman stops by for an interview. Vince says that he was every bit as good an outfielder as Joe, maybe a little better. He just didn't have the same batting eye.

Are the brothers close?

"We don't see each other much and that's a shame. Families ought to stay close together. Joe maybe has some things that I'd like to have and I have some things he'd like."

Such as?

"A long, happy marriage."

Dominic, a Red Sox hero for more than a decade, stood five feet nine, wore spectacles, and was called "The Little Professor." He was swift, gifted, and lacked only his older brother's batting power. Red Sox fans made him the hero of a song they would chant from the bleachers at Fenway Park, to the tune of "Maryland My Maryland."

Oh, Dominic DiMaggio!
He's better than his brother, Joe.

After baseball, Dominic became the president of a New England company that manufactured fiber cushion materials and, it is said, is a millionaire. His name has appeared in Tanglewood programs as a significant contributor to the Boston Symphony Orchestra, an immigrant fisherman's son among Cabots and Lodges.

Joe was born on November 25, 1914, soon after the guns of August had hurled Europe into World War I. It must have been a comfort to Giuseppe, as it was to most Americans, to believe that his family was safely distant from Europe's ancient, bloody battlegrounds. Joe was the eighth of the nine DiMaggio siblings.

In 1915, the family moved from Martinez to San Francisco, where Giuseppe rented the bottom flat in a three-story frame-and-plaster building at 2047 Taylor Street on the slope of Russian Hill. The building was situated in the North Beach section of San Francisco, about a quarter of a mile from the wharf where Giuseppe docked his boat, the *Rosalie.* North Beach enjoyed national prominence in the 1960s as the site of erotic bars and nightclubs. For the price of a few drinks you could watch almost-naked women dance about on small stages.

But in DiMaggio's boyhood such license and such ostentatious sexuality were unknown. North Beach was Italian, insular, and as intensely puritan as a midwestern Bible Belt town. The neighborhood was dominated by the spires of the Church of St. Peter and St. Paul, at the intersection of Filbert and Powell streets, where Joe took his Roman Catholic sacraments and where, years later, he would marry Dorothy Arnold.

A reporter who visited the household long ago described the DiMaggios as "intensely competitive, independent, family loyal and athletic." The DiMaggios had never heard of his employer, *Time* magazine. The reporter asserted that the DiMaggios were "uninterested" in his assignment and *"uninteresting"* (emphasis added).

All the DiMaggio boys were assigned to one bedroom. The girls had another. Then, as the children grew older, a few spilled out onto sofa beds in the living room and dining room. The household was crowded with energetic young people, without the blessing of privacy.

The family was poor. DiMaggio makes much of this in his reflective talks today. But they were not impoverished. No one went hungry. No one had to go to school barefoot. In a famous passage from *The Old Man and the Sea,* Ernest Hemingway has his protagonist, the Cuban fisherman Santiago, declaim: "I would like to take the great DiMaggio fishing. They say his father was a fisherman. Maybe he was as poor as we are and would understand."

The DiMaggios of Taylor Street were hardly as poor as Santiago of Cuba, but all the boys were expected to work. They sold newspapers and gave their proceeds to Rosalie when they came home. (Actually, what is assuredly valid in Hemingway's passage is its implicit endorsement of DiMaggio as the greatest ballplayer of his time. Hemingway was careful with such things. His favorite sportswriter, Red Smith, drew a mention in *Across the River and Into the Trees*.)

As a small child, DiMaggio had to wear steel leg braces. "I don't really remember it myself," he says, "but my parents told me that I was knock-kneed. Anyway, it was some kind of a deformity. The braces fixed it, but they left my ankles weak. For a time, when I was a kid, weak ankles gave me some trouble."

According to Tom, Joe was, quite simply, a natural ball-player. Tom did not remember long practice sessions. In his memory Joe just picked up a bat at the age of seven or eight, and, easy as that, began to hit.

Mickey Mantle's family was dominated by a miner-father, nicknamed "Mutt," who saw baseball as a freedom road, leading his family up and out of the mines. Each twilight, he worked with his son, teaching him what he knew about the game so that, as someone has pointed out, "when the old man came home, Mickey had to stop playing and start practicing." Giuseppe's household was notably different; Zio Pepe had no use for baseball until the sport began to support his household.

A paved alley opened behind the DiMaggio flat on Taylor Street. There Frances DiMaggio began pitching to her brother Joe, who swung whatever form of bat that he could find. A broken paddle became his particular favorite. Frances, who was four years older, worked out the rules of the children's competition. She threw to different spots—high outside, low inside—looking for a zone where Joe could not make contact.

Like a legion of major league pitchers twenty years later, she never found one.

When Tom DiMaggio talked about these times, he stressed that Joe had never *worked* at baseball. He simply played. Joe had marvelous hand-to-eye coordination, and he'd pound his sister's best stuff for a while until they tired of paddle-and-ball and switched to another activity, say pitching pennies.

In that old city game, children toss pennies toward a wall. Whoever places a penny closest to the wall wins, and hauls in all his rivals' coins. The home run, so to speak, is a "leaner," a penny that comes to rest actually leaning against that wall. According to one of the DiMaggio clan, "We all got so we could do pretty well at pitching pennies. We won a lot of pennies from other kids."

Vince, Joe, and Dom collected baseball cards that came in boxes of Zenith Cracker Jack, which advertised, "The more you eat the more you want." There was another game, flipping cards, in which you tried to match—face up or face down—the card another child had flipped. Winner gets to keep both cards. This was the early childhood then: school, church, family competitive street games, and hitting baseballs in an alley. Although DiMaggio evolved into baseball royalty, there was nothing regal in his early years.

A block and a half away from the house on Taylor, the children found the North Beach playground. As they grew older, the boys played baseball there. The girls played basketball. Joe tried his hand at tennis. He was good. For a time, he says, he dreamed of becoming a great tennis player, like Big Bill Tilden, or, later, Don Budge. Dominic played checkers in the park and became a neighborhood champion. Vince had a good singing voice and talked about finding a career in opera. But as they grew older, Vince and Joe and Dom all developed a common dream. The dream was baseball.

"My father had a rule," Tom said, "and it applied to all nine of us. Everybody had to be home for supper on time;

otherwise you didn't get to eat. Or that was supposed to be the rule. Mom wouldn't let us go hungry.

"You see, if we were playing ball in a pickup game and dinnertime came and it was the seventh inning, there wasn't a one of us who'd quit and hurry home.

"So when we did get back, maybe talking about our hits, Papa would start to shout and scold us. 'Baseball. What is that? A bum's game. A no-good game. Whoever made a living playing baseball?'"

And Mama?

"She would only scold when one of us came home with a tear in his pants."

Clothes were handed down from son to son. Mama's kitchen specialty—which later appeared in the family restaurant—was *cioppino,* a dish made of crabs, tomatoes, sherry, and garlic.

Sometimes over dinner the boys ragged at each other. They sold copies of the *San Francisco Chronicle* on the corner of First and Howard and they'd argue: Who could sell newspapers best? (In the end, of course, it was Joe, selling millions of papers that carried accounts of his slugging.)

Papa walked down the hill to the wharf each morning and set off in the *Rosalie.* Mama ironed and cleaned and washed. The boys grew and secretly sought out stars to follow. DiMaggio remembers lingering outside the Lido café, at Columbus and Lombard, waiting for Francis (Lefty) O'Doul to emerge, then calling out, "Hey, Lefty. Gimme a ball." Private lives of one American family during the Roaring Twenties. Obscurity in a safe corner of San Francisco.

Four hundred miles down the coast, a fair-haired little girl, who would become Marilyn Monroe, was looking for a safe corner in the ever more sprawling neighborhoods of Los Angeles. Her mother was already going mad.

"Look," Tom DiMaggio said, in an unusually contemplative moment, "I guess all us DiMaggios had our hopes for what we'd do with our lives. We wanted, you know, to move up. But we didn't sit around and talk about what we were going to do, even among ourselves." (If there was no physical privacy on Taylor Street, you then guarded the privacy of your fantasies.) "I knew what I wanted to be."

A ballplayer?

Silence. An injury to his left shoulder had robbed Tom of his powerful swing. It always seemed to pain him to discuss the injury. He became not a major leaguer, with his name borne on the snapping banners of fame, but a vice-president of the Crab Fisherman's Protective Association, a group less ominous than it sounds. It was the organization through which the fishermen sold their daily catch. Later he managed the DiMaggio family restaurant on Fisherman's Wharf.

"I had to figure out two things," Tom said. "What I wanted to be and what I *could* be. Then I went out and did what I could."

The fisherman's life, through which Giuseppe supported the family, was demanding and dangerously competitive. The men went for salmon or crab, depending on the season, and each dawn the small boats sailed out to the point where the ocean met the bay, and beyond. The seas were cold and the water was rough.

With a day's haul netted, the fishermen raced back to the dock. They raced because the first sailors back had the best chance of selling their catch. According to old-timers, forty or fifty boats would contend with one another to gain the single channel that led to shore. The crews shouted and cursed and threatened one another. Fistfights broke out between the fishermen. Sometimes one crew would slash another's nets. Or a crew would pour gasoline over another crew's catch, ruining it. On occasion someone would leave flowers at the door of someone else's home. This was not a greeting but a warning. The flowers were intended to suggest a funeral. If this sounds like the plot of a B movie—*Toilers of the Sea*—it is nonetheless true. Only after years of these fierce and sometimes bloody confrontations did the Italian fishermen of San Fran-

cisco organize themselves into groups, like the Crab Fisherman's Protective Association, which curtailed the internecine
battles. The associations established quotas, determining how
much each fisherman could catch and sell. Order appeared
and the B-movie plot came to an end.

By his own accounts, Joe DiMaggio had an ordinary and
landlocked lower-middle-class boyhood. Although late in life
he bought a boat and named it for himself (*The Yankee Clipper*), DiMaggio remembers that as a child he hated fishing.
"First," he says, "I'd get seasick when the water was rough.
Then, I couldn't stand the smell of the fish and the crabs. It
must have upset my father, but I never went out on his boat,
unless they dragged me."

He attended Hancock Grammar School and San Francisco
Junior High, without achieving or aspiring to academic distinction. He never traveled far from his neighborhood and
had few friends beyond the sheltering family. His late sister
Marie, a willful and assertive young woman, once remarked
that she wondered what would become of Joe, if anything. He
refused to fish. His schoolwork was dilatory. He seemed de-
void of any real ambition. "I used to wonder if he was backward," she said. "Not quick. I wondered what was the matter
with him. Then I decided it was mostly that he was a very shy
person."

He grew tall, skinny, and strong. A neighborhood game
that he enjoyed was known as horse-lot baseball. Boys gathered in a large fenced area near the wharf, where a dairy company parked its milk wagons. The horses that pulled the
wagons roamed the lot untethered. The boys picked up rocks
and scaled them at the animals, which, of course, retreated,
clearing a wide area. Then the boys used rocks for bases and
home plate and began pickup games, playing with an old
baseball held together by rolls of friction tape.

"Funny thing," DiMaggio says. "When I first started playing on the lot I couldn't throw at all. I tried the infield, but I
was a real scatterarm. That didn't straighten out right away.
Hell, one day later on when I was trying to play shortstop for

the San Francisco Seals, I made eleven errors, all on throws. It was an exhibition game that didn't mean much, but it got so that every time someone hit a grounder at me, the people sitting back of first base got up and ran.

"Anyway, when I was a young kid, I had this wild arm and I couldn't run much either. Probably that was from the braces I'd had to wear. But after a while my arm got better, except for lapses, and my legs came around, too. After that I was all right."

According to Marie, who shared a house with him for decades in their maturity, Joe was such a bashful boy that when one of the four DiMaggio daughters brought a girlfriend home to visit, he usually left the house rather than face the embarrassment of an introduction. He attended dances at a local lodge, but is remembered as a male wallflower, nervously puffing a cigarette and throwing brief glances at the prettier girls. He would devote many ardent adult years to making up for his lost time with the ladies.

Giuseppe variously urged and ordered his tallest son to learn the fisherman's trade. Joe, in sullen rebellion, resisted until at last the father, struggling to make a living, raising eight other children, simply gave up.

Tom, the first of the family ballplayers, set about convincing his father that baseball could provide a better living than fishing, if you were good enough. Giuseppe remained skeptical. How could the adventurous Sicilian fisherman, who had traveled so far and worked so hard and sired so many offspring, comprehend what Tom was saying? There was no John McGraw or Christy Mathewson in his background. The sport the old man knew was boccie, a kind of bowling, which you played on Sunday afternoons for a little recreation. Baseball in America is a passion, a pastime that rises to an art form, a game that stirs bubbles in the blood, if you are tuned to its particular bars of music. Giuseppe was tone-deaf to baseball, but one senses also that he was becoming a weary man, growing tired of arguing with his children.

Tom preached the gospel of baseball and Giuseppe weakened. All right. They were going to play anyway. What could you do? At least Michael, the third son, liked the fisherman's life. There is no record of angry battles over baseball in Giuseppe Paolo's home. Just years of resolute disagreement, with Giuseppe weakening and then resigning himself as people have to do when they grow older.

After carrying the brunt of the baseball effort, Tom lost his career with the shoulder injury, but in 1932 Vince signed a contract to play for the San Francisco Seals. That contract stopped the discussions for good. It guaranteed Vince $250 a month, a windfall during the Great Depression. Although Giuseppe never really learned to read English, he set about trying to understand a box score, and in a few months could tell whether Vince had gotten his hits. How? "We were never sure ourselves," one of the sisters said, "but Papa could certainly make out the family name. Then he must have figured out what the columns were. Times at bat. Runs. Hits. Anyway, he *could* read a box score and he learned how to follow a ball game on the radio."

Sealed off by his profound shyness and unwilling to fish, Joe followed Tom and Vince and found his pleasure on local ball fields. He played for the Salesian Boys Club team, called the Jolly Knights, and in every weekend pickup game he could find. It would take some time for Joe to discover his natural defensive position, but, Tom said, "Joe could always hit like hell."

It is an oft-told story. A shy and lonely boy, the social-club wallflower, steps onto a ball field and suddenly assumes the mantle of grace and confidence and strength. The game becomes his escape and in a sense his love. It offers a small world in which he tastes the mead of triumph. Everything in his young life but this game came hard to Joe DiMaggio: schoolwork, friendship, dating, and resisting his father's insistence that he fish for a living. Baseball came with delight and ease. He could feel the stardom within him even before he understood quite what it might become.

He dropped out of Galileo High School and then he had to contribute to his father's household. The only work he could find was in a factory that bottled orange juice. "Peeling oranges eight hours a day," DiMaggio says, "is one lousy way to make a living."

According to one story, Joe won a job with the San Francisco Seals solely on the recommendation of his brother Vince. Actually, a sandlot coach and scout named Edward "Spike" Hennessy had been watching Joe for years. Hennessy brought him to Charles Graham, who owned the Seals, during the summer of 1932, when the team was mired in last place. Graham watched Joe hit and run and throw and signed him. It was late in a losing year and DiMaggio only played in 3 games. But the next season, when he was eighteen, DiMaggio proceeded directly from obscurity to California fame. There were no stops on this particular express train. Joe became a wonder of the Pacific Coast League with a suddenness that startled and delighted everyone, including himself.

Minor league teams today are stocked with ballplayers provided by major league organizations. That is to say, an outfielder playing for the Oneonta Yankees in upstate New York is already the contractual property of the New York Yankees. The major league team positions him in Oneonta to develop his skills. He will advance to more demanding teams according to the patterns of his development and the whims of the Yankee farm director.

In DiMaggio's youth minor league teams were independent. They hired the best talent they could find—much was local—and then sold the contracts of their best players to major league teams, the profits going into the minor league club's bank account. DiMaggio's advancement would depend first on his success and second on the ability of Charley Graham to get the price he wanted from a major league club. The business side brought DiMaggio his first baseball storms.

At the age of eighteen, DiMaggio played 187 games for the Seals and batted .340. He hit safely in 61 consecutive games, breaking a Pacific Coast League record that had stood since 1915. He also hit 29 home runs and batted in 169 runs. Every one of the sixteen major league teams assigned at least one scout to consider him. He was quite suddenly the most sought-after minor league player in the country, and it would be a long time, if ever, before he had to peel oranges again.

His teammates admired his talent, liked him personally, but teased him for his solemn, withdrawn ways. Since he seldom changed expression, they nicknamed him "Dead-pan Dan." This faded quickly. In New York he became Joltin' Joe.

His slugging captured all of San Francisco, and when he broke the record for consecutive hits, one reporter remembered, "the entire North Beach Italian section was in the stands. When he got the hit, his mother and his sisters rushed onto the field at Seals Stadium and kissed him in front of the whole crowd."

Later, when DiMaggio was given an award, he had to make an acceptance speech at home plate. Trainer Bobby Johnson helped prepare it and the two rehearsed the lines over and over while Johnson gave DiMaggio a rubdown. But as DiMaggio walked to the plate, he began to tremble. He reddened, kicked his spikes, and muttered, "Thank you."

"That was a great speech, Joe," Bobby Johnson said. "Truly outstanding."

Where some eighteen-year-olds who are newly arrived might simply have ridden the fluffy crowds of glory, DiMaggio, always solemn and becoming calculating, wanted more than awards and kisses for his exploits. He wanted cash.

Tom DiMaggio called on Charley Graham in the Seals offices and said that his kid brother Joe was a helluva ballplayer and a helluva major league prospect. Graham agreed. "So when you sell Joe's contract to a major league team," Tom said. "Joe's gotta get a cut of what you get."

Graham said that was unthinkable. He would keep the profits. He had given Joe his chance.

"Unless Joe gets a fair cut," Tom said, "he'll just pull out of baseball."

"And do what?" Graham said.

"He'll be a crab fisherman and make his living doing that."

Joe, of course, despised crab fishing, but Tom, riding his formidable bluff, said, "I'll take my brother out of baseball. He does what I tell him. Then you won't have any contract to sell."

Cowed, Graham agreed to pay DiMaggio $6,500—the price of a comfortable house during the Depression—out of the proceeds of the sale. He then fixed a price tag of $75,000 on DiMaggio's contract and waited for bidders to call.

No major league team was anxious to spend that much money for one player during the Depression. Graham stuck to his figure and found no takers. Early in the 1934 season, DiMaggio's sophomore year in organized baseball, Joe played a doubleheader at Seals Stadium, dined with one of his married sisters, and caught a jitney to the family apartment on Taylor Street. The little bus was crowded and DiMaggio had to sit in a cramped position. When he got off his left knee "popped like a pistol shot." The pain was so fierce that he collapsed. He later described it as "a whole set of aching teeth in my knee."

He limped badly the next day and the knee was placed in a cast. DiMaggio would have to stay out of baseball for six weeks. Graham would have to discard the $75,000 price tag. DiMaggio was now a risk, damaged goods.

He recovered and batted .341 in 1934, but he missed more than 70 games. Some hard bargaining followed, and the Yankees finally agreed to buy DiMaggio that November for $25,000 and five journeymen athletes they would ship to the Seals. The names may be important only to trivia gamesmen, but they were pitchers Jim Densmore and Floyd Newkirk out-fielder Ted Norbert, first baseman Les Powers, and third baseman Ed Farrell.

It was an excellent sale for the time, but not the mammoth deal that Graham had anticipated. Since the price was so low, he told Ed Barrow of the Yankees that he wanted DiMaggio

to play one more season in San Francisco "to help the gate."
Barrow agreed.

DiMaggio batted .398 in 1935 and the Seals won the Pacific Coast League pennant. DiMaggio, now approaching his
twenty-first birthday, was voted the Most Valuable Player in
the league. That season the Yankees finished second to the
Detroit Tigers, and Barrow would subsequently insist "if we'd
had Joe, we would have won that one in 1935." Even so,
Barrow said that the $25,000 purchase of DiMaggio "was the
best single deal I ever made."

The season of 1935 was a golden one in DiMaggio's baseball history. Lefty O'Doul, his boyhood hero, became the
manager of the San Francisco club, and worked to show Di-
Maggio how to pull the ball sharply: hit it toward left field
rather than to more distant fences in center. To this day he
makes a point of thanking O'Doul for splendid batting coaching fifty years ago.

DiMaggio learned from O'Doul and some others what the
Yankees expected of their ballplayers. Play like hell and keep
your mouth shut. Tommy Laird, a San Francisco newspaperman, took it on himself to be DiMaggio's press adviser.
"When you get up to the big time," Laird said, "don't let
those New York newspaper guys, who're going to grab hold of
you as soon as you show up, put words in your mouth. They'll
make you sound like a blowhard. Don't say a word. Don't put
yourself on a spot. And don't let the newspapermen put you
on a spot."

DiMaggio listened and nodded. He did not say a word.

Two star Yankee ballplayers with Italian-American backgrounds lived in the San Francisco area: second baseman
Tony (Poosh 'Em Up) Lazzeri and Frank Crosetti, a notably
skillful shortstop. Lazzeri bought what Crosetti remembers as
"a beautiful Ford sedan" to drive to spring training at St. Petersburg, Florida, in 1936. With some urging from the Yankee
front office, the two veterans agreed to take DiMaggio with

them on the long adventure of the motor trip. Each man had to put up $15 for his share. "I think we had to add another five dollars to make it," Crosetti says. "Anyway, we got by on fifty bucks, three guys, eating, sleeping, gas, everything for the whole damn way."

Lazzerri and Crosetti shared the driving and then—it may have been in Texas; it may have been in Alabama—Lazzerri turned to DiMaggio in the backseat and said, "Okay, champ. It's your turn to drive."

"I don't know how to drive," DiMaggio said.

Lazzeri turned to Crosetti. "Let's throw the bum out and let him walk the rest of the way."

DiMaggio took it with a forced grin. He was a superstar rookie, but a rookie still.

Lazzeri timed his driving so that they would not arrive in St. Petersburg until late on the evening of March 1. That way, he thought, DiMaggio would be protected from an immediate onslaught by reporters. The idea was to ease DiMaggio's entry into the major leagues, to keep him free from the pressures of the aggressive New York press.

But hiding DiMaggio's baseball greatness was as difficult as hiding Marilyn Monroe's beauty.

After watching DiMaggio take batting practice the next day, Joe's first day in a major league camp, Dan M. Daniel of the *New York World-Telegram* wrote: "Here is the replacement for Babe Ruth."

Chapter ★ 3

The Dead Have No Secrets

She has given up her closest secrets in death. We know, because one of her housemaids has informed us with bubbling lechery, that her pubic hair was dark, not blond, and that this troubled her inordinately. Marilyn told reporters that she liked to feel "blond all over." Sometimes she used a toothbrush to apply peroxide to the offending curls, fulfilling her pursuit for golden fleece. We know on another level, because a number of intellectuals including Arthur Miller have confirmed it, that she seriously doubted her own intelligence, which was both quick and high, without being either formally shaped or disciplined. She tried to write good free verse, without much success, and she lusted like a true daughter of art to become A Serious Actress. But stepping beyond the dizzy-blonde roles that made her famous undid her poise in embarrassing ways. Once, when she agreed to play a scene from Eugene O'Neill's *Anna Christie* at the Actors Studio in New York, she became so frightened that she urinated into her underpants.

She was chronically late, generally hyperactive, willful, impulsive, tender, and tough, and incapable of having children. This last failing troubled the innermost places of her psyche. During her marriage to Miller, she suffered an ectopic pregnancy, the lodging of an embryo in a fallopian tube. When the condition erupted into a medical emergency on one charged night in Manhattan, she lay in bed crying out, not only in pain, but in misery. An ectopic pregnancy can hurt fiercely, but as she waited for an ambulance in an elegant apartment on East Fifty-seventh Street, she suffered because she felt she was a flawed and incomplete woman. Movie star, love goddess, the very embodiment of one American image of sexuality, she could not, as the doctors put it, carry a child to term. Was her femininity, indeed her person, really whole?

An eager and babbling procession of psychiatric professionals has speculated that she was sexually frigid. That is a common-enough game among certain analysts, standing behind a professional mask and theorizing about patients they have never met, let alone treated. More conservative therapists dismiss such comments as pop psych that demeans the craft. But the pop psych still persists, along with her legend.

As this specific variety is applied to Marilyn (and to some others of surpassing beauty), the woman is expected to conduct herself as a sexual paradigm, in public appearances, in films, in all her working life. She is coiffed and clothed to a smoothness beyond reality. All this becomes a burden, a kind of emotional pressure more acute than that imposed by dark pubic hair. Away from the public and the cameras, alone in bed with one man, the woman feels that she must deliver at a superhuman level of eroticism. Of course, she cannot. Result: blocked neural paths and distorted emotional patterns. The woman remains frozen at a high level of sexual excitement, but is quite unable to crest. Her adventure ends in writhing anticlimax. After the man has quit her side, and perhaps returned to the less exotic lady who is his wife, the love object lies alone.

But men who slept with Marilyn did not simply return to their other lives, their other women, privately congratulating themselves on having made a notable conquest. They returned to their other lives, all right, but a fair percentage of Marilyn's extensive collection of bedmates could not resist the urge to boast.

I met one of her lovers on a recent California trip and asked him directly about the frigidity reports. We were seated at the bar of a Los Angeles version of an English pub.

"We went at it for about six months," said the man, now white-haired and round of belly. "Let me tell you this. Marilyn was the best cocksucker in Hollywood."

Certainly in the late stages of her life, Marilyn loved having intercourse. Along with talking to her analyst, it was a favorite form of recreation. On the testimony of many, she reached orgasm quite normally, which is to say much of the time when her lover had reasonably proficient technique and displayed a decent concern for her desires. (Countertestimony, so to speak, from several women who knew him, suggests that DiMaggio was an adroit, compassionate, and notably arousing lover.)

Marilyn turned cold when men approached her as a slab of beef, or tried to order her into bed, announcing in an arrogant way that a fast romp would further her career. She despised being treated like a tramp. But there is nothing abnormal about that. She wanted always, desperately and in the end pathetically, for others to understand "my feelings."

We know that when she killed herself on August 4, 1962, Marilyn needed a pedicure. Polish had flaked from her toenails. A dark patch showed near the part in her hair. There was dirt under her fingernails. One of her friends, Ruppert Allan, who handled her publicity for several years, says semiseriously that Marilyn could not have intended to kill herself that night "because she was too vain to have allowed herself to lie in a coffin with a dark patch in that blond hair." But before the final, defiant, hysterical deed that is suicide, no one, not even Marilyn Monroe, is necessarily concerned with grooming. If you can think rationally in the circumstance, itself a sort of contradiction, you know that there will be ample time after your last faltering gasp for beauticians to busy themselves with sprucing up your corpse.

Marilyn died not by accident. She had been obsessed with suicide for at least five years and had played with the idea when she was little more than a teenager. She had made a pact with her friend Norman Rosten, a poet and playwright. If either ever felt inclined to jump from a high ledge, one would call the other. She did telephone Rosten on the day before she died, but chattered with incessant gaiety. Rosten says in sorrow today, "Maybe I missed a signal."

Indeed, Marilyn had tried suicide at least twice before she died. On one occasion, she shoved clumps of sleeping pills into her mouth, but then the terror of death so clutched her that her mouth dried and she could not swallow properly. She lay on her back, waiting for her natural body heat to melt the pills concealed within her mouth and for the drug—it was Nembutal—to drip slowly into her gullet. She was lying that way when someone found her and called an ambulance.

So she was, to say the least, a handful, rife with conflicts and terrors, famished for praise, but capable of arrogance and rage, the infinitely beautiful and infinitely lost American Blonde. "When she came to visit us in Brooklyn Heights," Norman Rosten recalls, "she always insisted on helping out with the dishes. She wanted very much to be regarded as a regular person, one of the family, you might say. But"— Rosten pauses to select his words—"she never quite could let you forget that she was a movie star."

Curiously, although we know so many of her intimacies, certain hard facts about her beginnings remain clouded. She was buffeted about during childhood and she told that part of her life story in many different ways at many times. She lived in eleven foster homes. Or she lived in six. She didn't really remember; there were so many. Someone, "a deranged neighbor," tried to smother her with a pillow when she was two. Or maybe not. Someone molested her when she was six, or was it twelve, or, no, it was not mere molestation. It was actual rape. That was how she lost her virginity. She loved her first husband, Jim Dougherty; in fact, DiMaggio reminded her of Jim. Or else, she never loved Dougherty at all. She only married him to avoid being sent back to a Los Angeles orphanage. One frustrated reporter who interviewed Marilyn across a number of years concluded that she was a mythomaniac.

She liked to recount one persistent childhood dream. "I was standing up in church," she said, "without any clothes on, and all the people there were lying on the floor of the church and I walked naked with a sense of freedom over their prostrate forms, being careful not to step on anyone." The dream leaps out to the practitioners of pop psych. Simply regard Hollywood, which someone called a pagan pantheon, as the church. Cover her nakedness but only slightly. And it would seem that her girlhood dream came true.

Naked? Marilyn never appeared before her public any more naked than a discreet Renaissance nude. She worked in an era when filmmakers and even *Playboy* art directors followed the airbrush school of nudity. Women's bodies were as hairless and smooth as the body of a marble sculpture. But in her last movie, *Something's Got to Give,* she did strip naked for a swimming scene, a development that was shocking or at least startling in Hollywood in 1962.

She was depressed and physically ill, or at least thought that she was physically ill. She missed twelve of the first seventeen scheduled shooting days for *Something's Got to Give* and then the heads of Twentieth Century-Fox simply fired her. The cost of a missed shooting day is enormous. The whole film crew, electricians, lighting men, actors who do show up, and everyone else must still be paid, whether a scene gets to film or not.

So after she finally appeared naked before the cameras, she was thrown out of work. Nakedness, real nakedness, and then rejection.

What a hard, sad life.

Marilyn's family traces to Missouri, where her grandmother Della Hogan was born on a farm. Della ventured west during the 1890s, and in 1899 married one Otis Elmer Monroe. Marilyn's mother, Gladys, was born in California the next year.

Like one of those grizzled, beaten-up adventurers in *The Treasure of Sierra Madre,* Otis went off to Mexico to find his fortune. He never did. Della moved back to California and soon the long-ago marriage of Marilyn's grandparents unraveled.

Gladys married a man named Jack Baker, a native of Kentucky, and in this generation, too, there were marital storms. Gladys gave birth to a boy and a girl—the boy would die in childhood—before the daughter she called Norma Jeane entered the world at Los Angeles General Hospital on June 1, 1926. Norma Jeane would evolve into Marilyn Monroe.

Out of her restless background, Gladys Monroe Baker became a restless woman herself. She had numerous affairs, and by all the available testimony, Jack Baker was not the father of her third child. The real father may have been a salesman named C. Stanley Gifford. Or he may have been Gladys's second husband, Martin Edward Mortensen. He may have been a casual lover of whom we know nothing. Marilyn told the people who prepared her publicity biography for Fox that her father had died soon after her birth. Later, when Marilyn became famous, Mortensen bobbed up, alive and well, claiming fatherhood. Whatever, Norma Jeane Baker never knew a father when she was a child.

A woman named Jody Lawrence, who shared a foster

home with Marilyn for several years when both were in their early teens, offered a chilling account of the circumstances surrounding Marilyn's birth, which Marilyn had confided to her in youthful intimacy.

"After Gladys had her son and daughter by her first marriage," Jody Lawrence said, "she fell in love with a man—I won't name him—who was very prominent in the motion-picture business. They made love and had an illegitimate daughter, Norma Jeane.

"Gladys was a beautiful young woman, very warm and very vital. Jack Baker was cold and businesslike and reticent. I guess Gladys wasn't all that guarded because all of a sudden, Baker confronted her and said, 'That baby you're carrying is not mine.'

"One day Gladys went to work [as a film cutter at a studio] and left the little boy and girl with a baby-sitter. When she got home she found both the children and her husband gone. Baker left her a note that said, 'I've taken the children and you'll never find them again.'

"She gave birth to Norma Jeane, but after that, Gladys had a nervous breakdown. They had to put her in a sanitorium. That's what really happened when Marilyn Monroe was born."

Della Monroe, Gladys Baker—all the women we know in Marilyn's line—never had more than a precarious hold on mental health. Both would have to be confined in psychiatric wards along their difficult journeys through life. But there were also long periods when Della and her daughter seemed able to function normally.

By the time Marilyn was born in 1926, her grandmother Della was married for a second time, to a man called Grainger, who was connected to an oil company. They lived in Hawthorne, a Los Angeles suburb near what is now the Los Angeles International Airport. Gladys, possessed of a new baby but missing her husband and the other two children, reacted in a predictable way. She asked her mother to take her in. Della declined. She was having problems of her own with her new husband, and what this particular marriage did not need at this particular time was a troubled young woman with an infant child.

But Della knew someone who could help—for a fee. Across the street at 418 East Rhode Island Avenue lived a tall, dark-haired, very pious woman named Ida Bolender. The name of the street has since been changed and the address has become 459 East 134th Street. The sense of the neighborhood has altered, too. Sixty years ago it consisted mostly of bungalows, populated by the families of oil riggers and truck drivers. "Semirural and semipoor," was how Marilyn described it.

On June 12, 1926, eleven days after she was born, Marilyn was deposited at the home of Ida Bolender and Albert Wayne Bolender, a postman. The Bolenders ran what county officials called a "registered home for foster children." That is, they were legally entitled to take in strays and to charge the biologic parents a reasonable amount for room and board. Over the years, Ida Bolender "accommodated" more than forty homeless children. Before Gladys checked herself into a sanitorium, she agreed to pay $25 monthly to the Bolenders to provide for her infant daughter.

Dickensian. The foster home has a California-Dickensian ring. Ida Bolender was a woman who liked to read in a limited way—she especially admired the poetry of Edna St. Vincent Millay. But that fondness for a sensual lyric poetess played against a background of severe religiosity. Ida Bolender passionately despised sin.

She would not tolerate sin in any form and you had to be ever careful, ever watchful, because sin could appear in many ways. Smoking. Drinking. Swearing. Playing cards. Dancing. Those were the devil's ways and children had to be protected from them. Playacting. That was another of the devil's pastimes. If the children fell into sin, they would surely burn forever in the sulfurous fires of hell. To protect them, the most spirited children simply had to be spanked. It wasn't a question of giving pain. It was a question of saving the children.

Across the street, Della Grainger wanted to keep an eye on her new granddaughter, but Della herself was something of a religious zealot. She became a disciple of Aimee Semple McPherson, an evangelist who enjoyed great currency in the 1920s and might have been even more successful if hormones had run less fiercely through her blood.

McPherson founded the Four Square Gospel Church, where she preached, with riveting intensity, the glories of embracing the Lord, Jesus Christ, and the ways of saintliness on earth. She ran a roofed-in equivalent of the old gospel tent shows, holding up the bright promises of heaven, warning of the alternative, and collecting thousands and thousands of dollars for her crusade. The Los Angeles area in the 1920s was an inchoate mix—some say it still is—of moviemakers and adventurers, roustabouts and poets, and others simply tired of snow. Although old Los Angeles attracted its share of gifted and practical people, it also drew hundreds of thousands from the East and the Midwest who came armed only with an illusion of what life would be in the golden West. ("Heaven can wait, honey. We're going to California.")

Jewish pharmacists from Brooklyn found themselves living next to Baptist laborers from Tennessee. The collection of cities that developed in the Los Angeles basin was as disparate as any American area has ever been. The dreams of California gold died painfully when it turned out you had to work in Los Angeles just as hard as you had worked in Chicago or Des Moines. There was no gold waiting to be panned, except for a few who found it figuratively in films or real estate or oil or the developing aircraft industry. Swarms of dreamily ambitious people discovered that you could be as broke in Los Angeles as you had been back home. You had gained warmer weather. You had lost your roots.

In that setting, religion became one's last best hope. Skeptics might sing, "You'll eat pie in the sky when you die," but most people cannot stand very much skepticism. Aimee McPherson, Sister Aimee, swore from her Four Square Pulpit that all you had to do was love the Lord, accept the Lord, embrace the Lord, and happiness would be your lot. Shun sin. Abjure fornication. Contribute to the Four Square Gospel Church and thou shalt be saved.

Unfortunately for Sister Aimee, she herself could not abjure fornication. She went off to a California desert retreat for a few weeks of carnal romping with a married employee of her church. (He was married, all right, but not to Sister Aimee.) Her sudden disappearance caused a furor, and when she returned Sister Aimee claimed that she had been kidnapped. Even in Los Angeles of the 1920s that story did not wash, and in time truth, in its persistent way, surfaced. The great gospel preacher was both an adulteress and a liar. Sister Aimee and her church faded. In 1944 she died from an overdose of sleeping pills. This was the woman Della and Gladys picked to baptize the infant who would become Marilyn Monroe.

Ida Bolender had a great deal to say about her most illustrious ward when a journalist tracked her down late in her life. (This was a splendid piece of reporting since Marilyn had never mentioned Ida to the press until that time.) The reporter found a "tall, gray-haired woman, with horn-rimmed glasses, who wore false teeth." She still lived in Hawthorne, just next door to the bungalow in which she had served as foster mother to Marilyn.

"I've often thought of telling somebody about Marilyn," Ida began, "but I just didn't know whom to get in touch with. Marilyn, or Norma Jeane as we called her, that being her name, was a rather quiet child, but full of personality. My husband, Albert Wayne, and I had adopted a boy named Lester, and Norma Jeane and Lester were very bright children. She lived with me till she was eight, you know.

"They'd sit in high chairs and jabber back and forth to each other before they were even a year old. Norma Jeane had her first teeth early, at three or four months. She walked in her crib when she was only seven months. She was precocious. She called me Aunt Ida."

At this point, Aunt Ida Bolender became defensive. "I can't understand stories about Marilyn being an ugly duckling, or being abandoned, or anything like that. She was never neglected. I looked after her and her mother, Gladys, provided the means for her support. Gladys also bought her clothes, beautiful things, made of taffeta and fine materials. We sent her to Washington School here in Hawthorne until she was eight. She made good grades in school. Lots of folks in Hawthorne still remember Norma Jeane."

The old lady brightened and even made a faintly risqué joke. "Now that Norma Jeane is such a big movie star, I joke with my adopted son Lester.

"I tell him that when he was one year old he rode around in the same perambulator with Marilyn Monroe."

Descriptions of the Bolender household from Marilyn and others are less bland. The couple made ends meet not only on Albert's salary but on the child-support checks they received. At times as many as six children boarded with the Bolenders, which meant an extra $150 a month.

It was good to have the money, there was a certain profit in a career of foster-parenting, but there was also a problem. The children were noisy, demanding, active—in short, children. After a day of delivering mail, Albert wanted quiet in his crowded bungalow home. When a child became boisterous, Albert went for his leather razor strap, bent the child over his knees, pulled off the clothing, and whipped. Marilyn said that she could always remember the feel of Albert's leather on her bare buttocks.

The Bolenders insisted on ritual churchgoing—twice each Sunday and once or twice during the week. There were constant lectures, they were more like sermons, against all the forms of sin that the Bolenders could imagine. The children had to be taught to work. Marilyn said she washed dishes and scrubbed floors before she was five.

Marilyn always liked games of pretend—"playacting," Ida Bolender called it—and when the Bolenders forbade such innocent activity, Marilyn retreated to a woodshed. If she was caught playacting there, she might be strapped.

At five or six, she said she began to hear "a noise in my head at night," and she became "quieter and more withdrawn."

"We have to watch that one very carefully," Ida told Albert Wayne one evening, indicating Marilyn. Ida pointed toward her own head, and made a circular gesture indicating insanity. "It's in her family, you know."

There is some reason to suspect that Albert Bolender did not strap Marilyn purely to save her from a future of brimstone. Amid all the noise of children, amid all the repressions of fundamentalist religiosity, he may have enjoyed having his way with the abandoned little blond girl. In later years Marilyn retained a particular sensitivity about her backside, that backside Groucho Marx proclaimed as the greatest of all the bottom ends of Hollywood. Discussing her figure, of which she was understandably proud, Marilyn sometimes added a cautionary, "Except my ass is too big."

Ida Bolender seemed glad to talk to a reporter, happy for the attention he offered her. There were more things, she said, that she wanted to get off her chest.

"Della [the grandmother] lived nearby," Aunt Ida said, "and no, she wasn't much help in bringing up Norma Jeane. You see about the time that Norma Jeane was one year old, Della just went insane. I remember it very clearly. Della ran down the sidewalk one day naked. She didn't have a stitch of clothing on. She came up to our house and tried to kick the door down, I don't know why. They had to take her away. So that was that for Della. I'm told she died violent in a straitjacket at Norwalk Hospital.

"Gladys [the mother] had a real bad breakdown when Norma Jeane was about nine. She tried to take her life with sleeping pills. Even though it ran in the family, I think Gladys got crazy from overwork. She always worked real hard. She drove herself. Anyway, this friend of hers named Grace

McKee [a film librarian] told me the doctors at Norwalk Hospital found out that a part of Gladys's brain had collapsed. It was worn out like the inner tube from a tire. Something like that can never be really repaired.

"Well, Grace was Gladys's friend, so she took things into her own hands and got herself appointed the legal guardian of Norma Jeane, who you call Marilyn Monroe. Grace McKee worked hard, too, and she couldn't look after Norma Jeane all the time, but Grace McKee's aunt, whose name was Ana Lower, did. Most of the time, until she got married, Norma Jeane lived with Grace or Ana Lower. I don't know where all those stories come from about Norma Jeane being in eleven different foster homes."

Some came from Marilyn herself.

"Well maybe she doesn't exactly remember everything. She always was one to make up stories."

Through Ida Bolender's primarily cheerful and even caring manner, traces of severity broke through. "Have you seen many of Norma Jeane's movies?" the reporter asked.

"No. I haven't seen any. I'm not a moviegoer. I'm a churchgoer. And most churchgoers don't go to the movies."

What did Ida think of Norma Jeane, as Marilyn Monroe, becoming a famous star?

A slight shrug. The thin lips pressed together over the false teeth. "It's her life. If she wants to live it that way . . . well, you can't tell other people what to do. I'd like to see her. I love her," Ida Bolender said, but there was not much love in Ida's tone.

The tale is strange and wrenching. Ida emerges not simply as a survivor, in the midst of other people's woe, but as an American gothic, grim as a midwestern prairie under February winds. The foster home, which Ida tried to portray as a houseful of love, was a constantly changing scene, with vagrant children shuttling in and out, each with his own dreams and problems and needs. Marilyn would remember occasionally having to take her bath last "after five other kids had used that same bath water." Penury, godliness, and low water bills were watchwords to the Bolenders. And then, of course, there was the leather razor strap.

Norma Jeane Baker was the four-thousand-four-hundred-and-sixty-third child admitted to the Los Angeles Orphans' Society Home when she was accepted there at the age of nine on September 13, 1935. (That was the year Joe DiMaggio batted .398 for the San Francisco Seals.) Gladys was off in the haze of mental illness. Della was dead. And the Bolenders simply would not look after her anymore.

Margaret Ingram, a former superintendent of the orphanage, pulled out a file some time ago and began, "Baker. Mortensen. DiMaggio. Monroe. You can choose any name you like. She's had so many."

The home itself consisted of a grouping of colonial-style red-brick buildings near the old RKO studio in Hollywood. The orphanage was privately endowed. It was opened first in downtown Los Angeles in 1911, and could provide reasonably attentive care for the children who found themselves grouped there. Attentive care, but group living still, more of the group living that Marilyn had tried to contend with at the Bolenders. In the girls' dormitory the children slept, twelve metal beds to a room.

Miss Ingram poured through Marilyn's case history, reading off comments first dryly and then with a touch of controlled passion.

"Behavior normal. Slept well. Bright. Smiling. Considered normal child. Well liked by others. Friendly. Appeared to have poise and self-assurance. Mother ill. Mentally ill. In hospital. That worried her."

As Miss Ingram continued to review the file, her face became troubled. "I can't show you everything in here," she said. "Our files are confidential, but you know some of these family cases are hurtful even to read. And this one. Marilyn. Well, with no father and the mental illness and the spankings

and the rest, this is about the saddest background of any child
I've ever seen."

Marilyn remembered "my mother getting sick, so the
Bolenders couldn't keep me anymore. And I had to go in this
car to the orphanage and when I got out of the car my feet
absolutely wouldn't move on the sidewalk. I saw a big black
sign with bright gold lettering. I thought it said 'Orphan.' I
don't know what it really said. I never could spell very well.
They had to drag me in by force and all the time I was trying
to tell them that I was *not* an orphan."

According to Marilyn she was assigned to wash dishes: a
hundred plates, a hundred cups, a hundred knives, forks, and
spoons. "I did that three times a day," she said, "seven days a
week. They paid me five cents a month. I had to give most of the
pennies back in the chapel on Sunday, but I always kept one—a
penny a month—so I could buy a ribbon for my hair."

Miss Ingram said that Marilyn exaggerated the demands of
life in the orphanage. "Children were never paid for chores,"
she said. "If the parents or guardians did not provide spending money, our society would. I think it was five cents a day—
not a week—when Marilyn was there. All the children, not
only Marilyn, shared the jobs that had to be done. Kitchen
chores, making their own beds, keeping the dormitory clean."

Whatever, Marilyn always said she hated her life in the
orphanage. She left on June 26, 1937. (DiMaggio was by then
a prince of New York in his sophomore season with the Yankees.) The reason, Miss Ingram said, was that "this particular
child had had enough of group living and badly needed some
family life. She went from us to her appointed guardian,
Grace McKee Goddard."

Once, in 1948, when Marilyn was living at the Studio
Club, a residence for actresses at 1215 Lodi Place in Los Angeles, she returned for a visit to the orphanage. She signed
the register in a neat hand: "Marilyn Monroe; maiden name,
Norma Jeane Baker."

Miss Ingram remarked to a reporter that Marilyn "was
certainly our most glamorous child. She's gotten far more

publicity than any of the judges we've turned out." Then Miss Ingram mentioned the orphanage's building program. "Tell Marilyn," she said, "that we want to make the place all that it wasn't when she was a little girl here."

Unalloyed compassion? Not quite. "Also tell Marilyn," Miss Ingram said, "that we need another hundred thousand dollars."

The late Grace McKee Goddard, who stepped forward as Marilyn's legal guardian in 1937, was a warm-spirited woman whose passion for good deeds exceeded her ability to accomplish them. She worked at various studio jobs, including her hitch as a film librarian, never getting very far ahead. Her husband, Ervin Sillaman "Doc" Goddard, was employed in an aircraft factory and at home he tinkered with a variety of inventions. He liked to talk about the day when all his patents came through and "everybody would be rich." Of course, that day never arrived. When Grace died, Doc Goddard had to take a job as a construction worker in Bakersfield.

Marilyn was released into the care of these rather kindly people. Kind but improvident. They did not feel they could afford to take her in. So Marilyn was, so to speak, farmed out. She was sent to live with a family in Compton for a time. She later complained that the Compton family "kept traveling. I was always on the road. I never had a sense of where home was." It was across the period from 1937 until her marriage to James Dougherty on June 19, 1942, that Marilyn suffered her most battering years of drift. She may have lived in as many as six different homes. She saw alcoholism, felt neglect, and was almost certainly fondled by men who were supposed to be foster fathers. It was difficult for her to speak about those years.

Exactly what happened to the abandoned child called Norma Jeane in the casual way stations where she had to live carries us onto the turf of novelists. Marilyn, never a reliable source about herself, regarded this period with a sense of shame. So complex piled upon complex. Nobody really wanted to take her in; nobody would keep her. What was wrong? What was wrong with *her*? "I always had to try to please the people that I lived with," she said once, "because otherwise I was afraid they might throw me out. And I was a good girl, but a lot of the time, the people didn't notice." She shook her head, looked sad, and very quickly began to speak of something else.

When at length the Goddards decided that they could afford to take Marilyn into their home, she entered Van Nuys High School and grew close to Doc Goddard's daughter, who became the starlet at Paramount who called herself Jody Lawrence. "My stepmother," Jody said, "couldn't have children herself, so she offered to take in almost every baby that her friends or relatives couldn't handle. She meant well, but she couldn't pull off everything she wanted to. And the house was a dump."

It was also a place of implausible dreams. Each day Grace came back from her job at Columbia Pictures with stories of the studio and stars. Most nights Doc went into his little workshop to create that one invention that would carry him to El Dorado. A household large on dreams and short on cash.

Marilyn fantasized about meeting real movie stars. Clark Gable was her special favorite. She hung a picture of Gable in the room she shared with Jody. "We were both neurotic children," Jody said later. (Could Marilyn have been anything else, given her background?) "That's the reason why we both were drawn to Hollywood as a way of life. Look, we lived in this household where there were some stresses. At times we were supposed to be, I don't know, invisible. We couldn't accept the way things really were, so we pretended things were different, and when the adults were around we mostly clammed up.

"I remember there were two huge pepper trees on the front lawn. Marilyn and I built a tree house. We used to crawl up there when we thought we'd done something that might get us into trouble. We knew my father and my stepmother couldn't climb after us. The tree house was our escape. We called it our 'safe place.'"

Jody was an attractive, sad-eyed young woman who wore her hair drawn back in a prim style. "Marilyn and I," she said, "don't really like to put on makeup when we aren't working. Makeup is for our business, the movies. We both have nice skins. We both believe, Why destroy our skins with makeup when we don't have to? And all that talk, that you have to sleep around to get ahead in the business . . . well, I'd certainly never do that myself."

There was a strain of Hollywood's peculiar schizophrenia in the talk of the young actress with the Puritan hairstyle. (As far as I know, her career never met with much success.) Along the way to making money, the principal business of Hollywood is marketing and selling sex, putting up on the big screen men and women whose images titillate the rest of us. In Marilyn's movie time, the sex was glossy and not quite real, the matings of gods and goddesses whom we never saw undressed and who seldom perspired. Sophisticated European filmmakers derided the sex in Hollywood movies as an enactment of childish fantasies and little more.

But the American industry called Hollywood reflected the American times, and the country was not yet ready for mass, public earthiness. The studios even set up their own film review board (called the Hays office), censoring themselves to ward off censorship from without. The Hays office decreed that no couple, married or not, could appear together in a double bed. Hollywood was twin-bed country, even for such wholesome bumpkins as Blondie and Dagwood Bumstead. No actress could appear more than briefly in a nightgown. So Hollywood lovers, in their twin beds, always slept with bathrobes placed within a forearm's reach. Kisses had to be brief—less than five seconds—and while kissing, the couples kept their mouths closed. No director could show the inside of a woman's thigh, much less her navel. The language the actors used could have passed in Aimee McPherson's Four

Square Gospel Church. Allowing Clark Gable to pronounce the word "damn" in the final reel of *Gone With the Wind* became a minor national issue. (Gable said it and the nation survived.)

An appearance of propriety was the order of the era on film, but it was a teasing propriety. One of the horny moviegoers of my own youth liked to say, "I want to see what happens *between* the dissolves."

Off camera, on the other hand, no Hays office issued Protestant-ethic decrees. In mansions at Holmby Hills and in beach houses at Malibu, bedsprings creaked under all the rolling bodies as studio executives demanded what were, to say the least, fringe benefits, and the young actresses pumped away toward what they hoped would be the top. The distinction between glossy film sex and real sex and the distinction between public ethics and private behavior would have been difficult to sort out for anyone. It was excruciating for Marilyn Monroe, who had grown up without consistent guidance.

Today, to be sure, Hollywood is a different country and the sex has literally become more hairy. A somewhat gamey Suzanne Somers poses naked for *Playboy* and Julie Andrews, with her refined Christmas-morning appeal, bares firm breasts to the camera in a movie called *S.O.B.*, directed by, of all people, her husband.

The movie Marilyn that would emerge combined the innocence of old Hollywood films with a suggestion that her blood ran hot off camera. The interviewer came away with a similar impression of Jody Lawrence, Marilyn's one-time best friend, who said she would not sleep with producers—which may well be true, because the road Jody traveled led to obscurity.

Pictures of Marilyn at Van Nuys High School show a pretty girl with fluffy light-brown hair, who is beautifully constructed but whose face is less than a classic model of beauty. Against perfectionist standards, the tip of her nose appears a bit too fleshy and her jaw is not quite symmetrical. In molding her movie face, Marilyn underwent plastic surgery at least once. But in high school she was extremely attractive. Boys noticed her. She seems to have thrived.

The next major episode on Marilyn's path toward Joe the Slugger was her marriage to Jim Dougherty, a handsome, outgoing young man who had been a leader of his class at Van Nuys High and was a next-door neighbor of Doc and Grace McKee Goddard. According to Dougherty, it was a love match. According to Marilyn, she was pushed. The Goddards, she said, were going through another of their recurrent financial crises as Marilyn passed her sixteenth birthday in 1942. One charged evening they said they could no longer afford to keep Marilyn in their household. "Grace told me what she wanted in a nice way. But it came down to the fact that I had to either marry Jim or go back to living in the orphanage. I'd had enough of the orphanage. More than enough. What could I do? I got married."

Marriage frightened Marilyn. She was streetwise, or perhaps foster-homewise, but despite her looks and build and the various molestations, still a sexual innocent. "How can I get married?" she said to Grace. "I don't know anything about sex."

Grace told her not to worry. "Jim," she said, "will teach you everything you need to know."

When they married, Marilyn was sixteen. Dougherty was twenty-one and employed in an aircraft factory. They settled first with Dougherty's family, and Marilyn was so childlike that she brought several dolls into her new home. One of Dougherty's brothers undertook to teach her dice and in the learning process Marilyn bet and lost a favorite doll. Dougherty found her in tears. "I lost my doll at crappies," she said, amid sobs. Dougherty had to reclaim it for her before she was able to stop crying.

After she was introduced to the rudiments of sex, she developed a passion for making love in a parked car. Dougherty found this somewhat vexing. A car was uncomfortable and besides, there was always the possibility of a passerby looking in through a window.

"What difference does it make?" Marilyn said. "We're *married.*"

They moved into a studio apartment, "a little fold-up bed place," Marilyn called it, and she found work in a defense plant as a paint sprayer. She was a bride and at the same time a child, trying to catch up with the world all at once, and she suffered from mood swings: Crying fits alternated with manic periods. In a moment of despair, she said afterward, she made a suicide attempt, "but not a very serious one." Dougherty, finding himself living with a real-life manic-depressive doll, joined the merchant marine in 1943. That was in effect the end of Marilyn's first marriage, although she and Dougherty were not divorced until 1946.

She was a teenager on her own, but now her good looks and her glorious figure began to assert themselves in positive ways. A photographer took publicity pictures of her at the defense plant, then guided her to the Blue Book School of Charm and Modeling in Hollywood, presided over by a woman with a name straight out of a B-movie boarding school: Miss Emmeline Snively. Miss Emmeline taught Marilyn how to strut and pivot. She told her to bleach her hair and to lower both her voice and her smile. "She smiled high," Miss Emmeline said, "and that made wrinkles." Miss Emmeline circulated sample photos and quickly Marilyn became a very busy model.

"I mostly answered calls for a girl in a bathing suit," Marilyn said, "but one month I was on five magazine covers: *U.S. Camera, Pageant, Family Circle,* where they had me hold a baby lamb, and men's magazines called *Hit or Miss* or something." She then stood five feet five and a half, weighed 118 pounds, and topped her beautifully sculpted figure with a look of innocence. She bought herself her first car, a 1935 Ford coupe, and promptly wrecked it. She began to be introduced to the rough-and-tumble inelegance of second-class sex in Hollywood.

"One day," she said, "after I smashed my car, I was waiting for a bus and this long dark-green Cadillac pulled up and the fellow said, 'Miss, I don't want you to think this is a pickup, but you could be a Goldwyn Girl.'"

Marilyn caught her breath. She said she thought, Good God, what I would give to be a Goldwyn Girl. (Not enough, as it would develop.)

It was a Saturday. Marilyn wore a $1.98 hat over her newly blonded hair and a wool dress that clung to her body. The man drove her to an office at the Goldwyn studios, which were all but deserted, found a script in a desk, and suggested that they read from a scene.

"This was one of those goddamned corny things," Marilyn said, "but I swear it happened just the way I'm telling it. He asked me to lift up my wool skirt so he could see my legs. Okay. Then he asked me to stretch out on the couch. Okay, but I insisted I had to keep on my little hat. He kept trying to get me to take my hat off.

"The hat and the wool dress stayed on. He made a long slow pass. I made a fast exit right back to Miss Emmeline Snively. And that's how I never became a Goldwyn Girl."

Marilyn enjoyed telling that sort of little coquette story, in which she emerged with her chastity intact. Sometimes she could confront darker experiences.

Once, when she was walking on Hollywood Boulevard, she found herself short of money. Confused, she approached a policeman and asked if he could help her cash a check. The policeman said he could, if she showed him suitable identification. He noted her address—she was living alone in a Burbank apartment—and escorted her into a shop where he was known.

That night Marilyn woke up in wild alarm. "I had just taken a sleeping pill"—she was having sleep difficulties before she was twenty years old—"and it sounded like someone was cutting the screen. I was wearing this very short nightgown. I'd had this dream once that somebody was cutting the screen and I thought this was still the dream. But it was really happening. I jumped out of bed, very groggy, and I saw this fellow. He had cut the screen and he was climbing through the window into my bedroom. I went running into the street in just my nightgown and the first place where I saw a light I asked them to call the police."

The neighbors obliged. When the police finally collared the intruder, he turned out to be the cop who had helped Marilyn cash the check. According to Marilyn, "he was taken off the police force." For years, she said, she would remember how the rogue cop looked when he was breaking in: "His eyes burning at me, his two eyes so close together."

After Marilyn told this story to a friend named Lucille Ryman, who worked at MGM, Ryman said, "You had to smile at that cop."

"I didn't," Marilyn said. "I mean I did. But in this business you have to smile at every man you see."

Ryman helped Marilyn find safer quarters at the Studio Club, where Marilyn shared a room with a young singer named Clarice Evans.

Despite the magazine covers, which made her the star of the Blue Book School of Charm, Marilyn was playing in the equivalent of the low minor leagues. To earn the closest thing that she could approximate to a steady living, she posed repeatedly for a calendar artist named Earl Moran. "He'd paint me in brief little costumes with red hair or black hair, whatever his mood was. He did a whole series of calendars and paid me five dollars an hour. That kept me eating."

Her forays to the studios produced bit parts, nothing more, and her struggle to manage her finances, and to have some finances to manage, led her to strip naked for the most famous of all the Monroe calendars. Here she posed for a man named Tom Kelley in what would become a staple of pop eroticism. Marilyn stretched out on red velvet, lying on her left side, looking over a shoulder with her mouth slightly open, in what can be read either as passion or as show of fearful embarrassment at having been caught naked by a stranger. Kelley sold his work to the John Baumgarth Company, which eventually peddled six million copies to the

American public. The company cleared about $750,000. Kelley earned $900. Marilyn earned $50.

As a star many years later—stardom struck Joe and Marilyn with different degrees of suddenness—she felt compelled to explain why she had stripped for Kelley. "I just couldn't keep up with my rent at the Studio Club," she said, "and they're pretty firm about rent over there. If you're two weeks behind, you can get kicked out. I was four weeks behind. So I called the photographer Tom Kelley for which [sic] I had modeled before and he had offered me the fifty dollars to pose nude. And I did it. And I paid my rent. Tom assured me that I'd never be recognized, and I wasn't much, until I became well known."

Her plea of need would seem to be enough to explain the airbrushed calendar photo, but Marilyn, caught between Hollywood sex and a puritan background, felt she had to explain further. There was absolutely nothing obscene or vulgar about the posing, she insisted. "Tom Kelley's wife was there all the time." She seemed to be missing the point. No one had accused her of having an affair with Kelley. The eventual appeal of the calendar, aside from Marilyn's beauty, was that a *movie star* had been caught naked. There were no similar portraits of Betty Grable or Rita Hayworth or Ava Gardner, at least no similar portraits that the public saw.

At length, Marilyn could look back on the adventure with a bit of humor, once she had learned how to mix, in her bewitching way, humor and sex. She autographed one of the six million calendars to a studio hand with these words: "Do you like me better with short hair?"

She would call her struggling years of modeling "just terribly morbid," a strange, foreshadowing phrase. A journalist described her at that time as "smothered by feelings of inferiority, swept by panics, countered by instincts as solid as an anvil. She took blows that would have smashed many people, but she did not fall apart."

She was driven not simply by the terrors of her childhood, but by cold, unrelenting ambition. Had she chosen, she could have remained Mrs. James E. Dougherty and become one more attractive housewife in the San Fernando Valley. Dougherty became a policeman in Van Nuys after World War II. (He since has moved to Maine.) He made one or two attempts to rebuild his crumbled marriage before he gave up and married somebody else.

Marilyn would have no more of her first husband. She pressed ahead, using her body, as surely as an athlete uses his, and then, when anyone suspected—how could anyone *not* suspect—that she was using breasts and bottom to move forward, she felt the weight of the old religiosity of Ida and Albert Wayne Bolender.

When she was pressed beyond those deflecting witty jokes about sex, she protested her own propriety with great seriousness and even a sense of hurt. How could anyone believe that little Norma Jeane, the diligent waif who went to church twice on Sundays, would ever do anything improper?

Tom Kelley's wife was there.

It wasn't vulgar.

But then, bobbing up like the sex drive itself, were the other jokes, the kind that no one made in Sunday School. *Do you like me better in short hair?*

She was experiencing a young womanhood in Los Angeles remarkably distinct from the youth of Joe DiMaggio in San Francisco. He had family, Roman Catholicism, and very tame dances at an Italian-American social club. She had foster homes, fundamentalism, modeling, pickups, rape attempts, and nudity.

But there was a subtle tie-in that allied them. He used his physique to play baseball. She used her body to get ahead.

The great future junction of Joe and Marilyn would not entirely be a meeting of minds.

When she wasn't modeling, Marilyn was tapping a tentative tap at Hollywood doors, trying, like ten thousand other pretty girls, to crack the movies. No one at first offered to wrap her splendid figure in a fat contract. Hollywood seldom, if ever, worked that simply. Rather, her wanderings and her ambitions led her into a gray country, between obscurity and fame, that is more or less policed by Hollywood agents.

In Beverly Hills one meets numbers of Hollywood agents who are scrupulous and hardworking, if always a little insecure. Then there are those who are not so scrupulous. The breed and indeed the entire ambience was summed up once by the late comedian Fred Allen. "You can take all of the compassion of the studios," Allen remarked, "put it into a thimble, and still have room for the heart of an agent."

Her modeling photos won Marilyn an interview with one Helen Ainsworth, a two-hundred-pound figure of a woman who was the head of the National Concert and Artist Corporation. (Hollywood agencies like to use the word "artist" in their titles, lest you conclude that they are peddling flesh.) Miss Ainsworth looked down at Marilyn from her vastness and proclaimed, "You'll go far. You have a virginal look."

Marilyn said thank you and found herself assigned by the agency to a man named Harry Lipton, who would later resurface in Hollywood's water-wheel life as the proprietor of Noel's Candies on La Cienega Boulevard. Lipton escorted her to all the studios where he had contacts and was able to get her interviewed for a minor film called *The Red House,* which would star Lon McCallister.

A director considered her and gave a quick no. "Your head," he said, "and Lon's head wouldn't be right together."

Howard Hughes, recovering from an airplane accident, saw a magazine picture of Marilyn and sent word that he might be interested in signing her. But for what? Agents draw no specific commissions from affairs.

Lipton was thinking that one over when one of his telephone calls was returned by Ben Lyon, the casting director at Twentieth Century-Fox. Marilyn later recounted the meeting.

Lyon looked at her professionally, then suddenly cried out, "It's like seeing Jean Harlow over again."

Marilyn blinked.

"Just looking at you," Lyon said, "I can tell. You're going to be one of the biggest stars in Hollywood someday."

Uncertain with praise, the waif suddenly pronounced a princess, Marilyn thought: "What is the matter with him?" Then, slowly and as it would turn out significantly, "This is like one of my dreams . . . or is it a nightmare?"

Lyon's next response was to tell the young woman that the name she was using, Norma Jeane Baker, lacked zest, oomph, star quality.

"For some of the magazines," Marilyn said, "I used another name. Jean Norman."

"Better," Lyon said, "but not much."

Marilyn mentioned that her mother's maiden name was Monroe. Lyon thought that was good. He decided that her grandfather was a descendant of President James Monroe. He looked at her carefully again and said, "you remind me of Harlow and Marilyn Miller. You know. The old singer." He played with combinations until he came up with Marilyn Monroe. Thus Norma Jeane, baptized in the Four Square Gospel Church, was rechristened in the less-than-holy offices of a studio.

"Well, I don't know," Norma Jeane said at the instant of the incarnation of Marilyn Monroe.

"The new name is great," Lyon insisted. "Very euphonious."

"Well, I don't know," she repeated. She later explained that one thing she *really* didn't know was what the word *euphonious* meant. She went on, "When I actually signed my first autograph, I had to go slow. I wasn't too sure how you spelled *Marilyn*. You know. Where the *i* went and where you put the *y*."

Lyon signed her to a contract at $75 a week. She posed for still more processions of photographers, now with studio people advising her on clothing and her firm young bosom: how to display it and how much to display. She was even cast in the movie *Scudda Hoo! Scudda Hay!* and given a single word of dialogue. Her reading of the word—it was "hello"—later was cut.

Within a year, Fox dropped her. A studio executive said

he simply didn't like the way she photographed. There were thousands of other blondes, desperate for $75-a-week contracts, so Marilyn, who had almost gotten to say hello, now got to say good-bye.

There is a story, supported by Marilyn, that the reason Fox dropped her was that she refused to go to bed with Darryl Zanuck, the moustachioed, autocratic president of the studio. Zanuck's publicity people denied it, but Marilyn insisted there had been a meeting in his office. Zanuck mentioned that he maintained a little apartment behind the office where he stayed after he'd had to work late. The apartment was comfortable, really cozy and . . .

Marilyn claimed she told him off. That broke a reasonable rule of Hollywood survival. Don't tell Darryl Zanuck to go to hell today if you expect to work for Fox tomorrow. She was dismissed.

But she was developing ways of meeting prominent men. Indeed, after Zanuck released her, she managed to encounter Joseph Schenck, the board chairman at Fox. (Despite his title, Schenck had only an advisory role at the studio. Zanuck ran it.) She said she liked Schenck, by then a bearish man approaching the age of seventy. Marilyn: "I used to go to dinner at Schenck's house. That was important because after Fox let me go, I was not eating so good on my own. He was always nice and friendly and open and warm to me, but I was not Schenck's girl [bedmate], not ever. He was genuinely fond of me as a person."

Other sources dispute Marilyn's prim version of the adventures of the bear and the blonde. At the least, they insist, there was both fondling and fellatio. One Los Angeles newspaperman recalled that he was visiting Schenck, sitting at poolside on the older man's estate in Holmby Hills. Marilyn appeared in a one-piece, skintight bathing suit, looking as she usually did in such attire, perfectly splendid. She began collecting drink orders from the guests. The newspaper man gaped at the blond actress-model-waitress and Schenck noticed his panting stare.

"Go ahead," Schenck said. "Take her upstairs to a bedroom if you want."

Press relations in the old Hollywood were somewhat intimate.

By a variety of accounts, including her own, Marilyn was developing a doctrine toward sex that accommodated both her own ambivalence and the nature of the community in which she worked. If someone came on to her with the manners of King Kong and said, "Take off your clothes and I'll get you a movie part," her reaction was severe and negative. She stayed vertical and dressed, sometimes protesting, "What sort of girl do you think I am?"

But with others who seemed to take an interest in her as a person, or better still as an actress, her barriers dropped quickly. She wanted to be taken seriously. She liked men—usually older men—who showed concern for her aspirations and her feelings, or at least acted as though they did. She was a living, wriggling embodiment of one of the primary rules sensible males follow in seduction. If you want to get a woman into bed, treat her like a lady.

If indeed Joe Schenck offered her around on his estate, she could accept that as a reality of doing business in Hollywood. Years afterward, when she stepped naked from the pool on the set of *Something's Got to Give* into the stares of a large and masculine film crew, she said both vulnerably and defiantly, "Oh, well. It's for art."

Her sometimes pragmatic use of her own body is what may have led to rumors that Marilyn was a prostitute. But in order to make some sense of her sexual behavior, one must come to grips with the sexual mores of Hollywood in her time. It wasn't, as publicity people protested, just like Cedar Rapids, "except in California." Hollywood was a factory, packaging and selling sex.

I remember attending a Hollywood party in the days of the big studios where I met a dark-haired, rather hard-faced actress who was noted for having had an affair with Joe Di-Maggio and talking about it. She was between studio contracts, out of work.

I remember even more vividly her opening remarks to me. "There must be something wrong with me," the actress said, considering me across a Scotch and water. Only a certain brassy toughness marred her pretty face.

"What might that be?"

"I'm afraid I'm a nymphomaniac. I was supposed to go out on a casting call today, but I felt so horny I stayed home and masturbated with my vibrator."

I assured her that there was nothing wrong with her, on the basis of what I knew, and went to fetch myself another drink. The actress then began to tell me about an evening, real or imagined, that she had spent with Cary Grant, and in time, not very much time, I was assuring her that if nymphomania was really her problem, I would do everything I could to help.

"Okay," she said, "but there's one thing. I got this hang-up."

"What's that?"

"I've got to charge."

She asked the name of my hotel and when I told her the Beverly Hilton, she said, "Then you can afford forty dollars."

"I can afford it," I said, "but I'm not spending it."

"Well, your hotel is out of the way for me," the actress said. "Come over to my place and it will only be twenty dollars."

Later, when the crowd had thinned, I confronted the host, a sometime producer, sometime movie columnist, and said I didn't think too much of a party where the most attractive guest turned out to be a hooker.

"Who?"

I pointed.

"She's not a hooker," the host said, managing to freight his tone with indignation. "You just don't understand how we do things out here. She's an actress looking for work. Right now she doesn't *have* twenty bucks. When you sleep with one of those, you leave fifty dollars on the night table. That's not a charge. That's a tip."

Marilyn always had a difficult time sorting out herself and the prevailing and perplexing sexuality of Hollywood. She had no family behind her, no stable girlhood where she learned to become comfortable with herself, her sexual needs, and a sense of propriety. Pragmatically, she was an available lady if the conditions were right, but Hollywood was full of available ladies, and to her dismay her movie career stalled and stuttered and seemed to be leading nowhere.

She played a bit part in an early teenage film called *Dangerous Years.* Nobody noticed. That was when Fox dropped her. Joe Schenck made some calls and helped her land a contract at Columbia. There she played a featured role in *Ladies of the Chorus,* and sang a song called "Every Baby Needs a Da-Da-Daddy." Writing in *Motion Picture Herald,* a critic named Tibor Krekes reported that "one of the bright spots is Miss Monroe's singing. She is pretty and with her pleasing voice and style, she shows promise."

But now Hollywood's prevailing sexual practices and her reaction to them stalled her again. Harry Cohn, the president of Columbia, was famous as a crude and willful tyrant, a caricature of a mogul except that he was real. One of his nicknames (never uttered to his face) was "White Fang." Another was "the Jewish Hitler." When Cohn died and a large crowd showed up for the funeral, someone uttered one of Hollywood's most famous end lines: "They just wanted to make sure he was dead."

Cohn spotted Marilyn, sixth over from the left in a ten-girl line in *Ladies of the Chorus.* He made some calls. Max Arnow, Columbia's director of talent, then summoned Marilyn to his office. "I got all dressed very quickly," she said. "I thought he wanted to see me for another part."

Arnow greeted her, then stepped out of the office. Harry Cohn walked in through another door. Marilyn said she felt frightened. "Hey, you," Cohn said. "Come here."

"I'm waiting for Mr. Arnow," Marilyn said.

"Arnow works for me," Cohn said. "He knows."

"Knows what?"

"Come with me," Cohn ordered.

Marilyn followed Cohn down several corridors, through an anteroom, and into the largest office at Columbia Pictures. Cohn motioned for Marilyn to sit, and produced photographs of his yacht. "I'd like you to come on the boat with me." He told her where it was docked. "Be on the boat at seven o'clock on Friday."

"I'd love to," Marilyn said. "Are you having other people?"

"No."

"Like your wife?"

"Hey," Cohn said, "what the hell are you trying to do? Be naïve?"

Marilyn, now twenty-two, retained remnants of naïveté. Besides that, Cohn's gorilla style offended her.

"Maybe some other time," she said, "when you *do* have other people."

Cohn fumed. "How dare you bring my wife into this conversation?"

Marilyn said nothing.

"This is your last chance."

To Marilyn this was more gorilla chest-beating. "I'm sorry," she said, "I'm just the wrong girl. Good-bye."

As usual, Harry Cohn made sure he had the *last* good-bye. A few days later Marilyn lost her Columbia contract.

She played a walk-on in the Marx Brothers' *Love Happy*. She appeared on camera, and complained to Groucho, "Men keep following me." The camera followed her bouncy bottom as she walked away. She played a slightly larger role in a Western. Then she was cast as house pet—Hollywood had not yet confronted the reality of mistresses—to a slick and sleazy lawyer, Alonzo Emmerich, in *The Asphalt Jungle*. Emmerich was played to a turn by Louis Calhern, a distinguished actor who had starred in *King Lear* on Broadway.

But *The Asphalt Jungle* turned out to be Marilyn's show. After it opened, the producers said, letters arrived by the sackful. All asked more or less the same question.

"Who was that blonde?"

Fox re-signed her for $500 a week. Marilyn was twenty-four. She was on her way.

She never really understood what he had done, how diffi-cult it had been, or what it had been like to be emperor of Yankee Stadium and Toots Shor's. She was not an ignorant woman. She had a slight passing knowledge of baseball. She had even played softball at the orphanage. But the magic of the game eluded her. She was interested in other things.

So his own great struggle, up from a poor and overcrowded life, might have taken place in another country, another world. She didn't understand it. She was not really interested in it, although she was aroused by his fame.

Now, if you are going to be friends with Joseph Paul Di-Maggio you had better recognize who it is whose friendship you are seeking. The Jolter. Joltin' Joe. The Yankee Clipper. After that, you can begin to get serious.

Marilyn set forth to be not merely his friend but something even more. His wife.

That was what she wanted, except, except, she never even knew who he was.

Chapter ★ 4

Baseball Joe
Captures New York

The Yankee team that Joe DiMaggio joined in 1936 was
worldly for a baseball club, arrogant, as old Yankee teams
tended to be, and quietly desperate for a superstar. They had
finished second, not first, for three consecutive seasons, and
New York was a city that worshiped winners but paid small
tribute to the second best. DiMaggio's greatest baseball accomplishment is generally held to be his 56-game hitting
streak of 1941. That strikes me as a rather limited view. As
I've mentioned, during his thirteen seasons of active play, the
Yankees won the American League pennant ten times. Ten
pennants out of thirteen against seven other ball clubs, some
backed by independent fortunes, all driving to finish first. A
DiMaggio team was a winning team, as only one had been
before him. That would be the Yankees of Babe Ruth.

Ruth swaggered and drank his way through fifteen seasons as a Yankee, a modern Rabelais whose lusts were a then-unwritten part of baseball legend. Hank Greenberg, now an exceedingly comfortable citizen of California, took me to lunch some time ago at the Beverly Hills Tennis Club and set about explaining the way things were when he broke in with the Detroit Tigers as a rangy, gifted, and somewhat shy young man from the Bronx. "In those days," Greenberg said, "you didn't talk much when you were a rookie. If you did, the veterans would sass you pretty hard. Take away your turn in batting practice. Things like that."

"Was that particularly because you were Jewish?" I asked.

"Hell, no," Greenberg said. "There were a lot of Southerners when I broke in and the big issue was the Civil War. That's what I remember about the needling. It was the South against the North and by the time they were done with that there wasn't time for other things, like anti-Semitism. Anyway, there were three big hitters in the league. Jimmie Foxx. They said that when Foxx squeezed a baseball bat, sawdust ran out between his fingers. Lou Gehrig. You know about him. You saw that movie *Pride of the Yankees*. And then there was the Babe.

"Now if you were a rookie, you didn't just go up to Foxx or Gehrig and say hello. You knew your place. Foxx, who was incredibly strong, had some problems with the bottle that got to him in later years. Gehrig was quiet, kind of aloof. But The Babe used to pull a chair into a runway that led up to the Yankee dugout and sit there and tell baseball stories. Or other stories. And Babe didn't care whether the other players were rookies or veterans. He liked people and he loved to tell his stories.

"When the Yankees were traveling, the ballplayers would come up to him and say, 'How's it going for you in this town, Babe?'

"And Ruth would say, 'Pussy good. Pussy good.' That was his sense of humor."

Greenberg and I were sitting among *very* expensive tennis

courts, where people who had invested thousands of dollars in lessons were playing competently, but no more than that, under a genial California winter sun. At other tables on the terrace, cool, elegant ladies sipped white wine and tanned, gray-haired men spoke seriously in quiet tones.

"Now," Greenberg said, shaking his head in self-reproach, "I told you that story and I'm going to come out sounding like a vulgar ballplayer."

We had been friends for many years. I grinned and said, "Only when you do." Greenberg moved on to mention a best-selling novel about professional football, which he said was reduced to junk by its focus on sex and its indiscriminate use of obscenities.

The Ruth, Heywood Broun wrote in the 1920s, is mighty and shall prevail. Despite an essentially protective press, a sense of the real George Herman Ruth sprang from the field at Yankee Stadium, seizing an era. Ruth set about drinking his way through the years of Prohibition, concentrating on ale, which he drank by the flagon until he had acquired the greatest ale belly in the annals of baseball. Falstaff with a bat. Ruth ran with an odd, mincing stride and the combination— that great jiggling belly atop skinny legs—was distinctive. When Ruth was running home one of his 714 home runs, the sight was equally incongruous and unforgettable.

Ruth loved big crowds and his own great fame, and his unflagging pursuit of women led to a classic baseball one-line joke. One of the first Italian-American major leaguers, Francesco Pezzolo of San Francisco, played under the name of Ping Bodie and for a time roomed with Ruth on the road.

"What's it like to room with Ruth?" a writer asked.

"I ain't rooming with Ruth," Bodie said. "I'm rooming with his suitcase."

In keeping with baseball mores of the time, the Yankee management worked to impose curfews and discipline on its ballplayers. Ruth, who liked almost everything, detested curfews—indeed, he seems to have hated only moderation. After one argument with the Yankee manager, a small serious man named Miller Huggins, Ruth wanted to emphasize that he did not like getting ragged about his habits. To do this, he held Huggins at arm's length off the rear end of a speeding train.

What goes round, the ballplayers say, comes round, and when time came round for Ruth and slowed his Herculean swing, the Yankees dumped him on the Boston Braves, for whom he played 28 games and then retired. Although the Yankees might have been well advised to bring him back—he wanted to manage—they never did. Except for a brief term as a coach for the Brooklyn Dodgers, George Herman Ruth, who all but created modern baseball as an extension of his own slugging style, spent his late years as an exile from both the Yankees and the game.

With Ruth declining after 1932, the Yankees stopped winning pennants. And with Ruth gone from the lineup in 1935, the Yankees had lost their ace drawing card. It was a remarkable bit of fortune for Joe DiMaggio to step onto a ball field recently vacated by The Babe.

Vernon (Lefty) Gomez, another Bay Area ballplayer and a contemporary of DiMaggio's, has quick perceptions and a fine wit. He said that a rival pitcher named Rube Melton, whose ears protruded, looked like a taxicab with both doors open.

"I felt sorry for Lou Gehrig," Gomez once told a newspaperman. "He had always played behind Ruth and finally he had it all to himself in 1935. Now in '36 DiMaggio comes along. Lou had another big year, but Joe was the rookie sensation so he got all the attention."

Gehrig was a polarity away from Ruth. He had attended Columbia and was a quiet, family-oriented man. As a young player, he was particularly close to his mother, a substantial German-American hausfrau, whose cooking delighted her son. Later Gehrig married Eleanor Twitchell, a well-born girl from Chicago, and proceeded into a life of quiet monogamy. Although he was a slugger of extraordinary strength, Gehrig was not quite a match for Ruth, who dominated any baseball scene he entered.

Where Ruth raised hell and spent money with bravado, Gehrig was quiet, serious, and frugal. One writer remembers having a malted milk with Gehrig during the Depression, then hearing Gehrig ask the waitress, "Can I have *my* check?" The writer adds, "Lou was making thirty-five thousand dollars, which was a Depression fortune. I thought he could have offered to pick up both checks. Thirty cents."

"Ruth was a leader," said George (Twinkletoes) Selkirk, who broke into the Yankee outfield in 1934 and played there until 1942. "Gehrig was not. Lou was just a good old plowhorse. He went about his way, played his game, took his shower, got dressed, and went home."

A few writers, aware of Gehrig's Columbia background, tried to dab color on him by depicting him as an intellectual. But Gehrig, while intelligent, was not a scholar, not even much of a talker. "Put him in a room," someone said, "and he won't be able to fill it with conversation."

It is one of baseball's sad ironies that Gehrig finally captured the fans and the press only when he was stricken with amyotrophic lateral sclerosis, a paralyzing disease that killed him in 1941 when he was thirty-seven. Gehrig faced his own premature death with great dignity, and at a farewell day for him at Yankee Stadium he spoke one of his generation's most famous farewell lines. Stricken by fatal illness, Gehrig told a crowd of seventy thousand people, "I consider myself the luckiest man on the face of the earth."

After that the Yankee players gave him a silver bowl, on which a poem by John Kieran was inscribed.

> Let this be a silent tribute
> To friendship's lasting gleam
> And all that we left unspoken—
> Your friends of the Yankee team.

Few, if any, rookies came into New York baseball with the drum rolls of publicity that accompanied the entrance of Joseph Paul DiMaggio in the spring of 1936. At the urging of his brother Tom, Joe bargained hard before finally signing a Yankee contract that called for $8,500 for his rookie season. This produced a banner headline in *The New York Times:* DI-MAGGIO, OUTFIELD RECRUIT, WIRES ACCEPTANCE OF TERMS. Writers who had never seen him play described his throwing arm as an "elephant gun."

This was an era when newspapers covered baseball year round, with off-season baseball stories often taking the play away from basketball and hockey. In January, while snows still lay about, the *Times* reported:

> A hurricane finish on the closing day of the Pacific Coast League pennant race last September, which saw him crack out seven hits in nine times at bat in a dou-ble-header, enabled Joe DiMaggio of the San Francisco Seals, who will make his debut under the Yankee ban-ner this spring, to come within a point of tying for the league's batting championship. DiMaggio's spurt gave him a fine batting mark of .398 . . . Oscar Eckhardt car-ried off the crown with .399.

(Eckhardt signed with the Dodgers in 1936, played sixteen games, batted .182, and vanished from the major leagues.)

Other newspapers billed DiMaggio as the man whose tal-ents had saved the San Francisco Seals and indeed the whole Pacific Coast League from bankruptcy. Although Mussolini's troops were invading Ethiopia and employing mustard gas against native forces fighting with spears, although the Jap-anese had lit the fuse of Asian conflict, although Hitler was demanding a German union with Austria, the future looked hopeful in America. This time, Americans said, we need have no truck with foreign wars. The wide expanse of oceans will protect us. President Roosevelt's New Deal seemed to be working, slowly lifting the country out of the Depression. It was an upbeat moment for a hero to arrive.

On March 1, 1936, DiMaggio appeared at the spring-training ballpark in St. Petersburg, Florida, that had been named for Miller Huggins. (Babe Ruth's old adversary had died in 1929.) DiMaggio was assigned number 18, formerly worn by Johnny Allen, a hard-living pitcher from the Carolinas whom the Yankees had traded to Cleveland. Later, a more established DiMaggio was given number 5. Ruth had worn 3. Gehrig wore 4. All three numbers have been retired. As DiMaggio walked onto the field for his first major league batting practice, a troop of reporters materialized in his wake.

There was as yet no "media," just "the press," and precious little electronic journalism. Home television lay in the future, and none of the three New York teams permitted radio broadcasts of their home games, in a common fear that radio might curtail attendance. So reporters from a dozen newspapers held sway. Some simply echoed Yankee press agentry; probably the best on hand to see DiMaggio's debut was Stanley Woodward, later sports editor of the *New York Herald Tribune.*

Woodward worked to keep a sense of proportion about athletes. Even so, his story the next day ran under a rhapsodic headline:

RECRUIT OUTFIELDER BLASTS
THREE 'HOMERS' IN DEBUT

It was a pleasantly hot Florida day and DiMaggio waited among other ballplayers for his turn at batting practice. When he got into the batting cage to hit, he bounced the first three pitches to the left side of the infield. Photographers joined reporters in a swarm around the batting cage. After that, concentrating on the baseball, not the crowd, DiMaggio began to connect cleanly, and in the course of a two-hour drill and a number of turns at bat, he hit three balls over the fence in left field.

His batting style itself was distinctive. He stood with his legs wide apart in a so-called closed stance—facing more toward center field than left. He did not stride much as he swung, but simply shifted his weight from his back foot to his front foot, whipping his bat with great velocity. "In street clothes," Woodward wrote, "he looks tall and slim, probably because his face is inordinately thin. His profile comes to a point at the end of his nose." But on the field, in a Yankee uniform, "he is so well-proportioned that he looks rather undersized." (DiMaggio stood six feet one, and weighed a well-muscled 187 pounds.) Woodward explained his description with a counterreference to three other Yankees who had put on considerable blubber over the winter.

After the workout, DiMaggio sat down and gave an interview to fifteen reporters. No, he had never been east of the Rocky Mountains before. He had never seen New York, except in movies and newsreels. He was a little disappointed by his first look at Florida. It wasn't as pretty as he had expected. Usually he hit to left or left center, but he knew how to hit to right when he had to.

"Do you think you can hit big-league pitching, Joe?"

"I don't know that yet. I'm just glad to have the opportunity to try."

"The question still exists," Woodward wrote, "whether he can power the offerings of the American League brothers after they start cutting loose, whether he can go and get them in the outfield and whether he can throw as well as his enraptured ex-manager [at San Francisco], Lefty O'Doul says he can."

That then was one *good* reporter's account of DiMaggio's first day in the major leagues. It is a day that would become legendary as years passed and more and more journalists claimed to have been there. "The first time I saw Joe move on the field," goes the refrain, "I knew he was a great one."

Woodward really was there. Clearly, he didn't know.

The Yankees quickly assigned DiMaggio a nickname. Tony Lazzeri, the powerful second baseman, was "Big

Dago," Frank Crosetti, the sharp-featured shortstop, was "Little Dago." DiMaggio became simply "Dago." Baseball chatter, like baseball needling, was crammed with ethnic and sexual references. A ball club is not like a seminar on the lake poets. You have to accept the ambience to survive.

DiMaggio did not fawn on veteran Yankee players or try to ingratiate himself with the press. At twenty-one, he was reserved and tight-lipped. Early on, a rough-tough veteran Yankee pitcher named Charles "Red" Ruffing approached him and said, "So you're the great DiMaggio." The rookie simply nodded and held his tongue.

Vernon Louis Gomez, called "Lefty" and sometimes "Goofy," who had been a Yankee since 1930, took DiMaggio under his wing. He explained in later years, "I had to room with Joe if I ever wanted to see his face. Because the way they hit me, when I was pitching all I ever got to see was his back." (Actually, Gomez was a fine performer. He won 6 games without a loss across five different World Series.)

As spring training proceeded, it began to be clear that Di-Maggio was one impressive rookie. John Kieran, the erudite sportswriter who originated *The New York Times* column "Sports of the Times," reported that DiMaggio was "going about in lively fashion living up to all the advance notices about him from the California area. He is fast in the field, turns loose a good throwing arm and lines hits to all corners of the Florida ball parks."

During the Yankees' fifth exhibition game, against the Boston Braves, DiMaggio bruised his left foot sliding into second base. The trainer, "Doc" Painter, prescribed short-wave diathermy, and DiMaggio was told to put his foot into a machine that would focus heat on the area of the injury. They told him to put his foot in, but no one told him to take it out. DiMaggio, the rookie and the good soldier, did as he was ordered, even when he began feeling more pain. By the time the trainer got around to remembering his patient, the foot was badly burned. The team doctor, Harry G. Jacobi, looked at it and found "an area of ulceration [on the instep] quite similar to that seen following burns."

Baseball's rousing rookie, the twenty-one-year-old who couldn't miss, now had to sit out opening day in Washington, D.C. (The Senators beat the Yankees, 1–0.) It was not until May 1, when DiMaggio took a long session of batting practice at Yankee Stadium, that he reported to Manager Joe McCarthy, "No pain."

On May 3, DiMaggio walked the few blocks from his room in the Concourse Plaza hotel to the Stadium and worked out for a while. Then McCarthy said: "DiMaggio, you're in there today."

The Yankees were playing the St. Louis Browns, the only major league team that had never won a pennant. It was a cloudy afternoon. DiMaggio played left field and batted third, ahead of Gehrig. The Browns started a big right-hander from Texas named John Henry Knott. In the first inning, DiMaggio lined Knott's second pitch safely into left field. Then he singled, flied out, grounded out, tripled to left center, and popped up. The Yankees won, 14–4. DiMaggio had gotten 3 hits in 6 times at bat. He was batting .500. The Yankee Clipper was under way.

Later in the week, DiMaggio suffered through a mini-slump and made out ten times in a row. Someone wrote that "the cognescenti are beginning to whisper that he can't hit a curveball on the outside." Next day, batting against one George Turbeville of the Philadelphia Athletics, DiMaggio lined an outside curveball down the right-field line and into the stands. It snapped the slump. It won him an ovation. It was his first major league home run, the first of 29 he would hit that season, the first of 361 he would hit in his career.

The world of 1936, in which Joe DiMaggio appeared, hawk-faced, neatly dressed in dark double-breasted suits or Yankee pinstripes, was a more dangerous place than most Americans realized, moving relentlessly, if not that obviously, toward the Holocaust of World War II and the age of nuclear bombs. New Yorkers in the summer of '36 had preoccupations that were less global than Armageddon.

A woman named Helen L. Greek, swimming among schoolchildren in Cobleskill Creek upstate, decided she would be more comfortable without a bathing suit. The children, bluenoses whose names are lost to history, called the police, who found Mrs. Greek naked and arrested her. She was sentenced to an indeterminate term at the state farm in Bedford Hills.

President Roosevelt, beginning a campaign for a second term, which would bring him forty-six of the forty-eight states, visited Mount Rushmore, where he was shown the heads of other presidents, carved and blasted out of the rocky crest of the mountain. He was accompanied by the sculptor whose handiwork this was, a man named Gutzon Borglum. One of the Yankee writers commented that the name Gutzon Borglum "sounded like a fart in a bathtub."

Republicans were calling the New Deal "socialistic in principle and un-American in fact," but no one except other Republicans took that seriously. People were going back to work.

Television was still confined to the laboratories of electronic engineers, but the country was fascinated by radio. On Sunday nights families gathered to hear the Jack Benny show, featuring Benny, his wife, Mary Livingstone, his bluff and hearty announcer, Don Wilson, and a tenor named Kenny Baker, who always fumbled about in amusing ways until Benny said, in a marvelously exasperated manner, "Sing, Kenny!" Later in the evening listeners could hear more serious music, in the low-fi of the time, when "Leopold Stokowski led his orchestra, joined by the great Irish tenor John McCormack."

Blacks were then called Negroes and lynchings continued to occur in Southern states, often when it was suggested that "a nigra" had looked with lust at a white woman. Liberals and leftists pressed Roosevelt to push an antilynching law through Congress or, at the very least, a law barring the poll tax, the device Southern states used effectively to disenfranchise most blacks. But Roosevelt's great coalition, which combined trade unionists and northern liberals with the solidly Democratic conservative South, was his foremost concern. He concentrated on economic recovery programs. Civil rights would wait.

Women's liberation was not yet a phrase, much less a movement. The *Herald Tribune* ran a column called "A Woman's Place," full of household hints, and one of the few women active in politics, Ruth Bryan Owen, startled the country when she announced that she would marry a handsome guardsman from the Danish Royal Court. Mrs. Owen was Roosevelt's minister to Denmark, a position she had to resign for love since Danish law forbade a foreign emissary from being married to a Danish citizen. Mrs. Owen had to work for the rest of her days to support both herself and her tall Danish guardsman. This international romance grabbed the front pages until it was swept away by the royal lust of the Prince of Wales for Wallis Warfield of Baltimore, Maryland.

The country read *Gone With the Wind,* as well as *I Write as I Please,* a sympathetic account by Walter Duranty about his Moscow days as a *New York Times* correspondent. John Gunther warned of war clouds in *Inside Europe,* and for a lighter moment there was Robert Benchley's funny collection of pieces called *My Ten Years in a Quandary (and How They Grew).* The big Broadway movie houses were playing *The Last of the Mohicans* with Randolph Scott and *The General Died at Dawn,* starring Gary Cooper and Madeleine Carroll. The theater offered John Gielgud's memorable Hamlet and Alfred Lunt and Lynn Fontanne in *Idiot's Delight,* which advertised: 100 SEATS PRICED AT $1.

The pace of many things, including travel, was relatively leisurely. American Airlines offered nonstop service from New York to Chicago in a "luxury 21-seat plane," the DC-3. Scheduled flying time was four hours and forty-five minutes. Since the DC-3 did not have a pressurized cabin and seldom flew higher than five thousand feet, flights tended to be bumpy on cloudy or windy days. Airline stewardesses, not simply airborne waitresses, were required to be registered nurses, the better to deal with air sickness and panic.

The great French liner *Normandie* and the Cunard liner *Queen Mary* held dignified races for the fastest transatlantic crossing time. First one ship held the record, then the other. Sailing time from New York to Southampton hovered at about four and a half days.

By today's standards, this world, in which DiMaggio appeared as a thrilling $8,500-a-year rookie, was a place where one could survive on very little money. Child's, a New York restaurant chain, offered "veal cutlet with tomato sauce, mashed potatoes, bread or roll" as a special. The price was thirty cents. Peck and Peck, the capital of tweedy clothes for Ivy League women, ran a sale in which all dresses were priced from $7.95 to $16.95. Hearns department store offered fifths of imported Scotch whisky, two bottles for $4.79. Care for ice with your drink? Hearns sold the Williams Ice-o-Matic electric refrigerator for $77, delivered to your home.

Co-op apartments in good and safe Manhattan neighborhoods sold for $4,000. You could rent a six-room apartment in Tudor City, on East Forty-second Street, gaining free access to private parks and private tennis courts, for $190 a month. The Chrysler Corporation advertised its new Plymouth, with safety steel body and hydraulic brakes, for $510 f.o.b. (freight on board) Detroit. General Motors copywriters pointed out that the luxurious LaSalle, a car not for everyone but for the very select, could be had for $1,175. A rookie outfielder earning $8,500 was distinctly a young man of means.

Society and social restrictions were prominent and unabashed. *The New York Times,* run by Adolph Ochs, a descendant of German Jews, advertised lodges in the Poconos and the Hamptons that said in a heavy-handed subtlety "restricted," or more openly, "Christian resort." Despite Hitler's murderous assault—the concentration camps were already being constructed in Germany—anti-Semitism in America was current and indeed fashionable. And if you didn't want a Jew lying near you on a beach, probably you would not be much happier if the person on the next blanket was a child of Sicilians.

Social ladies that summer were partial to light wool knits that clung to hip and breast. The bodies of the models in department-store advertisements were a bit more rounded than the models you see today, a bit softer, less firmly muscled, and to many, more distinctly feminine. Although bathing suits were less revealing than today's string bikinis, Davega's sports and clothing store advertised knit styles modeled by "Radio City Rockette Lucille Bremer." Miss Bremer's vital parts were covered but the knit clung so closely that on a page of the *New York Herald Tribune* you could clearly see the outlines of her pubic triangle.

So then, as now, hair existed, along with sex and baseball. Indeed, no less a personage than Helen Hayes found herself hauled into court by Carol Frink, a Chicago newspaperwoman and the first wife of the playwright and screenwriter Charles MacArthur. MacArthur divorced Miss Frink to marry Miss Hayes, and Frink sued for $100,000 on the grounds of "alienation of affections."

Meanwhile, Hitler demanded a return of the free city of Danzig to his Third Reich, and in the Kremlin Stalin carefully plotted his Great Terror, the purge trials. Before those were through, the general secretary of the Communist party would sign death warrants for more than a million Russians.

Apart from politics, in grassy urban meadows, Joseph Paul DiMaggio played baseball brilliantly on sunlit afternoons. There were as yet no night games in the American League and the pace of baseball was brisker than today. Many games were completed in less than two hours.

The Yankees understood what they had in DiMaggio as, a generation later, the New York Giants would recognize what they had in Willie Mays. "Marse" (a sort of baseball corruption of Massah) Joe McCarthy managed the Yankees in a stern, efficient way. He was a short, stocky, flat-faced man, whose minor league playing career had begun in 1907, and he possessed strong ideas on major league decorum. He insisted that his ballplayers wear jackets and neckties—certain other clubs let their players wander about hotel lobbies in T-shirts— and he told the players not to talk much to the writers. "That can get you in trouble."

Marse Joe had a quiet fondness for the bottle, and one spring training he drank so heavily that he failed to show up at Huggins Field in St. Petersburg for four consecutive days. At length, Mark Roth, the Yankees' traveling secretary, telephoned rugged Ed Barrow in the Yankee offices in New York, with a report.

"Don't tell the writers," Barrow snapped.

The writers all knew. Indeed, some had written that the manager was suffering from flu.

But most of the time Marse Joe stayed sober and severe. Before his death at the age of ninety in 1978, he spoke warmly of the young DiMaggio he first saw. "Joe was a little timid when he broke in," McCarthy told the sportswriter Maury Allen. "He never bothered anybody and they didn't bother him either. I started him in left field after his burned foot got better and then I moved him over to right field for a while. I wanted to make sure he was comfortable before I put him in center field. He would never have become that great outfielder he was if I hadn't moved him there. He needed that room to roam in Yankee Stadium. [In the old Stadium configuration the center-field wall reached almost 470 feet distant from home plate.] Only the real great ones can play out there," McCarthy said. "It was the toughest centerfield in baseball."

The rookie DiMaggio was the sharp spur to a strong Yankee team. Gehrig, whose home-run production and batting average had sagged somewhat in 1935, responded in 1936 with one of his finest seasons: a .354 batting average, 49 home runs and 152 runs batted in. Red Rolfe, a third baseman who had played at Dartmouth, had a fine slugging season; Bill Dickey, the strong, rangy catcher from Arkansas, had the best batting year of a career that would span seventeen major league seasons. The 1936 Yankees began to take the American League apart.

By June 1, they were in first place by 4 games and DiMaggio was hitting .381. One day in June DiMaggio tied a game with a single in the seventh inning and won it by tripling home Red Rolfe in the twelfth. Stanley Woodward wrote in the *Herald Tribune* that a large Yankee Stadium crowd went home "babbling incoherently of Giuseppe Paolo DiMaggio." On June 24, DiMaggio hit 2 home runs in a 10-run fifth inning against the Chicago White Sox, only the fourth man to accomplish that—2 homers in 1 inning—in the history of the major leagues. "Colonel Jacob Ruppert" [president of the Yankees], reported John Drebinger in *The New York Times,* "was in Chicago essentially to attend a brewers' convention." DiMaggio's hitting, which also included two line-drive doubles, "gave our Colonel a marvelous appetite for an excellent repast."

Everyone noticed DiMaggio's long-legged grace in the outfield. He did not often make diving catches, but he seemed to know where the ball would go as soon as bat and ball made contact, and he raced off, covering enormous distances with seeming ease. "He does what you're supposed to do," Mc-Carthy said. "The idea is to catch the ball, not make catches that look exciting." In later years this graceful, gliding style was contrasted with the techniques of Willie Mays. (Mays and DiMaggio are generally regarded as the outstanding defensive outfielders of modern baseball.) "DiMaggio," someone said, "makes all the tough catches look easy. Willie [who was forever diving and running out from under his cap] makes the hard catch look hard."

Baseball observers noticed also that DiMaggio had an extraordinary throwing arm. One August day a reporter named Jake Hart wrote in the *New World-Telegram* that yesterday I saw Joe DiMaggio make the greatest throw I ever had the privilege to see go winging through the air. In high school baseball it is rare indeed to run into an outfielder who can make even a short throw to get a runner at the plate. This shortcoming is pronounced in the minor leagues as well . . . Lefty Grove was on second and when the ball was hit to deep right center Grove headed for home. He figured he had an easy chance to score [on the base hit]. But DiMaggio cut loose with one of those fancy throws of his and Grove was out by three steps. You should have seen the look on Lefty's face. He won't take any liberties with Di Mag in the future.

In addition, DiMaggio was a superb base runner. "The best I ever saw," said Joe McCarthy. "He wasn't the fastest man alive. He just knew how to run bases better than anybody. He could have stolen fifty, sixty bases a year if I had let him, but I didn't want him pounding into that hard dirt two, three times a game and tearing up his legs. So that's why I never let him steal."

Only once could McCarthy recall DiMaggio making a base-running mistake. DiMaggio cracked a line drive into left-center field, sped into second, turned toward third, and found himself tagged out.

After the trot back to the dugout, McCarthy said, "What happened out there, Joe?"

DiMaggio shook his head. "Skip, I got to second base and I'm watching for the relay and all of a sudden I think I see the ball. I figure it's getting away and I can make it to third. When I look again I realize it wasn't the ball I saw, it was a bird. By then they got the ball behind me and I'm dead."

That was about as amusing as any of the stories that came out of DiMaggio's baseball years. He was never as funny as Babe Ruth, ostentatious as Leo Durocher, excitable as Jackie Robinson, or as talkative as Casey Stengel. But he could hit and run and throw and field, which, in sum, is everything that a ballplayer is supposed to do during the working hours of his day.

With his $8,500 rookie salary in an era of thirty-cent blue-plate specials, DiMaggio was comfortably fixed, but he was hungry to make more. He signed an endorsement contract with Camel cigarettes, which then advertised:

> Heavy-hitting baseball star Joe DiMaggio feels the same way about Camels as so many millions of smokers do. Says Joe: "When I need a 'lift' in energy, Camels is the cigarette for me. I stick to Camels. They don't irritate my throat or get my nerves jumpy. Ball players really go for Camels in a big way."

He may have led the league in clubhouse cups of coffee, but curiously, no coffee commercial was forthcoming until a quarter century after his retirement, when he began reaping hundreds of thousands of Madison Avenue dollars as the spokesman for a drip-and-filter machine called Mr. Coffee. By that time, he'd had trouble with his marriages and a stomach ulcer and had switched from drinking coffee to sipping tea.

He also collaborated with Dan M. Daniel of the *World-Telegram* for a six-part series of newspaper articles, purporting to be his life story. In the stories he claims to have attended high school for three years, without making clear why, then, he never played on the baseball team. The series is, to put it quietly, suspect in matters of accuracy. Early on, when the putative author is explaining that the correct pronunciation is Di-Mahg-gio, he writes, "My name is Joseph Peter DiMaggio." Actually, of course, the middle name is Paul, not Peter. Thus DiMaggio becomes the only ballplayer to my knowledge who got his own name wrong in an autobiography.

Whatever, the articles brought him a paycheck.

*   *   *

Ignited by DiMaggio, the Yankees went on a tear that would carry them into an unmatched period of baseball dominance. In each of his first four seasons in New York, the Yankees won the American League pennant by more than 10 games. Three times they won more than 100 games. The other year, 1939, they won 99. There had never been before, nor would there have been again so consistently commanding a major league baseball team, although the Yankees of the early 1960s, the team of Mickey Mantle, Roger Maris, and Casey Stengel, came close.

As few other athletes, DiMaggio had a capacity to rouse, inspire, and carry a team. You find that quality frequently among great baseball managers, who generally are intensely verbal men and, in a sense, unlicensed psychologists. A great manager demands and cajoles, manipulates personnel, devises tactics and stratagems, and sets not only each order of the day but also establishes the overall morale of the club. John McGraw of the Giants was fierce, tightly disciplined, and imperious—his nickname was "Little Napoleon." Generations of Giant teams responded to McGraw's whip. Casey Stengel was funny with the press, tolerant with Mickey Mantle, but consistently severe with the rest of his Yankee athletes. He moved them in and out of the lineup for reasons of strategy, and when the players complained—most wanted to play every day—all Casey's clowning ceased. He kept his Yankee teams sullen but not mutinous, and the ballplayers took out their rage on perfectly innocent visiting pitchers.

But keeping a team inspired is part of a manager's job. For a ballplayer, particularly for a rather silent ballplayer like DiMaggio, to emerge as the inspirational leader is both remarkable and somewhat elusive of explanation. Joe hit and ran and fielded and threw with grace, intensity, and a pure sense of purpose. I sent questionnaires to more than fifty of DiMaggio's teammates and opponents and their answers fell into a reverent pattern. "Terrific competitor," commented Buddy Hassett, a one-time first baseman. "Joe was just about the best I ever saw," wrote Frank Crosetti. "A great ball-player who could do it all!" Ted Williams wrote in high enthusiasm. After the Yankees with DiMaggio started winning pennants, the late Joe Cronin, then managing the Red Sox, looked back on DiMaggio's early years and made an emphatic point. "Most of those seasons," Cronin said, "there were four American League clubs that could have won the pennant. The Yankees. The Red Sox. Cleveland. And Detroit. Well, whichever one of those teams had DiMaggio was going to win it. That's the kind of difference he made. The Yankees had him and the Yankees won."

The 1936 Yankees stretched their lead further in July, when DiMaggio hit safely in 18 consecutive games. "His life," wrote James M. Kahn in the New York *Sun,* "is a merry round of base hits, cheers, flag-wavings, presentations and generally flattering hoopla. Joe is averaging 20 fan letters a day. He is getting more mail than Lou Gehrig. Practically all have been letters of praise and encouragement. Old friends out on the Coast have written him cheering notes and others, from strangers, have come from all over the country."

"I don't suppose you remember me," wrote Jack Lutich of San Francisco, "but we played ball together for the LaSalle Juniors managed by our good friend Fat Thomas. I was the blond fellow that played second base. Keep going, Joe. They can't stop you."

Someone else wrote, "I have great esteem and admiration for you as has every other Italian. Congratulations on the great name you have made for yourself. You hold a very important place in the heart of every true Italian." (All this before the man had been a major league regular for three months.)

Concluding his epistolary column, James Kahn wrote, "Joe gets a few mash notes, too, most of them on colored stationery. The gals want Joe's picture and they never fail to mention that 'baseball is my favorite sport.'"

"Those," Kahn wrote, reflecting the protective, prudish

nature of sportswriting in those days, "are the ones that Joe doesn't answer."

He became such a big star so quickly that even his failures made headlines. The baseball all-star game was then a new and developing tradition, played first in 1933 as an adjunct to the Chicago World's Fair. Its appeal solidified a season later at the Polo Grounds when the great Giant left-hander Carl Hubbell struck out in succession Babe Ruth, Lou Gehrig, Jimmie Foxx, Al Simmons, and Joe Cronin. By 1936, fans were selecting the all-star team by vote, and DiMaggio, not yet established in center, won handily as the all-star right fielder.

July 7, the day of the game, broke overcast in Boston and the crowd at Fenway Park did not exceed twenty-five thousand. "When young Joe DiMaggio stepped up to the plate in the first inning [with a runner on first base]," reported Richards Vidmer in the *Herald Tribune*, "the fans let go a yell of delight." DiMaggio hit into a double play.

In the second inning, with one National Leaguer on base, Gabby Hartnett, a hearty sort who caught for the Chicago Cubs, smacked a hard line drive to right field. DiMaggio raced in, trying to catch the ball at his shoe tops. He missed. The ball skipped between his legs. Triple.

DiMaggio came to bat with a man on base in the fourth inning and popped out. In the fifth, Billy Herman sliced a single to right and DiMaggio scooped the ball and dropped it. Herman went to second on the error. Joe Medwick scored him with a single. DiMaggio, "the boy wonder," in Vidmer's phrase, had already stranded two runners and misplayed two balls in the outfield.

Between innings, Joe McCarthy, managing the American Leaguers, studied DiMaggio. He meant, he said later, to ask some questions. Was the strain of the all-star game too great? Did DiMaggio want to come out of the lineup?

"I had those questions," McCarthy said, "but I never asked them. I took a look at the way his jaw was set. He looked grim. Joe was mad. Mad at himself. He was impatient for a chance to show the other all-stars that he belonged."

In the sixth inning, with a man on first, DiMaggio bounced out to Carl Hubbell. The American League had fallen 4 runs behind. Gehrig homered in the seventh and when DiMaggio came to bat, the bases were loaded and two men were out. A home run would put his team ahead. Some cheers for DiMaggio came from the crowd but now Fenway fans added an obbligato of hoots. This, Vidmer noted, served only to make DiMaggio grip his bat more tightly and dig his spikes more firmly into Fenway soil. He hit the ball well, a line drive toward shortstop, where Leo Durocher caught it and the inning ended. DiMaggio finished his dismal day by popping out in the ninth inning with the tying run on base. He was "a fallen star among the stars."

Inside the American League clubhouse reporters and photographers left him alone. Joe Cronin of the Red Sox approached him and put a hand on his shoulder. "Don't take it too hard, kid," Cronin said, "I wish I had you on my team. Someday you'll be the greatest star of them all."

DiMaggio blinked back tears and looked at Cronin's square, friendly face. He was able to smile, but he could not speak.

There were not very many other bad days. The pennant race was settled by August; the Yankees clinched it by the extraordinary margin of 19½ games. And, guided by his friend Gomez, DiMaggio settled into a quiet life in New York. He lived in the Concourse Plaza, two blocks from Yankee Stadium, and his hobbies, he said, were listening to the radio and reading Westerns. He was also a great fan of comic books, following the adventures of cartoon characters with a distinct passion—but that revelation came not from DiMaggio but from Gomez.

In later years, he learned to take a drink, and the liquor would sometimes loose streams of anger, suspicion, and arrogance. But in these early days he was a coffee-and-Camels man.

Occasionally the Yankees pressed him into making a promotional appearance for the club. He says he never enjoyed that sort of thing. "Enjoy it?" Gomez says. "He'd be introduced, get a hand, stand up and say thank you, then introduce me and sit right down. I had to tell baseball stories for the two of us."

"I don't want to be dined," DiMaggio said, in a carefully humble way, "because I haven't done that much to be dined about. Besides, I'm a ballplayer. I can't afford to stay out late and I can't neglect my diet."

Actually, throughout his eight decades DiMaggio has shown consistent patterns of withdrawn, even antisocial, behavior. The boy who ran out of the Taylor Street apartment in San Francisco rather than meet his sisters' friends was something less than a gregarious, or even gracious, young person. In later years, he has affected an air of mystery about his comings and goings. While it may be excessive to describe him as reclusive, his late-life social contacts are generally limited to a few good golfing friends and business associates; and a number of women much younger than he, almost always physically attractive and never, after the Marilyn disaster, ladies who challenged him in any serious way.

People become professional baseball players for a narrow assortment of reasons. The drive may begin with a boy's effort to please his father. Bobby Feller, the great Cleveland pitcher, and Mickey Mantle both had fathers who worked at baseball with their offspring as diligently as parents from other worlds taught their children to play the piano. Both Feller and Mantle became baseball prodigies. Of course, for everyone who succeeds as a diamond wunderkind there are a million we never see or hear about, whose dreams, or whose fathers' dreams for them, are dead before their twentieth birthday arrives.

Some want to become ballplayers to achieve fame. The French *la gloire*. Some lust for the great salaries major league stars earn. Some simply loved to play baseball as children and want to go right on playing the game, to the exclusion of many other things, including maturation, for as many years as they can. And to be sure most, become ballplayers for an individual mixture of these assorted considerations.

As far as anyone, including DiMaggio himself, can tell, his strongest motivation to be a ballplayer was his healthy passion for money. He could do better hitting line drives than he had done peeling fruit in an orange-juice factory. Although he has said from time to time that he is thankful to Providence for having made him a Yankee, his comments—and his conduct in his playing years—reflect little of the sheer, bubbling joy of baseball. The young Willie Mays played brilliant center field for the New York Giants and then repaired to the streets of Harlem for a few hours of the city street game stickball. Dizzy Dean almost literally lived to pitch. Playing baseball was more of a job to DiMaggio—a job that pride drove him to perform with all the excellence at his command. But where Stan Musial mostly had great fun playing ball and batting was the enduring happiness of Ted Williams's life, DiMaggio was a solemn baseball genius. He was neither able nor willing to forget that this game, rhapsodized by some as America's native art form, was primarily a means whereby he could lift himself and his clan to ever-higher income levels. This cold financial ambition would get him into trouble before his major league career was three years old.

For outgoing people, major league life is a passport to paradise. As a star, you find bank presidents, politicians, lawyers, professors, doctors, and a whole horde of blue-collar types anxious to partake of your presence. Musial, now fixed in stone as a statue outside the St. Louis baseball park, loved meeting people and could drift happily from table to table in restaurants where people always asked, "How ya hitting 'em, Stan?" Musial would smile, sometimes accept a free drink, and make small, happy baseball talk with strangers who were soon convinced by his very geniality that Stan the Man was a true friend. I cannot remember ever hearing Musial booed.

Hank Greenberg, in his wealth at his tennis club, enjoys nothing more than meeting with baseball-wise people and talking about the way the game was and the way the game is. DiMaggio, who to this day brings a remote, aristocratic, almost papal demeanor to his public appearances, is fundamentally uncomfortable with and distrustful of strangers. This did not, in truth, make him a favorite of the press corps trooping after the great Yankee team of 1936.

He understood that he was paid to play, but he felt that telling reporters after the games what he had done was an imposition on his time. They had seen the game, hadn't they? What were they watching out there, the girls? Where Gehrig, another quiet man, would help a reporter who asked questions, and beyond that, answered fan mail from children with personally written, longhand letters, DiMaggio disliked being fussed over. In the early years he seldom made an effort to be cooperative or even courteous to the press. "He was," an old baseball writer told me once, "the kind of arrogant young man who wouldn't say hello to you unless you said hello to him first. He was a star right from the beginning, but you couldn't much like that attitude coming from a twenty-one-year-old kid."

After the games at Yankee Stadium, DiMaggio spent considerable time before a clubhouse mirror, getting the part in his straight black hair just so. There was, the reporter said, something intimidating about DiMaggio fussing with his hair. "It was clear that he didn't want to be interrupted with a question and it always seemed that the day you had the most to ask him, the longer he stood in front of that damn mirror. Deadlines? I don't think Joe D. gave a damn about other people's deadlines. They weren't his problem."

The words "surly" and "sullen" slip into some accounts of him as a rookie. Years later he finally began to relax with the fine columnist Jimmy Cannon, but only after receiving great gushings of idolatry from Cannon both verbally and in the papers. "Cannon," someone has remarked, "courted DiMaggio as if he were a broad."

When the rookie DiMaggio did speak, he did not say interesting things. No, he hadn't gotten excited when he came up with two men on base, "because it doesn't pay to get excited in baseball." Although his manner bespoke arrogance, he was careful to put out comments that rang with humility, however hollow. "I'm just a ballplayer trying to give all I've got to help my team win."

In the days before the dominance of television, the press conditioned the public's impression of ballplayers, but the image was built primarily by the player himself and his achievements. DiMaggio, the golden rookie, could indulge himself in silence or petulance. What was a reporter going to write: "Joe DiMaggio, who got three hits today, wouldn't chat with me after the game"?

With the Yankees, previously a second-place team, now tearing apart the American League, the golden rookie became the centerpiece of most accounts. DiMaggio certainly had to extend himself to play as well as he did. No one played harder. But he did not *have* to extend himself for the sportswriters.

He did not have to and he did not.

For the Yankees, 1936 was what the political writers refer to as a watershed year. (Indeed, politically it was a watershed year for Adolf Hitler, who sent German troops into the Rhineland, and for Francisco Franco, whose rebel forces landed in Spain from North Africa on July 19, starting the Spanish civil war.)

The Brooklyn Dodgers of 1936 were not a competitive team in the greater New York market. The Dodger management had mortgaged Ebbets Field, missed payments on the mortgage, and was offering the franchise for sale. The asking price, $2 million, succeeded in frightening away all entrepreneurs. But the New York Giants, under the severe and driving leadership of their playing manager "Memphis Bill" Terry, were a disciplined and attractive ball club. Mel Ott, their stumpy home-run-hitting right fielder, was one of the most popular players in the game. Their pitching staff was led by "King Carl" Hubbell, whose screwball was one of the wonders of baseball; "Prince Hal" Schumacher, a sinker-ball specialist and "Fat Freddie" Fitzsimmons, who threw knuckleballs out of a whirligig motion. While the Yankees were outclassing the American League, the Giants were narrowly winning the National League pennant over strong teams from St. Louis and Chicago.

So as autumn came in DiMaggio's first major league season, the New York press chattered excitedly about a World Series that would match the Yankees against the Giants for the championship of major league baseball coincidentally and the City of New York. Writers referred to that season's denouement as "a subway series" or a "nickel series." If you lived in upper Manhattan or on the Grand Concourse in the Bronx, you could get to all the games even without the nickel for fare. Both Yankee Stadium, at 161st and River Avenue, and the Polo Grounds, at 155th and Eighth, lay within an easy walk.

DiMaggio completed an outstanding rookie season, batting .323 with 206 hits and 29 home runs. All but two of the Yankee regulars batted over .300, the benchmark of hitting excellence. Did any Yankee resent that the publicity for this remarkable team always seemed to focus on the rookie from San Francisco? Certainly not Gehrig. "I've never gone overboard for a young ballplayer before," he said, "because too much can happen. But this kid, well, I'm going overboard for him."

That September, when the two fine New York ball clubs arrayed themselves against one another, Earl Browder, the presidential nominee of the American Communist party, was arrested in Terre Haute, Indiana, for attempting to make a campaign speech. The local chief of police said he had warned Browder that he would not tolerate Reds disturbing the peace. Other stories reported that the Dionne quintuplets had been permitted to play with their brothers for the first time. The Dionnes were big news in 1936. So was a fifty-seven-year-old San Francisco housewife named Mrs. Rosalie DiMaggio.

DiMaggio says that his first World Series lives with him as one of the highlights, perhaps *the* highlight, of his life in baseball. "Here I was," he says, "just a boy and getting to play in the biggest Series in the biggest city in the country." He arranged for his mother and his brother Tom to make the trip from San Francisco, four nights in Pullman cars. The New York press was waiting, but Mrs. DiMaggio spoke almost no English, making her an even more difficult interview than her son. The *New York World-Telegram,* publishers of the flawed autobiography, met this feature-desk crisis by dispatching a writer named Bart Paganini, who spoke Italian.

Paganini reported and the *Telegram* headlined Rosalie's World Series selection: THE YANKEES IN FOUR STRAIGHT. "My son Joe," she said, "will win." Paganini asked for an impression of Manhattan, and she said she was uncomfortable in the Mayflower hotel on Central Park West because "there's nothing to do, but sit by the window and think about the games. I wish I had some cleaning or some dishes I could wash or dry."

She had been in New York once before, passing through on the way from Sicily to San Francisco. She said she now missed real Italian food. Someone made a few phone calls and Rosalie and Tom were borne by taxi to Little Italy on the lower East Side. There they feasted at Papa Moneta's restaurant.

"It was so beautiful," she said later. "As soon as Papa Moneta found out who I was, Joe's mama, he went crazy. He ran around telling everyone I was there and people kept coming over to shake my hand. I wanted to eat my supper, but every time I tried to eat something, someone would want to shake my hand. It took me almost three hours to finish."

Then the patrons of the restaurant hired her a taxi for a sightseeing tour that lasted until midnight.

"Where was Joe?" Paganini asked.

"He told me, mama, I got to go out with the boys."

Well, what does one tell one's mother who has come three thousand miles—"Mom, I've got a date with a blonde"?

Elsewhere, however, several hints appeared that Joe the super rookie would have flunked out of a monastery. Someone asked if he liked the women of New York and he nodded tightly.

"With your grace on the field, you must be a terrific dancer."

"I can't dance a step," DiMaggio said.

Then what's your secret?

"I like the ladies," remarked twenty-one-year-old Joe Di-Maggio, "but I never fall in love with any of them."

Then, on September 30, it was time for the World Series to begin.

The Series opened on a day that was overcast; each team went with its finest pitcher. The Giants started Carl Hubbell, who was calm enough in pregame interviews to remark that New York's damp weather would be welcome near his farm in Oklahoma, where a drought was endangering his pecan crop. Hubbell was coming off his greatest season. He had won 26 games. The Yankees started "Red" Ruffing, who had won 20 and lost 12.

Reporters at the Polo Grounds noticed that the Giants ran through their pregame drills more precisely than the Yankees. Their infield practice was crisper. Warm-up throws from the outfield were more accurate. There was a sense in the old green horseshoe of a ballpark that the Giants represented old money, established, conservative New York. Their winning tradition traced from 1904, John McGraw's second full season as manager. The Yankee aura, largely formed by Babe Ruth, was louder, a bit more garrulous, somewhat more muscular, but still tainted by the suggestion of nouveau riche.

Hubbell pitched a characteristically commanding game, yielding a run only on George Selkirk's homer. He effectively defused the batting power of DiMaggio, Gehrig, and the slugging catcher Bill Dickey. The game was close until the eighth inning, when the Giants scored four times. Hubbell out-pitched Ruffing and the Giants won, 6–1.

DiMaggio was not a significant factor. With a chance to put the Yankees ahead with a home run in the eighth inning, he hit the ball sharply but directly at the Giants' second base-man, Burgess Whitehead. Afterward, reporters wanted to know how Hubbell's great pitching had impressed him.

Arthur Patterson wrote in the *Herald Tribune,* "DiMaggio was surly. He took a long time to part his jet-black hair, look-ing petulantly at himself in the mirror." At length, Patterson was able to catch his eye and ask about Carl Hubbell.

"I didn't think he was so tough," DiMaggio said grace-lessly.

Patterson blinked. "He wasn't invincible, anyway," Di-Maggio said.

Rain washed away the game scheduled for October 1 and the papers occupied themselves with cheerleading for Alf Landon and his Republican running mate, Colonel Frank Knox. Next day the sky cleared and the Yankees over-whelmed the Giants, 18–4, with a barrage of batting that broke twelve World Series records. DiMaggio got 3 hits, but the Yankee stars were Tony Lazzeri and Bill Dickey, who each batted in 5 runs.

The significant element was the overwhelming nature of the Yankee attack. The Giants started Hal Schumacher—and he never made it through the first inning. Giant fans, number-ing many of New York's elite, went into mild shock before all that unbridled Yankee power. Although no one knew it at the time, the date, October 2, 1936, marked the start of the era when DiMaggio and the Yankees would dominate New York, and indeed all baseball. This began not with a whimper but a bang.

The Series moved to Yankee Stadium for the third game, and DiMaggio drew wild cheering throughout the afternoon. He did not, however, make any hits. "Italian fans," Arthur Patterson wrote, "dominated the gathering of 64,842. There can be no doubt that Joe DiMaggio is fast taking the place of the one and only Babe Ruth as a drawing card for Colonel Ruppert."

The Yankees won, 2–1, when Frank Crosetti singled home a run in the eighth inning and the next day, powered by Lou Gehrig's home run, they won again 5–2, defeating Carl Hubbell. They now led the Series, 3 games to 1. But the Giants, tough competitors, salvaged Game Five, 5–4, behind Schumacher. The newspapers compared Schumacher to Horatius at the Bridge, and the scene moved a few blocks west to the Polo Grounds.

Game Six would end it, and DiMaggio was a dominating player. The Yankees moved ahead, but the Giants chipped at the lead until the ninth inning, when the Yankee margin was cut to a single run. DiMaggio opened the ninth with his third hit, a single. Gehrig singled him to third. Bill Dickey poked a bounding ball to Bill Terry at first base, and DiMaggio started for home plate.

That appeared to be a triumph of aggression over judgment. He braked and turned back toward third. But as soon as Terry threw the ball to the third baseman, DiMaggio changed direction again and scored with a head-first dive over the Giants' bulky catcher, "Harry the Horse" Danning. The Yankees kept on scoring until the game was out of the Giants' reach.

Then, with two out in the last half of the ninth inning, DiMaggio raced back into deep center field and caught Hank Leiber's drive almost 460 feet from home plate. The Yankees had won the game, 13–5, and the Series 4 games to 2.

DiMaggio stood alone in deep center field. All the players had been instructed to remain on the field until the president of the United States was driven off through the center-field gates. As Mr. Roosevelt's touring car rolled past DiMaggio, the president gave him a smile and a thumbs-up sign. DiMaggio has called this moment his greatest single thrill in sports.

Mrs. Rosalie DiMaggio, interviewed for a final time before she departed for San Francisco, said in Italian that she was proud of her son.

"Did he look like the best of the Yankees?"

"I couldn't say that. All the Yankees looked very good. And the Giants looked good, too. I feel sorry for them, playing so hard and losing."

Just before DiMaggio left for California he was finally able to relax with a reporter. "Well," he told Rud Rennie of the *Herald Tribune* while packing and moving about his hotel room, "it's back to San Francisco. I'm off to Columbus Avenue and Taylor."

Rennie asked how he had enjoyed his rookie season.

"It's been great," he said. "There's nothing like playing in a World Series. That's what makes baseball worthwhile. It gives you something to work for. There's nothing like it. A thrill was diving home safe in the ninth inning of the last game. It was a little risky, getting off third base as far as I did, but you take chances at a time like that. We needed the run. And the moment Terry started to throw behind me, I was gone."

"Any regrets, Joe?" Rennie asked. "Do you feel you made any mistakes?"

DiMaggio paused and turned away from a suitcase. "It was a great year, but I don't think I got swelled-headed," he said. "But, yeah, I did make one mistake, and I could kick myself for it. Not talking to anybody."

"Why didn't you talk to the press more?"

Joe looked serious and shrugged and said, "I dunno. But I'm sorry about it because the writers treated me great. Put in your story that I want to thank them a million."

DiMaggio seemed to have the country at his feet. His World Series share was $6,430.55; at twenty-one, in a Depression economy, he had earned more than $15,000. Soon he would be able to move his family from the cramped apartment on Taylor Street into the handsome stone house on Beach. He would invest wisely in a seafood restaurant on

Fisherman's Wharf, called Joe DiMaggio's Grotto, which his brother Tom managed profitably. He would wear expensively tailored suits, drive Cadillacs, and was said to find more willing show girls than even he knew what to do with. All this from playing baseball on sunlit summer afternoons.

The Yankees would dominate baseball and DiMaggio, everyone agreed, was the greatest Yankee of them all. As he aged and lines entered his long, strong face, he actually grew more handsome. His quiet manner bespoke a kind of elegance. He became The Yankee Clipper.

But tranquillity, if that was what he wanted, and he sometimes told intimates that it was, eluded him. He fought hard for higher salaries. He had already known a knee injury and the curiously scorched foot. Another injury, which might come at any time, could end his career overnight. You had to make as much as you could as fast as you could in a dicey business like baseball. But when he pressed for money the Yankees would beat him down and turn their friends in the press against him with suggestions that he was an arrogant and greedy young man. He would hear boos in every ballpark where he worked. The hoots wounded him both because he was proud and because he believed he had done nothing to warrant them.

Beyond that, he would never be able to make a happy marriage. Gehrig was happily married. Even Babe Ruth, once he settled down a bit, lived comfortably with his second wife, Claire. Joe's brothers and fellow center fielders, Vince and Dom, would marry loving, loyal wives.

But Joe, the idol of a country, found beds of thorns in marriage. Tranquillity would be a stranger to him. Loneliness would not. He would become, said Eddie Lopat, a fine pitcher on later Yankee teams, "the loneliest man I ever knew. He led the league in room service."

A columnist wrote that DiMaggio was the young man who had everything. Ahead for the golden rookie lay years not only of triumph, but ordeal.

Chapter ★ 5

Going for the Gold

*A*lthough historical perspective informs us that the late 1930s were memorable first for the nightmare ascendency of Adolf Hitler, Americans of the time were preoccupied with jobs and home relief—and whatever happened to the politician who promised a chicken in every pot?—during their staggering recovery from the Great Depression. How poor was the country? According to a Department of Commerce survey, 60 percent of all the automobiles sold in 1936 were purchased by families earning less than $2,000 a year. A car was, to be sure, both a symbol and symptom of affluence. Affluence on $40 a week.

In living rooms, on the radio, and in newspapers, economic debates became an order of the era. Were Roosevelt's social programs—the W.P.A., the C.C.C., and the rest of his mix that some called alphabet soup—helping the country to recover? (They were.) Wasn't the president pushing America down a red road toward socialism? (He was not.) When would the difficult business climate end so that American life could be as prosperous as it had appeared in the 1920s, with jobs abounding and profit charts climbing clear off the graphs? (Not until World War II shoved the economy into overdrive.)

But for the DiMaggios of San Francisco the Depression came to an end as soon as Joseph Paul established himself as a Yankee. He was a particularly generous son and brother. He bought the family a new house on Beach Street; he helped his brother Mike buy a fishing boat; he financed the family restaurant on Fisherman's Wharf. He was more than a great young ballplayer. He was a one-man economic-recovery program.

He does not usually speak about this particular burden and joy. He dislikes probing his own motivations, and besides, the whole area, DiMaggio family finances, strikes him as a matter almost as private as marriage. But even when he was a very young major leaguer he gave as much attention to the numbers typed into his contracts as he did to the flight of a fly ball.

A generation later, in the 1950s, a youthful Willie Mays agreed to sign a blank contract and let Horace Stoneham, the president of the New York Giants, fill in whatever amount struck Stoneham as fair. Young Willie approached life with a sense that as long as he was playing well, he would win appropriate rewards from God and his employer. DiMaggio tackled, and that is the suitable word, the Yankee management, with undisguised ferocity. Trust? Trust was merely the last name of a number of banks.

He skirmished with the Yankees after his rookie year and then, for his third season, 1938, loosed a categoric demand for $40,000, which would have made him the highest-paid player in baseball at the age of twenty-three.

Colonel Jacob Ruppert, the president of the Yankees, issued increasingly angry responses until he finally announced that DiMaggio would not get "a button more" than $25,000. DiMaggio responded with a number of wrathful statements. The battle of egos, wills, and dollars became ferocious.

Usually when contract arguments broke across sports pages in those long-ago days, fans sided with the player. No ballplayers' union existed, and contracts decreed that the athlete could either play for the team that had signed him the year before or, in effect, spend the summer working in a gas station, if he could find one to hire him. People identified with the athletes, not the owners.

But DiMaggio's demand for $40,000 a year when he was twenty-three ran against the American grain. It just seemed to be more money than any young ballplayer, maybe any young person, could be worth. It probably would have seemed too much even if DiMaggio had handled the negotiations with tact and a touch of humility, which he did not.

The Yankee management was able to marshal opposition in the press. In those days major league teams paid the traveling expenses and meals for reporters assigned to cover their games. This created an unhealthy alliance between the accounting departments of the clubs and the newspapers. In some, but not all, cases, baseball teams dictated the thrust of stories, saying, in one way or another: "You're our guest when we travel, you're our guest in spring training. Kindly write accordingly." A half-dozen writers followed the Yankee management line on every issue. The press-box term for such a character was "house man."

DiMaggio, the holdout, was portrayed as avaricious and headstrong by the ambient house men. But even reporters whose integrity and independence could not be stifled found the young DiMaggio excessive.

Ruppert insisted at one press conference that his offer of $25,000 was reasonable. From San Francisco, DiMaggio responded, like a pouting child: "That's what he thinks. I won't accept twenty-five thousand dollars. I'll stick right here until I get the salary I want."

A California newspaperman asked DiMaggio just where his Yankee contract was.

"In the city dump." Then, trying to soften that reply, Di-Maggio said it had been misplaced when the family moved. Too late. A twenty-three-year-old kid had thrown away an offer of $25,000.

These remarks reached a public trying to purchase a car on a family income of less than $2,000. The public, like the press, lost sympathy for DiMaggio. This hurt him, angered him, and reinforced the suspicious strains in his nature.

He was discovering in the late 1930s what Marilyn was to discover in the early 1950s: that even glory has its thorns. His first years as a public figure were frequently painful, in part because he made them so by overreaching. (He might respond, after long thought, that he was also overreaching when he caught Hank Greenberg's 460-foot drive.)

Judging from his responses at the time, he saw fans as inconstant and the press as less than trustworthy. From his viewpoint, and he has never been greatly sympathetic to other viewpoints, he was right.

An easier beginning with the Yankees might have encouraged him toward openness. But given his nature, and his proclivity for accident and injury, there would never be real ease to his baseball experiences, despite the illusion wrought by gliding grace. He seemed always to be fighting against injuries or being attacked for trying to earn what he believed he was worth.

Not even the press's gushing response to his first marriage, on November 19, 1939, cut through the layers of mistrust. By the time *that* relationship soured for good, after Marilyn entered his life in 1952, DiMaggio was locked into a complex, lifelong posture.

He knew who he was. Joe DiMaggio. If you were a crony, he'd share some baseball stories. If you were a stranger, you'd get a moment of civility. If you were somebody who wanted something from him, you drew suspicion.

Of course, everything was different, in the beginning, if you were a golden California blonde.

Everything proceeded from the ball field: fame, the opportunity to argue for real money, the sense of DiMaggio as a desirable and heroic young man. The ball field was his platform and in his time no one worked a ball field any better than, or perhaps as well as, Joe DiMaggio.

DiMaggio's performance during his second season with the Yankees was even more remarkable than his play as a rookie but it was then, in 1937, that the first storms accompanying his contract negotiations broke: clouds about a halo. He wintered quietly in San Francisco, playing a little basketball until the Yankees ordered him to desist. Too risky. With Tom's help he began to plan a more comfortable life. Money was the pathway there. He expressed disappointment, but kept his anger in check, when he could not get the Yankees to offer him a salary of more than $15,000 for the season of 1937. He was twenty-two.

But for weeks he refused to sign a contract, and he actually remained in San Francisco when the Yankees convened spring training at St. Petersburg in March. After the triumphant summer of 1936, it had been difficult for the Yankees to corral all their stars. Both Lou Gehrig and Red Ruffing turned down Colonel Ruppert's early offers, and by March the New York papers carried daily bulletins on the salary wars.

DiMaggio recognized, if grudgingly, that he could not do very well as the junior member of a holdout troika. In mid-March he accepted the $15,000, and when at length he arrived in Florida, he told reporters: "This holdout business is a lot tougher than playing ball. All I want to do is go back to work."

Curiously, or not so curiously, given his preoccupation with the possibilities of injury and disability, he developed pain in his right shoulder. He could swing a bat, but he could not throw. The badly burned foot of 1936 gave way to the mysteriously sore shoulder of 1937. He rested and stayed out of exhibition games. No progress. Finally, when the Yankees were barnstorming north, McCarthy sent DiMaggio to see a highly recommended physician in Knoxville, Tennessee. The doctor, one Reese Patterson, reported that DiMaggio was suffering from a decaying tooth and inflamed tonsils. Somehow poisons from the infections were settling into his right shoulder and causing pain.

DiMaggio was injured enough during his baseball career for some to suggest that he was accident-prone, but 1937 predates the popularity of psychosomatic medicine. DiMaggio was spared speculation that the bad shoulder and his response to it were rooted in emotional causes. However, tracing a bad throwing arm to tonsils, and indeed, missing the tonsil diagnosis for weeks, now seems like rather primitive medicine. Competent physicians today would spot tonsilitis promptly and, most likely, clear it up with an antibiotic.

Alarmed, DiMaggio left the team for New York, where Dr. Girard Oberrender, personal physician to Colonel Ruppert, confirmed Patterson's findings and conclusions. He removed both tonsils and adenoids at Lenox Hill Hospital. To DiMaggio's delight, the surgery worked splendidly. Almost as soon as he could swallow normally, the pain in his shoulder began to ease.

He made his way back into the Yankee lineup on May 1, with 3 hits. He was on his way to a superb season. He would lead the major leagues in home runs and a flock of other statistics and carry the Yankees along with him to another walkaway pennant.

Not much humor comes of the DiMaggio baseball years, but there is one light ethnic story that persists from 1937. During a Yankee romp over the St. Louis Browns, someone rapped a ground ball to Lefty Gomez with a man on first. Both Tony Lazzeri and Frankie Crosetti moved toward second base, but Gomez threw the baseball directly to DiMaggio, who was running in from center field to back up the play.

The runner, of course, was safe. After the inning ended, Joe McCarthy turned on Gomez and asked what the hell he was doing.

"Someone shouted, 'Throw it to the dago,'" Gomez said, "but nobody said which dago."

McCarthy's temper flared. He shouted to the entire Yankee bench, "From now on specify *which* dago."

The dugout erupted in laughter until even McCarthy realized that he was being teased.

Another light day, or light morning, saw DiMaggio travel to the Biograph studios on 175th Street in the Bronx to play a brief role in a movie called *Manhattan Merry-Go-Round.* Even though he had to report to the studio at 7 A.M., DiMaggio enjoyed himself because he was surrounded by beautiful women.

He was hitting .372 that August when he drew his three-line role. The lines were:

"Well, I'm here."

"What?"

"But I'm—"

A girl from the Kay Thompson chorus combed DiMaggio's hair for a publicity photograph. Another girl manicured his nails. DiMaggio smiled and remarked to William Birnie, a reporter from the *New York World-Telegram,* "This is hotter than a ball park."

"They seem to like you," Birnie said. "What's your recipe?"

"Never fall in love," DiMaggio said. "I just talk a good game with women."

Although Birnie pointedly described DiMaggio as a "buck-toothed Yankee outfielder," he also interviewed several chorus girls who, Birnie reported, thought that DiMaggio was "colossal."

DiMaggio's wardrobe consisted of white shoes, tan slacks, and a checkered sport jacket. He completed his scene in twelve takes, which the director, Richard Auer, said wasn't half bad for an amateur.

"The toughest part of acting," DiMaggio pronounced with great authority, "is being nonchalant."

He chatted not only with the reporters but with numbers of young women on the set. When he departed for batting practice at the Stadium he had made a date with a pretty, blond bit player who was new to the city from Minnesota.

This was the beginning of the end of DiMaggio's never-fall-in-love recipe. The Minnesota girl was Dorothy Arnold.

Between May 1 and July 4, DiMaggio hit no fewer than 20 home runs. A newspaper ran a cartoon of Yankee Stadium with the right-field stands labeled RUTHVILLE and the left-field seats, where most of DiMaggio's home runs landed, marked LITTLE ITALY. A catcher was quoted as saying that "DiMaggio's bat swinging makes the loudest swish of anybody since Babe Ruth." Sportswriters wrote that DiMaggio might well break Ruth's classic record of 60 home runs in a single season.

He never came close. The layout of Yankee Stadium handicapped right-handed hitters and besides, DiMaggio did not have Ruth's prodigious power, any more than he had Ruth's outgoing and dominating personality. Contrasts to Ruth are significant as a rite of passage: one superhero was replacing another.

After DiMaggio hit a grand-slam home run at the Stadium on July 4, a *New York Times* sportswriter set down the response:

"The stands shook with shouts and stomping, a deafening crescendo of shrieks, cheers, whistling and handclapping. At the plate there began a demonstration of affectionate mobbing that continued on the bench as every player pummeled and thumped the youth."

He became very quickly a prince of the city. Yankee management people considered the DiMaggio phenomenon, and Ed Barrow summoned the young star to his office and volunteered advice. "I know the fans are all for you, Joe," he said, "and that's great, but fans can turn around. The smartest thing is not to take all that applause too seriously."

DiMaggio was to echo this sentiment to Marilyn seventeen years later, but, of course, the hurrahs pleased him and contributed to his growing sense of himself. When sixty thousand people trumpet your name, humility, as well as the eardrums, suffers a beating.

Wherever DiMaggio walked in Manhattan, strangers greeted him. "How ya doing, Joe? Nice hitting, Joe. Hey, sign this for me, will ya?" He was civil to his idolators, even though he didn't smile very much.

DiMaggio insisted to reporters that he spent his hours away from the ballpark listening to a radio, or resting, or going to a movie. He was not a swaggerer like Ruth, nor did he drink with the abandon of his center-field successor Mickey Mantle, but he began to develop a set of macho friends with whom he could relax.

One was the fight manager, Joe Gould, who helped him find endorsements and reviewed DiMaggio's contract for *Manhattan Merry-Go-Round.* Another was Al Schacht, a onetime Washington pitcher who created a broad and funny baseball comedy act that he performed at ballparks. DiMaggio met Toots Shor and George Solotaire, who ran the Adelphi Theater Ticket Agency and is credited with devising such terms as "dullsville" for boring shows and "splitsville" for divorce. Solotaire made enough money in the ticket brokerage to move "from Brownsville [a poor neighborhood in Brooklyn] to Bronxville," and said that the Astors and the Vanderbilts were steady clients of his ticket business. But DiMaggio was Solotaire's particular hero.

What these new people brought DiMaggio was a tough-talking Broadway outlook, chatter about the rich and famous and, though they tried to mask it, unalloyed awe for the talents of their new young friend. Solotaire would spin out favorite stories. "You know, J. P. Morgan, the rich guy, once called for tickets to the same show for seven straight Saturday nights."

"How come?" DiMaggio said.

"It wasn't the music. He had an eye for a broad in the chorus line."

Shor told his stories about speakeasy days and the years he had spent working as a bouncer. Gould talked about his fighter Jimmy Braddock, who had to toil as a day laborer while making his way toward the heavyweight championship. But inevitably the conversation focused on the great Yankee team that was running away with the pennant and on the tall young center fielder who was, the Broadway crowd agreed, already the greatest player in baseball. It was heady stuff.

If he tired of the company of men, there were always show girls who were excited to meet a strapping, wide-shouldered, and heroic young man. DiMaggio continued to live in hotels—the New Yorker, the Edison, and the Madison at various times, but at this point in his life he was simply too busy, and too delighted with New York, his own career, the Broadway characters, and the willing show girls to feel loneliness. "I guess," he remarked to a friend, "I'm just a naturally lucky guy. Sometimes everything seems too good to be true—or to last. I mean, everything started out with so little promise. We were poor and I didn't like fishing for a living and it didn't seem that I'd ever be able to do anything else. Then, all of a sudden, everything is just right." DiMaggio made a small sigh of contentment.

He liked Dorothy Arnold. She was pretty, knew sports, adored him. But he wasn't rushing into anything there. When she announced on April 25, 1939, that they were engaged, he seemed a bit put off.

Although he could never approach Ruth's record, in 1937 he reached his own career high with a total of 46 home runs. The outfield at the old Yankee Stadium stretched to almost 470 feet at its deepest point and the cow-pasture acreage cut two ways. It did give DiMaggio ample room to run down long fly balls. He could have found no better setting to display his fielding skills. But the great depth, particularly in left-center field, converted many of his own long drives from home runs into doubles or triples, or, worst of all, fine running catches by other outfielders. Later, a popular baseball remark suggested that if Ted Williams had played in Yankee Stadium [with its short right field] he would have hit 60 home runs a year. "And if DiMaggio played in Fenway Park [with its short left], he'd hit seventy."

The Yankees won the 1937 pennant by 13 games and rolled over the Giants, 4 games to 1, in the World Series. The winning share was $6,471.10. DiMaggio headed back to San Francisco as a national hero.

His two years as a major leaguer had earned him $36,347 just from baseball. Side activities probably brought the total to more than $40,000, a fortune in the 1930s.

But the money he banked did not slake DiMaggio's thirst for more. The summer cheers resounded in his memory. Hundreds of thousands of people were paying to see him play. A growing number insisted that he was the best ballplayer in the game. Very well, DiMaggio decided. Very nice.

Now it was time for the Yankees to pay him accordingly.

A sense, a deep quivering anxiety, grew in America that the world was headed for terrible storms. In March of 1938, spring-training time, Hitler's soldiers occupied Austria, and in a Nazi "rite of purification," twenty thousand books were burned in Mozart's birthplace, Salzburg. The volumes burned, the *Herald Tribune* reported, consisted mostly of works by Jewish authors. This obscene ritual was organized by the National Socialist Teachers' Association. Arturo Toscanini, the great conductor, canceled an engagement in Salzburg and traveled instead to Haifa, where he conducted the newly formed Palestine Symphony Orchestra.

The Spanish Republic was falling before the onslaught of Francisco Franco's forces, supported by German bombers and Italian fascist troops. The Japanese swept south in China, raging through Nanking, and Japanese aircraft bombed and sank the U.S. Navy gunboat *Panay*. An American Nazi group, the

German-American Bund, held frightening rallies in the York-ville district of Manhattan and outdoors in northern New Jersey. After a few protestors appeared at a Yorkville meeting, Fritz Kuhn, the Bund leader, said from a podium, "We demand the protection of the Constitution while we organize to fight the Jews and communists." Then four Bundists beat a crippled Jewish pamphleteer named Charles Weiss and inked swastikas on his back and chest.

With the general news so grim and agitating, sports and the sports pages became more than ever a great escape. Base-ball's popularity tends to run in cyclic patterns, around a constant central core of glowing fans; DiMaggio, the handsome, hawk-faced newcomer, won enthusiasts for the game. Millions of Americans were relieved to turn away from headlines re-counting war and violence and plunge into the sports section. There they could read of DiMaggio's summertime heroics and soon thereafter, his wintertime bargaining with the Yankees. That was less disquieting than the front pages, somehow safer.

I don't mean to suggest the sports pages did not provoke passions. Clearly they did. But these were passions on a smaller scale than those created by the Nazis or the Japanese militarists, passions one could live with and enjoy. Much of the country preoccupied itself with heroes from Hollywood and the sports arenas. People complained that the hard news was depressing. The hell with Hitler. Maybe he'll go away. Let's see what's doing with DiMaggio.

Across the years, DiMaggio has had little to say about his extraordinary 1938 holdout. No one knows with certainty—he himself may not remember—exactly what prompted him to demand that the Yankees increase his salary from $15,000 to $40,000. Baseball salaries simply did not jump in such loga-rithmic progressions; his demand was both naïve and vain. DiMaggio remarked vaguely a few seasons later that "some of my friends told me I was worth it." Perhaps. But the ar-rogance he flashed while bickering was all his own.

The episode began innocuously with a report after the

1937 World Series that DiMaggio and the Yankee management had secretly agreed on his salary for 1938. The story was false but it proved good enough gossip to persist. When DiMaggio and the Yankee front office subsequently waged a furious struggle, certain newspapermen suggested that it was a device, just a show, to keep DiMaggio and the Yankees in the headlines. (DiMaggio himself later called the struggle "plain hell.")

On January 17, 1938, DiMaggio arrived in Manhattan to accept an award as "Player of the Year" from the New York chapter of the Baseball Writers Association of America. The occasion was a black-tie banquet at the Hotel Commodore that would conclude with a series of skits in which the sportswriters gave themselves a chance to impersonate famous baseball people and even to sing.

DiMaggio accepted his award with a few remarks of thanks both to the writers and his supporting cast of Yankees. There was no sense of impending controversy that night.

On January 20, Ed Barrow announced that the Yankees had mailed contracts to all twenty-eight players carried on the team roster. DiMaggio was offered $15,000 again, a bid the *Times* dismissed as "a mere formality. That the great Di-Madge is due for a substantial boost for his sensational second-year work," John Drebinger wrote, "seems to be accepted all the way around."

Then Drebinger raised a recurrent issue. "By reason of DiMaggio's close association with Joe Gould, the fight manager, who seems to be taking more than a friendly interest in the young player's financial affairs, it is quite certain that DiMaggio will enter his conference [with both Ed Barrow and Colonel Jacob Ruppert on January 21] well coached in setting forth his demands. Gould, however, emphatically denied that he was Joe's 'manager.'"

The last sentence gives the Drebinger story a ring of fairness. He seems to be giving readers both sides. But Drebinger's raising the suggestion that DiMaggio secretly worked with an agent, in violation of the rules baseball imposed on its players, points toward another conclusion. Several Yankee officials were close to Drebinger. It is reasonable to conclude that they talked to him about Gould, as a potential problem, possibly on the night of the baseball writers' dinner, at the dinner itself or during a cocktail party that preceded it. They would thus have been able to use Drebinger to plant an item in the *Times* that said in effect: The kid plays great, but watch out for his sneaky agent, who can make trouble. Gould was hardly the only person in New York or San Francisco offering DiMaggio free financial advice. He was, however, the one character Yankee executives would single out if they wanted to marshal public opinion against their star. Fight managers were by reputation cigar smokers, foul-mouthed and corrupt. Bad company.

DiMaggio was told to appear at 10 A.M. on January 21 in the colonel's offices at the Ruppert Brewery, a hamlet of red-brick buildings on the Upper East Side of Manhattan. Ruppert's fortune came from the family beer. His military title came from no more bellicose an assembly than the New York National Guard. If you wanted to get along with this rich and natty bachelor, you called him by the title. He considered himself, Ruppert once said, "a gentleman, a sportsman, and a Catholic." He took himself very seriously. It annoyed him when anyone called him "Jake."

DiMaggio was prompt. Ruppert and Barrow kept him waiting in a reception room for forty-five minutes. There DiMaggio posed for photographers and listened to the chatter of reporters, but he had enough sense not to comment on the meeting directly ahead.

After DiMaggio finally was led into Ruppert's office, Ed Barrow, a shaggy-browed character who was the chief defender of the Yankee exchequer, mentioned the figure of $15,000. But, he said, the Yankees appreciated DiMaggio's work and might be induced to go higher.

"How much higher?" DiMaggio said.

"What are you looking for, DiMaggio?" Ruppert said.

"What are you offering?"

Silence. It is a good negotiating tactic to force the opposing side to mention its serious figure first. Barrow and Ruppert were skilled at this particular game and when their silence persisted, DiMaggio recited some of his imposing statistics and mentioned the success he had helped bring to the team. More silence. Finally, he said $40,000.

"What would you say?" Ed Barrow asked carefully, "if I told you that Lou Gehrig, who's been a star for fifteen years, doesn't make forty thousand dollars himself."

"I'd say, Mr. Barrow," DiMaggio answered, "that Gehrig is grossly underpaid." The temperature in the room dropped 20 degrees.

After a time Ruppert said that he would pay DiMaggio $25,000 for 1938, but no more. That would "make you the highest-salaried third-year man in baseball history." DiMaggio said he was sticking to his demand. Forty thousand. The discussion hit a wall. Ruppert said DiMaggio would have to take $25,000 or stay home next summer. DiMaggio glared. Ruppert said that there was no sense in talking further, that he was not bargaining, that $25,000 was a final offer. "And one more thing, DiMaggio. Don't go talking about this meeting with the writers. It will do you no good."

DiMaggio said that the one thing they did agree on was not discussing his salary with reporters. Then, unspeaking and grim, he fled the brewery.

Ruppert called in the press and in his baronial way broke the code of silence. "I suppose there's no end of wild guessing among you fellows," Ruppert said, "so I might as well tell." He did, adding that $25,000 was "a fair salary for DiMaggio. I don't intend to go higher."

DiMaggio returned to San Francisco, where he spent some time helping Tom manage the restaurant and more time sweating out his cold war. Spring training began in Florida. DiMaggio worked out a few times in Hanford, California, with the San Francisco Seals. New York newspapermen covering the Yankees in St. Petersburg began to fire blowguns. Someone wrote that "DiMaggio is talking dollars, but making no sense." On March 12, Gehrig accepted a $3,000 raise and signed a contract for $39,000. A California newspaperman brought that news to DiMaggio.

"It makes no difference to me what Gehrig's done," Di-Maggio snapped. "I'm still dickering with Colonel Ruppert. I've returned my contract unsigned." (He probably had not. This was the contract he earlier said had ended in the San Francisco municipal dump.)

Ruppert hired a private Pullman car to carry him off to spring training. He did not, in that circumstance, plead poverty, but before boarding he fired a few more rounds at his center fielder. DiMaggio was "ungrateful and unfair to his teammates." He would not get "a button over twenty-five thousand dollars." All "the other boys" were working themselves into shape. DiMaggio was "just trying to get out of spring training." Then, attended by a valet and other servants, the Baron of Hops mounted his private Pullman.

Actually, Ruppert was both angry and worried. DiMaggio was threatening the entire structure of salaries that baseball owners had created: Young players, however gifted, were given increases slowly and with reluctance. Besides, if DiMaggio got away with $40,000 for 1938, what would other Yankees demand for 1939? Babe Ruth had lifted star salaries behind his own when he reached an outrageous $80,000 a season during the 1920s. This young man, Ruppert decided, had to be brought up short.

The colonel leaned on his field manager, and a few days later at St. Petersburg, Joe McCarthy entered the dispute. Managers, like ballplayers, are hired hands, and to this day try to remove themselves from their athletes' contract negotiations. The manager has to live with both sides, the front office and the ballplayers, all summer. But now McCarthy announced in the team's press room: "The Yankees can get along without DiMaggio. That twenty-five thousand dollars is final."

From San Francisco came a swaggering response. "Maybe McCarthy knows what he's talking about and maybe he doesn't. That contract for twenty-five thousand dollars is gone with the wind. The Yankees are going to pay my price or else."

Or else what? DiMaggio was negotiating against a tough company that held exclusive rights to services. Or else he'd quit and go fishing? Absurd. Or else he'd tell the world that the Yankees were tightwads? The world regarded $25,000 as a marvelous salary. DiMaggio was running on a treadmill.

In calm moments he conceded that he was not going to get his $40,000. He talked to his friend Tom Laird, the sports editor of the *San Francisco News,* and said that he didn't actually *have* to get that figure. He might take less. But, as a matter of personal pride and dignity, he had to extract an offer of more than $25,000.

"He can say anything he wants," Ruppert declaimed. "Twenty-five thousand and not a button more. This is one case in which I'm determined to be the winner."

DiMaggio lapsed back into silence. The Yankees finished their labors in St. Petersburg and Ruppert told the press, "I have nothing new on DiMaggio. I have forgotten all about him. Presidents go into eclipse. Kings have their thrones moved from under them. Great ballplayers pass on. If DiMaggio isn't out there, we have Myril Hoag for center field."

The Yankees barnstormed north. Little Rock. Atlanta. Knoxville. Spartanburg. Baltimore, the birthplace of Babe Ruth. A reporter picked up a tip that DiMaggio would accept the $25,000 contract if a $2,500 signing bonus was added to it. DiMaggio would not comment on the rumor.

Henry Ford celebrated the fiftieth anniversary of his marriage to Clara Bryant and said they had never had an argument. The great football player Slingin' Sammy Baugh married Miss Edmonia Smith in Sweetwater, Texas. Richard Whitney, a five-time president of the New York Stock Exchange, began a five-year prison sentence for grand larceny as Sing Sing convict number 94835. DiMaggio was out of the headlines now, drawing only occasional mentions at the bottom of the sports pages.

Jack Doyle, described by the *Herald Tribune* as a "Broadway betting man," installed the Yankees as 7-to-10 favorites to win their third straight pennant. Myril Hoag batted .352 in spring training. The *Herald Tribune* ran an editorial welcoming the return of major league baseball to New York.

"The Yankees, led by the popular Mr. Joseph McCarthy, are, as usual, very strong. The immortal Lou Gehrig will be at first base. To be sure the Yankees will miss the brilliant California youngster, Joseph DiMaggio, until he decides to be reasonable about his salary demands. [He] will eventually come to terms. They nearly always do. But even so he has hurt himself with his New York admirers, trying to get too much money out of poor [sic] dear Colonel Ruppert."

In the 1930s ballplayers drew expense money for spring training, but salary started only with the onset of the regular season. Ruppert took pains to explain this after sportswriters wondered if he was docking DiMaggio for the days that the star was missing. "The best way," Ruppert said, "might be to start salaries when training begins. Personally I would favor that. But the poorer clubs oppose it. They don't want to have to pay salaries until the regular season begins and they start getting their share of gate receipts.

"But be assured of this. If DiMaggio is not ready to play for the Yankees on opening day, we will start docking his salary then."

On Easter Sunday, April 17, the St. Louis Cardinals stole headlines by selling Dizzy Dean, the flamboyant fastball pitcher, to the Chicago Cubs for $185,000 and three lesser ballplayers. A smaller story in the *Herald Tribune* reported that "beginning tomorrow, when the Yankees open in Boston, DiMaggio's stubborn behavior will start costing him $162 a day." (The figure was based on a per-diem calculation of a $25,000 seasonal salary.) The *Tribune*'s sports columnist Richards Vidmer published his pennant selections. "The American League race will not be so close as to cause sustained excitement. And the winner? The Yankees, with or without Joe DiMaggio."

DiMaggio talked to Tom, talked to friends. The issue, pride versus cash, yielded no solution. Donald Barnes, the president of the St. Louis Browns, that ball club of staggering ineptitude, telephoned Ruppert and offered $150,000 cash for the rights to DiMaggio. "My thinking," Barnes said, "is that you might be willing to dispose of a fellow who is quite likely to be a disturbing influence on a great ball club."

Ruppert was curt. "DiMaggio is not for sale at any price."

The Yankees traveled to Boston and lost to the Red Sox, 8–4, on opening day. Arthur Patterson of the *Herald Tribune* interviewed ballplayers in the clubhouse about DiMaggio. No one wanted to be quoted by name but the anonymous comments mixed sorrow and anger. Joe didn't understand the way things worked. He didn't seem to be worrying about the team. Mostly, one ballplayer snapped, "he wants to get rich quick."

The Yankees split 2 games with the Red Sox on Tuesday, Patriot's Day, in Boston, and now the season was 3 games old. The Yankees were indeed playing without DiMaggio. Two days. DiMaggio was out $324 Depression dollars. The debit meter was running.

Tom couldn't help him. Ruppert would not let him save face. DiMaggio composed a wire of capitulation and sent it to the Yankees:

YOUR TERMS ACCEPTED. LEAVE AT 2:40 P.M. [Wednesday] ARRIVE 7:30 SATURDAY MORNING.

He was angry and he was powerless. He told a San Francisco reporter that he was conceding. Then, trying to say something positive about his defeat, he added: "This year I'm going to have such a good season that there won't be any room for argument next year."

The nature of economics being what it is, no ballplayer has ever had that good a season.

The Yankee management and the natty Colonel Ruppert cackled in triumph. They had pinned DiMaggio to their terms as a butterfly is pinned against a post. Now they wanted to make him squirm.

The Yankees released his wire to the New York press. That meant reporters would assemble to meet his train Saturday morning among the old marble pillars of Pennsylvania Station. Let him explain himself to a bunch of newspapermen who weren't even making $100 a week.

Then, on the matter of salary, a Yankee spokesman explained that, of course, salary could not commence until DiMaggio actually was ready to play. Joe McCarthy would be the arbiter there. No pay for DiMaggio until McCarthy decided that he was in shape.

Before boarding a train in San Francisco, DiMaggio offered diplomatic statements to a local newspaperman. He was excited to be heading for New York, where he could "start rapping the ball again. I'd sure rather play ball than hold out." The Yankees were "a championship club" and "a swell bunch of fellows." Diplomacy all right, but the war had been lost.

A dozen reporters and photographers gathered at Penn Station early that Saturday morning. DiMaggio, whose sense of public relations was still somewhat primitive, ducked the press by leaving the train in Newark. There he was met by, of all people, Joe Gould, the fight manager, the agent who was not an agent. Reporters finally found them having breakfast at a restaurant, Jimmy Braddock's, which, may have been owned by Gould, and was, to be sure, named for Gould's brave fighter. Headstrong DiMaggio defiance. He's not my agent on baseball matters but when I arrive in New York to sign a contract, he's the first feller that I see.

The Yankees at once allowed DiMaggio to take batting practice and sit on the bench, but pointedly waited two days, until April 25, before presenting him with his $25,000 contract. Ruppert met DiMaggio privately for a few minutes, then invited in the press. "We're going to review this thing right in front of your eyes," he told reporters.

"DiMaggio," Ruppert said, "is there any bonus for you here?"

DiMaggio shook his head. Ruppert picked up the contract and considered it. "DiMaggio," he said, "put in your full address." DiMaggio had printed the address of his new home on Beach Street, neglecting to add "San Francisco, California."

"That's so we'll know where to get in touch with you," said Ruppert the conqueror.

"Joe," a reporter said, "when you met with the colonel alone, was he peeved?"

"If he was, so was I," DiMaggio answered. Ruppert shook his head, like the father of a talented, spirited, but poorly disciplined child. He explained again that DiMaggio would not start to earn money until he was "in playing condition."

"Suppose he makes a trip with the team?" a reporter asked.

"Until he's in condition," Ruppert said, "if he wants to travel with the Yankees, he'll have to pay his own way."

DiMaggio paled but held his tongue. He elected to skip a Yankee trip to Philadelphia and organized what must have been a wonderfully comical batting practice for himself at Yankee Stadium. Al Schacht, who had last pitched in the major leagues seventeen years before, did the throwing. A collection of youngsters and Broadway characters, including Joe Gould, who appeared under a beret, shagged flies. DiMaggio neglected only to hire Groucho Marx as public-address announcer.

By the time the comedy ran down and McCarthy elected to start him in center field, DiMaggio had lost eleven days' pay, roughly $1,800.

On DiMaggio's first day back at work, April 30, in Washington, Taft Wright hit a fly ball into short center field. DiMaggio and the fine rookie second baseman Joe Gordon went for the ball. DiMaggio was standing under it when Gordon ran into him. Coming out of left field, Myril Hoag caught the fly. DiMaggio and Gordon spent the night in Garfield Hospital.

But the next day, DiMaggio was well enough to play again. Another day. Another $162. He hit a home run.

Ruppert had made his point with a force DiMaggio has never forgotten nor perhaps forgiven. Kenesaw Mountain Landis, the commissioner of baseball, had yet to make his. He called DiMaggio into his office and pressed him sharply on the Joe Gould connection. Landis, a former federal judge, had been hired to supervise baseball operations by the club owners after the Chicago White Sox had thrown the 1919 World Series for a gambling group directed by the late Arnold Rothstein. Landis was white-haired, craggy-faced, bony, and severe.

The meeting was secret. No word of it escaped for almost a year. DiMaggio insisted to Landis that Gould was simply a friend who gave him business advice on matters beyond his Yankee contract. Landis warned DiMaggio that if Gould was getting a percentage of Yankee money, DiMaggio might be suspended or banished from major league baseball for life.

DiMaggio repeated his disclaimer. He must have been terrified.

The Sunday *Herald Tribune* ran an advertising cartoon in its comics section that made it appear as if baseball life for DiMaggio were just as it had been. Two young men, finding they can have the afternoon off, decide to visit Yankee Stadium. DiMaggio hits a game-winning home run and one of them catches it. They tramp to the players' gate so they can ask DiMaggio to autograph the baseball.

One says, "I caught the ball you socked into the stands, Joe! Would you autograph it for me?"

The cartoon DiMaggio is smiling as he says: "Sure, fella! Just wait until Lou [Gehrig] and I light up a couple of Camels!"

But things were not as they had been. Fans booed DiMaggio in the Stadium and all around the American League. They threw so much debris at him that one Yankee suggested he wear a catcher's mask in center field. His fan mail turned angry, even hateful.

DiMaggio played well but he was upset and confused. After the season, he unburdened himself to columnist Joe Williams of the *New York World-Telegram*.

"The fans," Williams wrote, "have decided the Colonel was right and the player was wrong and they, let [DiMaggio] have it every time he stuck his patrician schnozzle out of the dugout."

"All I was doing," DiMaggio said, "was trying to get as much as I could. Is that so terrible? I had a great season and some of my friends"—he was careful not to name them—"said I ought to be worth $40,000 to a team like the Yankees. I guess they were wrong. I *know* I was wrong holding out as long as I did.

"I hear the boos and I read in the paper that the cheers offset them, but you can't prove that by me. All I ever hear is boos. At first I thought it would wear off, but every town I'd go into I'd get a fresh batch of razberries right between the eyes. It didn't seem to matter whether I had a good day or a bad one. Pretty soon I got the idea that the only reason people came to a game at all was to boo DiMaggio.

"And the mail. You would have thought I kidnapped Lindbergh's baby the way some of the letters read. Boy, did they tell me where to get off."

Late in the season of 1938, DiMaggio drove himself in a race with Jimmie Foxx, the massive first baseman of the Boston Red Sox, for the league batting championship. Foxx was hitting .347; DiMaggio was at .341. The fans, particularly Yankee fans, were caught up in the struggle and at last forgave DiMaggio his holdout and stopped booing. "Then I couldn't hit a lick," DiMaggio said, "because I started trying too hard. I sensed that the fans were coming back to me and I wanted to keep them on my side. I tried so hard I tightened up. I lost the naturalness of my swing and instead of creeping up on Foxx, I slipped further away from him each day." (Foxx won the batting championship with .349. He also batted in 175 runs and hit 50 homers. Those 50 were second best. Hank Greenberg hit 58.)

The Yankees won their third straight pennant easily and swept the World Series from the Chicago Cubs with disdainful ease. People began to say, "Break up the Yankees."

One of DiMaggio's basic qualities in baseball was an ability to learn from his own mistakes, even though he had a hard time admitting them. As no young ballplayer before him, he had elected to challenge the Yankees and with them the full feudal power of organized baseball. When he was feeling talkative he justified his action to friends. He had already hurt a knee, come up with a sore arm, and been knocked unconscious by the collision in Washington. A fine pitcher, Monty Stratton, had lost a leg and his career in a hunting accident. "Look," DiMaggio said, "a ballplayer shouldn't be selfish or try to put a price on his services that's way too high. But you never know when something will happen and you won't be able to play ball anymore. I know it looks easy, but it's rough out there. You can break a leg. A fastball can hit you in the head. So any ballplayer who doesn't try to get all he can while he can get it is a sucker."

Good tough pragmatism. But in trying to become the highest-paid player in baseball at the age of twenty-three, DiMaggio had put a price on his own services that was, in the context of the times, "way too high." He would never be easy for the Yankees to sign until the last few seasons of his baseball life, when he and the Yankees both seemed content with $100,000. But he never again made such unrealistic demands, nor did he issue so many arrogant public statements. He wanted to be paid $30,000 in 1939, a $5,000 raise. The Yankees offered him $27,500. He ground his teeth, said nothing, and signed in March.

Jacob Ruppert died at seventy-one on January 13, 1939, and leadership of the organization passed on to Ed Barrow, also seventy-one, and, if anything, more severe than Ruppert. Even though Ruppert always called his players by their last names, by way of underscoring the matter of class distinction, even though he could be ugly when crossed, Ruppert was a rich man with a marvelous toy, the Yankees. For all his imperious bluster, there remained about him a suggestion that he was a fan.

Barrow was strictly business, strictly professional. After he assumed command, he mentioned to friends that three interesting rookie outfielders were coming to spring training in 1939. (The best would be Charlie "King Kong" Keller.) If DiMaggio made any more outrageous salary demands, or again attacked his employers in the press, Barrow said, the Yankees might do best simply to sell his contract to the highest bidder. Remarks of this impact travel with great speed. During the winter of 1938–39, the last winter before the onset of World War II, there was talk in New York that the Yankees now regarded DiMaggio as expendable.

The Cardinals had disposed of Dizzy Dean, who soon developed arm trouble in Chicago. Barrow considered one baseball rule ineluctable. There was no such thing as an indispensable ballplayer. The good of the organization always came first.

Barrow was no one to trifle with. Indeed, after DiMaggio's so-called Golden Year of 1941, when he hit safely in 56 consecutive games, Barrow suggested that DiMaggio take a pay cut—the salary by then was $37,500—"because there's a war on." DiMaggio's answer was brief and accurate: "Preposterous."

But with Barrow in ascendancy in 1939, DiMaggio's New York friends heard stories that the Yankees might sell their brightest star and they urged him to be careful. He took them seriously.

For one thing, he did not want to endure all those hoots again. The booing made baseball such an ordeal, he said, that at one point he was smoking a full pack of cigarettes before each game.

Beyond that, he did not want to find himself playing center field for the St. Louis Browns. No pitcher's curveball could make DiMaggio cringe at home plate, but something in Ed Barrow's cold, gruff manner set off signals of alarm.

Barrow must have frightened him.

Each year's salary moved up in relatively small, orderly increments for some time. He was raised from $27,500 to $32,000 in 1940; to $37,500 in 1941; and after the batting streak, to $43,750 in 1942.

There remains a particularly current relevance to DiMaggio's experience as a holdout in his embattled season of 1938. Once he defied the organization, the Yankees treated him in a merciless and autocratic way. A ballplayer had few baseball rights and the Yankee management, possessed of the most glorious star in the game, came down on him with a cataract of power. They were telling DiMaggio, and with him every other major leaguer, Know your place.

After the team won its third consecutive World Series, the Yankees could comfortably have returned the $1,800 docked from DiMaggio's 1938 salary. Imagine how nicely that would have played. Back to the brewery. Summon the press. Ruppert announces: "DiMaggio has given us another splendid performance, so we've decided to pay him as though he played the full year."

DiMaggio: "Thank you, Colonel."

Smiles. Press cheers good-naturedly. Flashbulbs light up the room. Ruppert offers drinks all around. Mellow glow.

But the Yankee management did not behave that generously. Now, five decades later, the men who own ball clubs complain that the athletes have *too* many rights, the athletes are merciless, and the athletes' agents don't care about the game. Sooner or later, former commissioner Bowie Kuhn maintained, a major league team will go bankrupt. (Actually, for more than fifteen years, the prices of major league franchises have moved up in a perpetual inflationary spiral.)

In his seventies, Joe DiMaggio has become carefully noncontroversial with public statements. He says mostly that in his own case he truly believes a long-term multimillion-dollar-contract would have increased the level of his performance by relieving him of a certain amount of stress.

That's it. That's all he has to say. But looking at the tight-lipped, solemn face and remembering the ferocity of his salary wars fifty years ago, you can almost hear a sentence that is unuttered.

The bastard owners brought it on themselves.

Chapter ★ 6

Joe and Dorothy

The character, the true ambitions and the most secret heart of Dorothy Arnoldine Olson are somewhat veiled by time. The first Mrs. Joe DiMaggio comes down to us in photographs as a smiling and rather athletic-looking blonde with plucked and penciled eyebrows, a fine, healthy figure, and a face that makes you think: "I know her. She was third from the left last year in the chorus line at Caesar's Palace." Without question, Dorothy was an attractive woman, but the brow is a bit too wide and the jaw a touch too strong for classic beauty. She looks like what she was: a jazzy show girl.

Dorothy's comments on Joe were conflicted, which of course tells us something about herself, and she seems to have spent her own life divided by cross ambitions. She wanted to have a successful show-business career. This eluded her. As

Dorothy Arnold she never became a major movie star, although she did come close enough to keep that ambition at a boil. She wanted a happy marriage and this also proved elusive until her later years when, in the classic phrase, the heyday in the blood is tame.

She liked to tell Broadway columnists that she had been "captivated" by DiMaggio on the set of *Manhattan Merry-Go-Round* after taking in his angular good looks with a single and ultimately devouring glance. "I fell in love with him," Dorothy insisted, "before I even knew who he was."

Perhaps. But some of the later interplay between them and her own independent conduct suggests that she knew perfectly well who he was before surrendering to love. Indeed, her marriage to the most famous baseball player on earth may have been impelled as much by her drive for fame, even borrowed fame, as it was by passion.

Dorothy and Joe were involved in flirtation and romance, separation and divorce, then more flirtation and romance from 1939 clear up to 1952, when DiMaggio's love affair with Marilyn split them for good and all. She liked to say that she wished Joe only the best, but Dorothy's concept of the best for a former husband did not include a blonde who was more glamorous than she. Most of her public statements on Joe were tempered, even ladylike, except that once in a while traces of vitriol appeared about the edges of her public smile. When Joe's affair with Marilyn heated up in 1952, Dorothy came charging into court with angry allegations that Joe was exposing their son to people and places unsuitable for a child. And, because Dorothy and her lawyers were twentieth-century Americans, her caterwauling was accompanied by court papers in which she tried to terminate the father's visitation rights and increase the child-support payments she received. (The adversarial system never works mischief more powerfully than in an angry divorce and its long aftermath.)

In her anger Dorothy now insisted that Joe had been a cold and insensitive husband. He and domesticity were strangers. He had never really worked at being married. He pre-

ferred staying up all hours and running around with the boys
(and, implicitly, the girls). The difference between the words
of Dorothy angry and those of Dorothy dormant is a matter
of shading and tone. That is to say, in earlier, measured statements she depicted herself as a loving, stable woman, a
builder of nests, who had fallen in love with a man who had a
great deal of difficulty in knowing how really to be a husband
and a parent. Imagine a faint clucking sound here, somewhat
regretful, somewhat sympathetic, and also somewhat patronizing. But it was Dorothy who left Joe, not the other way
around, and before her death in Palm Springs in 1984, she
married two more times. Dorothy Arnoldine Olson, the nest-
maker, leaped out of a number of nests herself.

To couch love in plain baseball language, DiMaggio's
romance with Dorothy served as spring training for his yet-
more-painful romance with Monroe. In both instances passionate coupling yielded quickly to hard-eyed separation.
And, in both instances, after separation and lawyers, the de-
positions and the testimony, the old lovers found out that passion and fondness still endured. Divorce had been a
parenthesis, not a finality. Afterward, the old lovers continued to work powerfully on each other's lives.

From Dorothy's side comes a picture, too carefully
wrought to be wholly believable, of a gentle, loving woman
who was willing to abandon or at least delay a show-business
career to build a home, to raise a child, to love a man. Even
when she was suing Joe in 1952, she insisted that she was
acting for *everybody's* good.

"I'm only trying to make a better father out of Joe," she
told a tabloid reporter named Jess Stearn. "Joe has never
really exercised his privilege to see the child. When he did, he
never spent more than a few minutes with him, sometimes
shoving him off on his men friends to take him to the movies.

"Over a period of years there has been a culmination of
things done by Joe in relation to our child and, although,
good heavens, I'm not a jealous woman, the straw that broke

the camel's back was when he took him to the Bel Air Hotel pool with Marilyn Monroe."

DiMaggio's confidants insisted that he was a devoted father. "He loved that kid," one old Yankee insisted, "even more than he loved base hits." And some of DiMaggio's old teammates suggest a different portrait of Dorothy.

"The truth," one former Yankee said, requesting anonymity, "is that she could be tough as nails. She wanted to be Mrs. Joe D. and she wanted to be a star. When she found out that it was a tall order to be Joe's bride, and when she never did become a star, there got to be a lot of anger in her. I think if she'd been more patient, the way Lefty Gomez's wife was patient, they might have made it. A fellow like Joe, who was so intense about his baseball and who loved to sort of cool out with the boys, just took a lot of taming. Who knows what goes on between two people, but my impression is that over the years most of the love was coming from Joe's side."

During the late 1930s, the *San Francisco Chronicle,* a staid, serious, and generally excellent newspaper, indulged in a persistent flippancy on its front page. Rather than simply provide each day's weather forecast, the *Chronicle*'s editors invented two characters, Anemometer and Barometer, who conversed on winds and clouds and temperature. If this sounds a bit arch, it is nothing compared to the aggressive cuteness inflicted on us today by television weathermen and -women.

Discussing the San Francisco weather for Sunday, November 19, 1939, Anemometer and Barometer chattered at one another across two paragraphs before agreeing that the wedding day of Joseph Paul DiMaggio and Dorothy Arnoldine Olson would be fair and mild. So it was, but the relationship that it portended was only briefly fair and seldom mild. A more appropriate weather term is *stormy.*

The ceremony, at DiMaggio's boyhood church of St. Peter and St. Paul, stalled traffic for many blocks and drew a throng that police estimated at ten thousand people. As far as I can learn, this was the best-attended coupling in the history of San Francisco. It was a measure of DiMaggio's unique stature, part of baseball and yet distinct from it, a sports hero who transcended sports, that he could attract a huge, adulatory crowd without carrying a ball, a bat, or a glove and this during the football season to boot.

Within three years, Dorothy would move to Reno, establishing residence for the quick and scandal-free divorce that was one of Nevada's major businesses at the time. Pleas from DiMaggio and some of his friends and from people in the Yankee offices who were concerned about his morale convinced her to relent. But she moved to Reno again before finally getting a divorce—the prideful DiMaggio declined to contest it legally—in 1944.

Subsequently they talked reconciliation. Joe's comments to friends about Dorothy were tentative, particularly for such an assertive man. He said, "Maybe we can get back together and maybe we can't. I don't want to say too much about it because I'd really be sticking my neck out there." He focused on his son—he would send the boy to Lawrenceville, and a military school and Yale. He didn't want the boy to know the barbs that tear at children who shuttle between the fragments of broken homes. Aside from that, he continued to love Dorothy Arnold, as he would continue to love Marilyn Monroe, long after a divorce decree was signed.

He was not monastic, but the daisy chains from Broadway were never much more than dalliances. Dorothy remained the central woman in his life. He even pursued her, as best he could, until her marriage in 1946 to New York stockbroker George Schubert. One of his teammates attributes his relatively poor season in 1946—he batted only .290—to the pangs of unrequited love. "Joe was pining," says the ballplayer, "that whole season."

But Dorothy divorced Schubert in 1950, and the following Christmas she, Joe, and their son gathered in a ski chalet near Reno for a family celebration. A winter storm struck and left them snowbound in a mountain lodge for four days. Hollywood stuff. A sky full of snow. A crackling fire. A few drinks. After a while, the little fellow tramps off to sleep, leaving the old lovers by themselves . . .

When they came down from the hills, a reporter asked DiMaggio if there was any chance of his remarrying Dorothy.

"I don't know what's going to happen," he said. "I haven't asked her yet."

But before very much longer, Joe met Marilyn Monroe at a restaurant called Villa Nova, and by Marilyn's account they were making love a few hours later in, of all places, the back of a car. Joe telephoned the next day, Marilyn told her friend Ben Hecht. "You know," Joe said, "this is the first time I ever called up a girl the morning after I laid her to see how she was."

Joe's in-person style is direct. The baseball world in which he spent his greatest years in no way resembled finishing school. But the earthy comment to Marilyn was intended as a major compliment. After a single evening he quickly came to feel that Marilyn was someone more than just another bleached show-business blonde. She made him feel not only passionate, but serious.

The famous couple felt one another out, liked what they found, and soon included Joe junior on a number of their dates. But including the boy in the developing romance turned Dorothy nasty. All this lay far ahead on that fair, mild, wedding day in the San Francisco autumn of 1939. The next morning the *Chronicle* described Dorothy Arnoldine DiMaggio as "a blonde Hollywood princess."

Dorothy Arnold was one of that legion of pretty girls who marched out of the Midwest fresh-faced, firm-bosomed, with a modicum of talent, an innate sense of the power of sex, and a limitless ambition to conquer show business. Such women often glow with a kind of sweetness that suggests dirndl, sun-splashed mornings, and flapjacks for Sunday breakfast on the old farm home. Usually that impression is deceptive. Girls who are happy in dirndl, cooking flapjacks, never have to leave the prairie. The others, the ones who target Hollywood, are impelled by fires of ambition burning under the soft curves of their bellies. Such women make gorgeous wives and troubled marriages.

As Lady Macbeth instructs us in high school English classes, raw ambition is unattractive and somewhat frightening. So shrewd young women with their eyes on stardom learn to conceal their drive behind the smiles and charm that are part of the acting craft. An irony in old Hollywood was that several actresses made fortunes by playing the very dirndl, flapjack, kitchen-princess roles that they had, in real life, rejected.

Dorothy was born not on a farm, but in Duluth, Minnesota, on November 21, 1917. Her father worked as an official for a railroad company. She seems to have been the most favored of the four daughters in the middle-class family of Mr. and Mrs. V. A. Olson. When still quite small, she took lessons in singing, dancing, and—that staple of ladylike breeding long ago—elocution. Young women who wanted to act first had to be taught how to enunciate, although this sometimes led to aberrations and an affected pseudo-English intonation best described as midwestern Oxonian. Dorothy survived elocution without affectation.

She grew into an attractive and athletic young woman who stood five feet five and enjoyed swimming, horseback riding, tennis, and even tried her hand at softball. "I wasn't bad," she said later, as Mrs. Joe DiMaggio, "but tennis was probably my best sport. I won a lot of tennis tournaments when I was growing up." Sports were no more than a pastime. Her passions turned toward the theater and, she said, she starred "in a few student productions" during her few years at Denfield High School in Duluth.

By the time she was fifteen acting had infatuated her, and she left school to join a traveling musical-comedy company on the Balaban and Katz "wheel," or theater circuit. Were there storms in the Olsons' proper Scandinavian home when the pretty teenager left a schoolgirl's life for the roustabout existence of the road? Not according to Dorothy. "My parents knew how much I wanted to act and sing. We had some good talks. If that was what I wanted to do to be happy, then that was all right with them."

She traveled from Minnesota out through the Northwest, rooming with another girl, singing, dancing, playing small parts, and hoping for bigger ones. The suitcase life, with its boarding houses, skimpy meals, and drafty dressing rooms, was not what she had expected. At length, she quit a production called the Bandbox Revue and returned to her parents' home. She found some work in little theater and dramatic clubs around Duluth, then left again and played summer stock in New England. By the time she was eighteen, a three-year veteran of show business, she decided to settle in New York City. She found a small apartment and, she said, proceeded to "sing for buttons. I sang wherever I could find a job. Night clubs. Radio. Dance orchestras. I was a kid. I kept hoping I would be discovered."

A talent scout from Universal Pictures noticed her when she was nineteen and signed her to "a very small stock contract." She was hazy about the numbers, but probably earned $50, or at most $75, a week. She was cast as a bit player in *Manhattan Merry-Go-Round* and, as she later told it, saw "a very nice-looking fellow" on the set one August morning in 1937.

"Who's that?" Dorothy asked another young actress.

"Why that's just Joe DiMaggio from the New York Yankees."

The other girl seemed so awed that Dorothy made a sharp snap. "So what?" Long afterward she insisted that he had appealed to her at once. "It sort of happened," she said, "with my first look. He asked for my number. We started going around together and the first thing we knew—at least, I knew—it was getting hotter."

This was a willful lady, who was sufficiently courageous and determined to challenge life on her own while still an adolescent. When both her marriage to DiMaggio and her

movie-star dreams came crashing at her feet, she grew disin-
clined to talk about either at any length or in any depth. Possibly there never was much depth to Dorothy Arnold. But her
early knockabout show-business years define a woman who
could focus on a goal.

Stardom was one goal.

DiMaggio was another.

In a witticism that was popular in New York during their
courtship, he chased her and he chased her, until she finally
caught him.

The young DiMaggio was not a man to hurry headlong
into marriage or, for that matter, an engagement. His career
had taken wings. The world lay naked before him. His great
baseball skills charged his life with money and fame, idolatrous fans, more show girls than any mortal could accommo-
date, a gentle press (now that the acerbic 1938 holdout had
been forgiven), and for his cooling-out nights, a crowd at
Toots Shor's that was ever more impressed with his high
deeds at Yankee Stadium. Solotaire, the ticket broker, once
complained that a journalist portrayed him as "a coat hanger
for Joe." But George was always available to carry sand-
wiches to DiMaggio's hotel room, help with packing for a
Yankee trip, find out which dancer in which show was most
anxious to meet the great ballplayer, or, in fact, to hang Di-
Maggio's coat. Gould, the bereted fight manager, wanted to
help wring the last buffalo nickel out of each endorsement
contract. Beyond them, two excellent journalists, Jimmy Cannon and Bob Considine, essentially sophisticated men, dis-
carded their sophistication whenever it came time to write
about DiMaggio. To them (and later to Red Smith) DiMaggio
became not just a column subject, but a personal hero.

The phenomenon is understandable, considering how brilliantly DiMaggio played baseball, but it does not always make
for the best of journalism. While DiMaggio was mocked by
Life magazine's Ivy Leaguers for his Sicilian background,
which ultimately is embarrassing mostly to the *Life* jour-

nalists, he moved through the columns of Considine and Cannon as flawless, a black-haired god. Good mythology. Fine
reading. Inferior reporting.

Cannon, a short, intense, gabby New York Irishman, was
developing a writing style suggestive of works by Hemingway
and Runyon, which had its full blossoming after World War
II. No newspaperman has surpassed him at a particular breed
of sports column, personal and sonorous, that cries out, "I
was there and here is all I saw and heard and felt!" At another extreme, Cannon could create a nice, lean piece, il-
lumined by bright perceptions, propelled by accurately
rendered conversation, out of a simple walk through Times
Square with DiMaggio.

Considine was a tall, droll, bulbous-nosed character, a
Hearst syndicate star, who became less the pure columnist
and more the protean scribbler. He eventually wrote books
and screenplays, including *The Babe Ruth Story,* which, Considine said in his disarming way, was such a bad movie "that
when I gave my kid a print so he could show it in assembly at
Cardinal Hayes High School, the kid said, no thanks the reels
were too bulky for him to carry them all the way to school."

Whenever a crisis, or even a wrinkle, appeared to furrow
DiMaggio's brow, Considine and Cannon would turn over
their columns to the ballplayer. They might quote him, if that
seemed appropriate, or they might simply expound his viewpoint as their own. DiMaggio never demanded that sort of
tame, house-organ press. Rather, it was offered to him, after
which he learned quickly how to use it.

DiMaggio's penchant for holding out did not end in the
spring of 1938, although he never again conducted himself
with such public arrogance. He would fight later grim salary
wars but now he learned to present a more modest public
image and to make the harsh points indirectly through Considine or Cannon.

The Yankee front office continued to be troubled by what
the executives described among themselves as "DiMaggio's
greed." Kenesaw Mountain Landis continued to be troubled

by DiMaggio's friendship with the fight manager and gambling man Joe Gould, clear into the season of 1940. At that time, Landis announced through a spokesman that he intended to "inquire further" into the relationship, and later to report his findings.

DiMaggio was infuriated. He had already assured Landis once that Gould was not getting a percentage of his baseball salary ($32,000 in 1940). Once ought to be enough. The Landis statement, on top of the Yankees' glacial resistance to his financial demands, was, DiMaggio felt, one more instance of baseball powers banding together to intimidate, and incidentally, to humiliate, a fellow who was just trying to make the best living that he could playing ball. A younger DiMaggio would have spat out such comments to ambient reporters. But by this time—1940 was his fifth season as a major leaguer—he had learned that it was a loser's game for a ballplayer to attack baseball at large. So he simply griped briefly and quietly to Bob Considine at Table One in Toots Shor's.

"This isn't just about me, Bob," DiMaggio said. "Landis is using me to get a message to all the ballplayers. Stay dumb."

"Do you talk to Gould about your Yankee contracts?" Considine asked.

"You won't print it?"

"No."

"Sure I talk to Joe. I talk to my brother Tom. I've talked to Lefty O'Doul and I've even talked to Ty Cobb. I'll talk to anybody who I think can help me get paid what I deserve. It's a free country, isn't it? But Joe Gould isn't getting a cut, any more than you are."

That Sunday in the *Daily Mirror,* a splashy tabloid that was created in the hoydenish image of the *Daily News,* Considine's column bore this headline:

DIMAG CASE SHOWS
HAND OF MANAGERS
THEY DON'T WANT
BOYS TO SMARTEN UP

"If you were puzzled," Considine wrote, "because Judge Landis said he would 'inquire further' into the report that Joe DiMaggio is kicking back a piece of his salary to Joe Gould, the fight manager, even though DiMaggio and Gould both hotly denied it, the answer is that baseball has a perfect horror of any player's ever getting a mouthpiece.

"And Landis—prodded by the owners—wants to be sure that he muffs no chance to make an example of DiMag, if he can ferret out the flimsiest business relationship between the outfielder and the manager of Jim Braddock.

"The reason the average owner wants no part of a player's agent or manager is that it would cost the owner more money. It stands to reason when a green kid from Walla Walla comes face to face with an owner who has been around the baseball business for a generation, the kid winds up taking whatever the owner wants to pay him. . . . Whereas if he had someone in there talking for him—as agents know how to talk—he could do a lot better. . . .

"DiMaggio and Gould are good friends. I don't believe Gould distilled any of DiMaggio's baseball demands. These were prompted more by his friends Lefty O'Doul and Ty Cobb and, in light of future happenings, were pretty reasonable. Gould has helped DiMaggio make money from outside interests. DiMag got tied up with a large firm of agents when he first came to New York and he and Gould felt the firm lost track of the player. . . . When his contract with them ran out, Gould began to hustle business for him. At no fee, I understand. . . .

"Why this heavy rightousness in Landis' office? If Joe Gould dug up some easy endorsement dough for DiMaggio . . . it's none of Landis' business. . . . The lackadaying, of course, is a front. The big league bosses are afraid that the ball players will smarten up enough to hire fast-talking tough-bargaining agents to speak for them. . . .

"And if that ever comes to pass the ball clubs would have to pay all the blokes what they're actually worth."

(It has come to pass.)

Recently, when someone asked what he thought he'd be

earning if he were playing major league baseball in this era, DiMaggio allowed himself the suggestion of a smile. Then he said he would open his discussion with the mercurial Mr. Steinbrenner this way: "As a starter, George, I'll take half the Yankee franchise."

The old Considine column is an excellent summation of DiMaggio's position and never once quotes DiMaggio. In essence, you can't get mad at Joe. He didn't *say* anything. You can get mad at Considine, if you are partial to the position of baseball's ancien régime, but that doesn't matter much because people are always getting mad at columnists anyway.

In the two brief years between the Great Holdout of 1938 and the Gould Storm of 1940, DiMaggio had mastered a sophisticated device for contending with controversy. Use the press to make his points, as though the columnists were his hired attorneys. (The public at large was surely a jury.) Stay above the battle himself. John Kennedy knew how to get certain writers to articulate his positions without attribution when he wanted to get them across. In return, he offered writers the friendship of a president. That melted such reasonably rugged journalists as Ben Bradlee of the *Washington Post*. DiMaggio had learned to play this expedient game a generation earlier, when he was only twenty-five years old. Like Kennedy, he offered only a curiously personal reward to those who played the game with him. Friendship with the greatest center fielder on earth.

Actually, Landis was motivated by several concerns about DiMaggio's business with tough-talking, cigar-smoking little Joe Gould. The first, as Considine reported, was the question of a ballplayer employing an agent. In DiMaggio's playing days, organized baseball still enjoyed immunity from all anti-trust laws—and, some said, the First Amendment. The legal rationale for this, no less a figure than Justice Oliver Wendell Holmes intoned in one of his most perplexing decisions, was "the peculiar nature of the business." Glorious game. Tight little monopoly.

Ed Barrow of the New York Yankees spoke for the con-

servative baseball establishment when he said that if any ballplayer showed up at his office with an agent, he, Barrow,
general manager of the Yankees, elderly and gnarled though
he might be, would personally throw out the agent. More
than three decades passed before lawyers and agents forced
their way into baseball salary talks and created the new breed
of millionaire ballplayers, and, swarming about, the sub-
species of millionaire baseball agents.

Although Judge Landis showed occasional spasms of liber-
alism, he was employed by the owners to protect the status
quo. Rumors that Gould was masterminding DiMaggio's salary negotiations struck Landis and his employers as a genuine
threat. But quite beyond such hidebound thinking, Landis felt
concern for another reason. Joe Gould was not only a boxing
manager, but a gambling man. Gould liked to watch baseball
games, but not quite so much as he liked to bet on baseball
games, and he made no secret of his gambling penchant. Indeed, some of his best friends were bookmakers.

Publicly, at least, Landis looked upon gambling, any gambling, as unmitigated evil. He was ferocious in policing the
game. He would not tolerate ballplayers associating with
gamblers, or even with the friends of gamblers. An athlete
who went to a racetrack and made perfectly legal horse bets
risked fines and a suspension from the commissioner. Landis
reasoned that, in the words of J. Edgar Hoover, "it's not
enough for things to *be* right. They have to *look* right, too."

Now here was The Jolter, the prince of ballplayers, running with a boxing man who boasted about his betting (when
he won), and his betting on baseball games, at that. DiMaggio
always has enjoyed friendships in the fast lane. Landis's second concern, in retrospect, his legitimate concern—the young
superstar running with a gambling man—did not make the
newspapers of the day. Considine focused on an obvious and
sympathetic position—civil rights for ballplayers—and ig-
nored the rest.

Why, some ask, did the New York press come to protect
DiMaggio and even propagandize for him, while 250 miles

away the Boston press waged a twenty-year war with Ted Williams, the great Red Sox slugger? The answer, if there is an answer, approaches an enduring element of Joe DiMaggio: As attractive as he was to women, he also exerted an astonishing charismatic hold on men.

He was first of all a complete baseball player, matching his high dedication at the bat with equal dedication to every other aspect of his play. Among all the testimony by the teammates and opponents on his pursuit of excellence, only one small criticism appears. He would not willingly bunt, that is to say, tap the ball instead of swinging as a device to advance base runners. He felt he could hit a home run any time he swung. On the one occasion when a manager—it was Bill Dickey— ordered a bunt, DiMaggio erupted in anger. (But first he did bunt—and successfully.)

All the rest of his game, including his usual mental approach, approximated perfection. Effortless power. Strength without sweat. These were images that DiMaggio projected from the ball field. As he himself was forever pointing out, these impressions were illusory. He sweated like any other ballplayer and worked harder at his game than most. But the sense that DiMaggio was not only great but *effortlessly* great persisted. He appeared to be a cool performer, and cool works a commanding appeal whether you imagine it in ballplayers, actors, or blue-eyed Nordic blondes.

DiMaggio played a short center field, relatively close to second base. This enabled him to catch some line drives that otherwise might have dropped safely for singles. When a ball was hit deep, he turned and fled backward with such sure speed that sportswriters actually speculated whether it was possible to hit a ball over DiMaggio's head, as if he were a god with winged heels.

Willie Mays, Mickey Mantle, and Duke Snider, DiMaggio's successors as great center fielders in New York, were "hot" athletes. Mays was forever losing his cap in scampering pursuit of long fly balls. Mantle, who could hit a baseball farther than DiMaggio, had a long-striding swing that tore at his body when he missed a pitch. Snider, possessed of considerable physical grace, was an emotional fellow who once told an assemblage of sportswriters that the fans in Brooklyn were the worst in baseball, a comment of dubious accuracy and little wisdom for a man who played his home games at Ebbets Field, near Flatbush Avenue. The collective cool of Mays, Mantle, and Snider could not have filled one of DiMaggio's black spiked shoes.

Williams, the major contemporary rival to DiMaggio, was a somewhat better hitter—we are dealing here with levels of Olympian performance—but he was a limited outfielder without an outstanding throwing arm. Criticism made DiMaggio brood, glare, and retreat to silence. Williams responded to criticism with diatribe and tantrums, frequently directed against his home-team Boston Red Sox press. During a casual interview he once told me that every Boston sportswriter, every one, no exceptions, "would give his left nut to see me have a bad year. But it ain't gonna happen, because old T.S.W., he don't have bad years." Certain Boston journalists enjoyed goading Williams in the way children enjoy lighting the fuse to firecrackers.

Williams, who got along well with a few syndicated columnists, never developed a protective cadre among Boston journalists. On some levels he and the Boston reporters must have enjoyed feuding with one another, because once the relationship was pointed toward that direction nobody changed course. At length, Boston sportswriters would compete with one another in telling stories about the terrible-tempered Ted, and he would keep the lava bubbling by telling strangers (such as myself) that the Boston writers were unalloyed bastards.

Williams was more the natural man, the naked nerve ending, as it were. DiMaggio sized up the press coolly, dispensing a favor here, a background interview there, until the New York press was kept "like a broad," Joe might say off the record—and the New York writers boasted competitively about their friendships with the great DiMag.

Typical, both of the newspaper style of a departed era and

of the hold DiMaggio worked on newspapermen, is the beginning of a long article by the late Dan M. Daniel called "My friend—The Yankee Clipper." (Daniel wrote for the *New York World-Telegram* and *The Sporting News* and loved projecting absolute authority. In one of his columns, "Ask Daniel," he answered questions with imperious and sometimes grouchy expertise. "No, nobody has ever hit a fair ball out of Yankee Stadium and I am tired of you readers' submitting that question.")

"In writing about Joseph Paul DiMaggio, ball player par excellence, stylist and perfectionist," Daniel began, "I have undertaken the pleasant duty of reminiscing about and assaying the technical and personal values of one of the greatest exemplars it has been our national pastime's privilege to produce. . . .

"Here . . . was a picture athlete if ever there had been one in the major leagues, the very apotheosis of the poetry of motion."

On April 25, 1939, Dorothy Arnold announced in Hollywood that she and Joe DiMaggio would be married "this summer." Dorothy was speaking to wire-service reporters at a modest press conference arranged by Universal Pictures. A reporter looked at her left hand and noticed the absence of a gem. "Oh, I haven't got a ring or anything," Dorothy said. "It's just understood between Joe and me. We'll get married this summer and go on a honeymoon after the baseball season."

Dorothy was twenty-one years old. Joe had in fact asked her to marry him and she had agreed, but they had not decided on a date, nor, for that matter, on how the announcement should be made. In an effervescent mood, she mentioned her plans to someone at the studio. This created more attention than her acting ever had and led to the press conference. The repercussions tested DiMaggio's poise.

Sportswriters approached him at Yankee Stadium with the wire story from California. DiMaggio blinked, said nothing for a time, and when he did speak, he sounded surprised. As he spoke further, he appeared to grow annoyed.

Yes, it was true, he and Dorothy were engaged. But "the wedding positively will not be this summer."

"Then when, Joe?" a reporter asked.

DiMaggio looked irritated. "We may be married next winter," he said, "or even the following winter. The wedding definitely will not take place while the baseball season is on." That was as much as he would say. He did not intend to hold an extended interview on his personal life. He moved away from the reporters. There was a distinct sense that if Dorothy conducted any more press conferences on the romance, DiMaggio might reduce the romance to history. He would tolerate nothing that distracted him from his baseball career and a wedding is, among other things, a distraction. Save it for the off-season.

During their two years of intermittent courtship, baseball had brought him boundless success while Dorothy continued to knock about in the minor leagues of show business. Universal did, of course, bring her to Hollywood, but used her only to play blonde parts in B movies and in the suspense serials that supplemented double features at neighborhood movie houses on Saturday afternoons. In addition to *Secrets of a Nurse,* she appeared in *The Storm,* both with Edmund Lowe, and moved up to play a lead in *The Phantom Creeps.* As far as I can learn, none of these movies survives.

When Marilyn played bit parts, she always generated some excitement, if only for the way her buttocks jiggled as she walked (*Love Happy,* 1950) or for some amusing dumb-blonde routine as when Miss Caswell (*All About Eve,* 1950) needs another drink. At an elegant, high-powered party, Miss Caswell addresses the butler as "waiter," drawing an arch correction from her escort, Addison DeWitt, played by the elegant, low-keyed George Sanders.

No comparable electricity crackled from the acting efforts of Dorothy Arnold. When her engagement announcement brought flurries of press attention, a Universal executive remarked to a reporter, "She isn't anybody special. To tell you the truth, we doubt if she ever will be." Still, the following week, confirmed as DiMaggio's betrothed, she appeared in *Life* magazine. Dorothy posed in a tight one-piece bathing suit, white shoes, and a bright smile. She had made *Life* not as an actress but as the fiancée of a famous man.

The question of love and ambition persists. Dorothy herself never suggested that she would abandon show business for homemaking. She insisted that "marriage won't stand in the way of my career," then added tactfully, "and it won't get in the way of Joe's career either." Nothing ever would, but injuries and time.

She never became anything more than one more pretty blonde in Hollywood's regiments of ambitious, pretty blondes; she comes down to us mostly as the first woman who married DiMaggio and rejected him. As Joe declines to talk about Marilyn, the legendary blonde, he will not talk about Dorothy, the forgotten blonde, either. "The wounded veteran," someone remarks, "doesn't want to talk about how much it hurt."

With his engagement confirmed but placed on an indefinite hold, the man reporters described as "the Yankees' leading eligible bachelor" embarked on his fourth consecutive extraordinary season in 1939, a year that he would climax with World Series heroics. But first he suffered an injury that terrified him.

Roberto Estalella, a short, stocky Cuban outfielder with the Washington Senators, smacked a line single into left center field on April 29, a day when the playing surface at Yankee Stadium had been soaked by rains. DiMaggio ran hard to his right. The ball took an unusual spinning bounce to his left. As DiMaggio stopped short, he caught the spikes of his right shoe in the soggy turf. He fell in his tracks and lay writhing for fully eight minutes. The pain embraced him fiercely. The Yankee team physician, who ran onto the field, reported that he found DiMaggio in shock "with hardly any pulse."

The injury was diagnosed as severely torn muscles in the lower right leg. "Myself, I thought the bone was gone," Di-

Maggio said afterward. "I heard something make a loud crack." Although there was no fracture, once again the lean, muscled body had revealed its frailty. Once more the fragility of a ball-playing career impressed itself on the young hero. All his baseball days mixed holdouts and physical pain with glory. He never really found relief from his anxiety that an injury would come suddenly on a snarl of fortune and relegate the glory to the past. It was June before he could play again. When he did, he proceeded to dominate the American League.

DiMaggio's Yankees won the 1939 pennant by 17 games, with a winning percentage of .702, which is to say they averaged slightly better than 7 victories for every 10 games played. That is a phenomenal record in the major leagues and represents a pinnacle of team excellence among all the DiMaggio-Yankee years. In addition to DiMaggio's slugging, the team would get fine batting from Charlie (King Kong) Keller, the thick-browed muscular character in right field; Robert (Red) Rolfe, a thin, intense New Englander who played third base; catcher Bill Dickey, and left fielder George (Twinkletoes) Selkirk. As a team the Yankees batted .287 and hit 166 home runs, about 40 more than any other club. The defense was sure and the pitching staff was by far the finest in the league. The Yankee season of 1939, a model year of high-achieving, was short only on suspense. You always knew that they were going to win. They always knew that they were going to win. Which is not to suggest that the season lacked drama.

On May 2, while DiMaggio lay in Lenox Hill Hospital worrying about his right leg, Lou Gehrig, the captain of the Yankees, Larrupin' Lou, The Iron Horse, took himself out of the starting lineup. Since 1925, Gehrig had played in 2,130 consecutive games, a record that has not since been approached. But now, although he did not know it, he was dying.

Gehrig did recognize that he was not able to play well enough to help the team. In 8 games this once-mighty power hitter could manage only 4 hits, all singles. Nor could he move around first base. No one, not even manager Joe McCarthy, had the heart to bench Gehrig and thus conclude the

man's hard-bought endurance streak. At length, Gehrig himself directed McCarthy to take his name out of the lineup.

A moving scene ensued. As captain, Gehrig walked from
the dugout to home plate, where the umpires were gathered,
and handed them the Yankee lineup card with the name of
Ellsworth (Babe) Dahlgren penciled in at first base. Usually a
pregame meeting with umpires is cheerful and chatty. This
time nobody said much. Then Gehrig walked back to the dugout and over to the water cooler, where he took a long drink.
He was still bending over the spigot when he began to weep.

Johnny Murphy, a former Fordham star who was the Yankees' premiere relief pitcher, threw a white towel toward his
captain. The towel landed on Gehrig's head. Gehrig let the
towel stay there, hiding his face, his sorrow, and his tears.

Amyotrophic lateral sclerosis, a disease of the nervous system that is incurable to this day, had begun its relentless attack
on Gehrig's massive frame. Two years later, on a sun-splashed
June day when DiMaggio was rocketing along in his famous
batting streak, Lou Gehrig died at the age of thirty-seven.

His brief and generally admirable life would become the
subject of books and a flawed but touching movie called *The
Pride of the Yankees,* in which Gary Cooper played a suitably
stoic Gehrig and Teresa Wright was enchanting as Eleanor.
Fresh generations weep at television reruns. But nothing, not
even tragedy in their midst, slowed the Yankees of 1939. This is
not to imply heartlessness or lack of interest. At first, most of
the other ballplayers could not believe how gravely ill Gehrig
was. After leaving Lenox Hill Hospital, DiMaggio told reporters: "Don't count out Lou just because he's taking the first rest
he's had in years." There persisted an intense, personal, and
irrational hope that somehow Gehrig would recover.

Beyond that, these Yankee ballplayers were young men in
their prime, and life goes on. There was a new game to be
played every day. The Yankees raced away from the other
contenders (although Dahlgren never hit much and was
traded two seasons later) and six of their number filled start-

ing positions on the American League all-star team (DiMaggio, Rolfe, Selkirk, Dickey, Joe Gordon, and Red Ruffing).

Overall, combining power and average, DiMaggio hit better than he ever had. On September 8, he was batting a redoubtable .408 with a clear chance to finish above the magic and all-but-unattainable figure of .400. Then he developed an inflammation in one eye, related either to a head cold or an allergy. He could not bring himself to ask McCarthy for a few days off. It was part of baseball's old, rugged, macho ethic that you stayed in unless you had to be carried off on your shield. But with his vision reduced, his hitting fell off, and DiMaggio finished the season at .381, good enough to lead the league by a wide margin, but 19 points shy of his objective.

"Something was really wrong with my left eye," he recalled a few years ago. "I could hardly see out of it. But Joe McCarthy didn't believe in cheese champions [a boxing term for champions of little repute and less courage] so he kept me playing every day. He had to know the agony I was going through and I'll never understand why he didn't give me a couple of days off. But he didn't and I paid the price. You played in those days with anything short of a broken leg."

Resentment, or at the least disappointment, touches DiMaggio's tone. He never did bat .400, or, for that matter, reach .381 again. Two seasons later, in 1941, Ted Williams, the Red Sox's old T.S.W., batted .406. No major leaguer has since cracked the barrier of .400.

In a season of irresistible Yankee triumphs, the team swept the first 3 games of the 1939 World Series from the Cincinnati Reds. The Yankees had now won 8 consecutive World Series games against three different National League champions. They were trailing by 2 runs in the ninth inning of Game Four, but rallied—DiMaggio hit a critical single—and tied the score.

Facing a tall, dour, sinker-ball pitcher named Bucky Walters, who had won 27 games during the season, the Yankees put two men on base in the tenth inning. DiMaggio lined an outside sinker safely to right field, where Ival Goodman of the

Reds, hurrying to throw home, misplayed the ball. Frank Crosetti scored easily from second base. King Kong Keller never stopped running and scored all the way from first base with a hard slide that separated the Reds' large and hawknosed catcher, Ernie (Schnozzola) Lombardi, from both the ball and his senses. The ball rolled out of Lombardi's glove and the big catcher sat on the soil of Crosley Field without realizing where he was or what was going on around him.

DiMaggio, who never stopped running either, sized up the situation at once and, as *The New York Times* reported, "winged across home plate before the utterly befuddled Lombardi could do anything about it." A memorable photo of this play shows Lombardi lying on the ground and DiMaggio sliding past him. Lombardi later reported that Keller had accidentally kneed him in the groin, but sportswriters buzzed for months about Ernie Lombardi's snooze. They paid less attention to DiMaggio's swift and alert baserunning. He was a daring and adventurous young ballplayer. The Yankees defeated Bucky Walters and the Reds, 7–4. They had now won the World Series in each of DiMaggio's first four seasons in New York. It is doubtful, claim some old Yankee hands, if they would have won any without him. He was the centerpiece about which the Yankee ball club blossomed.

When the 1939 season was history, the Baseball Writers Association announced that it had voted DiMaggio the Most Valuable Player in the American League. (He won the award again in 1941 and 1949.) Flushed with victory and success, becoming wealthy by the standards of the time, DiMaggio put certain trepidations to rest and set about planning a November wedding for himself and Dorothy Arnold.

Despite four years of national fame, he was still a very young man. He would not reach his twenty-fifth birthday until November 25. He was also the product of a devoutly Roman Catholic household. (His religiosity grew less intense as he aged and experienced divorce.) He wanted, he explained to Dorothy, a wedding at his old neighborhood church.

Dorothy, raised as a Minnesota protestant, would have to agree at the least that any children would be raised as Catholics. Ecumenism was unknown in the 1930s and the inter-religious attitude of many Roman Catholic clergymen was a strong and even bellicose assertion that theirs was the one true church. Outside it lay only purgatory and damnation.

Dorothy, who had not been notably religious herself, met Joe's family, the three brothers and the five sisters, Mama and Papa, and said she found them all warm and receptive. Then she decided to become a Roman Catholic herself and took instructions from a San Francisco priest, Father F. Parolin. She and Joe were feeling happy and festive.

But the mood of the country and the city of San Francisco was somewhat uneasy. That August—another August darkened by the long shadows of guns—Adolf Hitler concluded a ten-year nonagression treaty with the Soviet Union. Thus stabilized, Nazi Germany unleashed its Blitzkrieg against Poland. Dashing Polish lancers were decimated by Tiger tanks and Stuka dive bombers. The Poles surrendered in twenty-seven days. Then, while the Wehrmacht regrouped, Hitler offered Britain and France "peace on my terms or a war of destruction." His terms were unacceptable, even to such weak leaders as Neville Chamberlain.

In Doorn, Holland, where he had settled in exile, Kaiser Wilhelm, the German ruler during World War I, had a private air-raid shelter built. The Russians, who had carved out a piece of fallen Poland, turned on the Finns and demanded territorial concessions north of Leningrad. None was forthcoming: The Russo-Finnish war broke out on November 30.

German officials in Poland announced to an international gathering of reporters that they had found a new solution to "the Jewish problem." An area of southern Poland, centered around Lublin, would become a Jewish reservation "similar to Indian reservations in the United States." Each day made the world at large more chilling.

Some Americans foresaw that the gathering European war would envelop the United States. Barely twenty years after

World War I, America would have to fight again. Others in an odd grab bag ranted for peace. These included America-First-ers such as Charles Lindbergh; the pro-Nazi German-Amer-ican Bund; and U.S. communists, who abruptly found themselves wedded to the Stalin-Hitler accord on non-belligerence. The three groups joined voices in denouncing American internationalists as "warmongers."

San Franciscans distracted themselves by following the for-tunes of a fine Santa Clara football team. On Saturday, No-vember 18, Santa Clara was to play UCLA and face a "terribly fast Negro running back. Lightning Jack Robinson." Lightning Jack would cross paths with Joe DiMaggio in a World Series eight years later. By that time Lightning Jack would be born again as Jackie Robinson, a dark arrow of fire, the first black to play in modern major league baseball and the first baseman DiMaggio declined to spike in that World Series. (In a small anticlimax, Robinson never got to play against Santa Clara. A leg injury kept him sidelined. UCLA and Santa Clara struggled to a scoreless tie.)

On Sunday, November 19, that fair, mild day, Mayor An-gelo Rossi, an honored wedding guest, felt sufficiently con-cerned about the vast crush of people outside the church to assign plainclothesmen to work inside as ushers. Spiritus Sanctus and the cops.

Admission was by invitation—no one remembers how many invitations were mailed—but uninvited DiMaggio root-ers came driving down that Sunday morning, anxious merely to see the young slugger and his blond bride-to-be. They milled outside the church, spilling over into nearby Washing-ton Square. Most of the onlookers were Italian-Americans from the North Beach section. They were friendly enough; the crowd became a smaller version of those throngs that gather outside St. Peter's to receive the blessings of a pope.

DiMaggio arrived with a police escort. He wore a well-tailored cutaway and was supposed to be attended by his ball-playing brothers, Dominic and Vincent. Dom, in a cutaway himself, said he felt embarrassed. "Isn't this outfit silly?" he

asked. "Someone just handed it to me and I had to put it on."
Dom's contract with the San Francisco Seals had just been
sold to the Boston Red Sox for $50,000. Vince, a wonderful
defensive outfielder, had been in the major leagues long
enough (three years) to have led the National League in
strikeouts. He had as much difficulty with the wedding crowd
as he did with curveballs. He became tangled in the mob and
did not reach the church until two o'clock, which is when the
wedding was scheduled to begin. But by that time the
plainclothesman-ushers, fearing a surge from the populace,
had locked the church doors shut. It took several minutes of
pounding and shouting before Vince DiMaggio could get in to
his brother's wedding.

DiMaggio's mother put on a new wine-colored dress of
velvet and chiffon. His father wore a tuxedo. People had been
arriving at St. Peter and St. Paul since late morning and by
two o'clock the naves were crowded with standees. Others
pressed between the communion rail and the altar. The wedding guests grew noisy and Father Parolin raised one hand.
"Remember that you are in a house of the Lord. I ask you in
His name to be silent." Excited buzzing persisted. When word
spread that Dorothy and her party were arriving, the buzzing
rose toward tumult.

"When the bride appears," the priest pleaded from the
pulpit, "let there be no commotion. Please keep your seats."

The ceremony started thirty minutes behind schedule.
Joe's sisters walked down the aisle first, followed by one of
Dorothy's sisters, Mrs. Irene Morris, who was matron of
honor. Then Dorothy appeared, looking poised, if pale, and
carrying a bouquet of gardenias and orchids. She wore a white
satin gown "designed by Barbara Ross of Hollywood," with a
V neck, a sculpted bodice, a five-yard train, and a coronet veil
tied with gold metallic lace. Understatement was not the
order of the day.

The couple kept their composure as they took their vows.
As soon as they were married, Marie DiMaggio, the sister

who was closest to Joe, began to cry. "I used to hold Joe in my arms," she said. "Why I *raised* him."

Joe noticed and offered her a warm smile. A newspaperman remarked, "He's sure not Deadpan Dan now." As the couple left the church and DiMaggio saw the huge crowd, his look turned bleak. Police guided Joe and Dorothy to a car that took them to a photo studio. Then they rode off to the family restaurant, DiMaggio's Grotto, where a wildly enthusiastic wedding reception had begun.

Guests at the Grotto included politicians (Mayor Rossi), baseball people (Lefty O'Doul), and immigrant fishermen, in a great revel of food and drink and music. A three-piece orchestra played Neapolitan songs. A local policeman, George Stinson, who advertised himself as "The Singing Cop," gave a full-voiced rendition of "Vesti la Giubba" from *Pagliacci*. The crowd at the bar became so thick and stationary that someone asked the restaurant bouncer to keep things moving. The bouncer stationed himself appropriately and repeated loudly, "Get your drink and get away from the bar."

When at length the party wound down, Pietro Pinoni, the maître d'hôtel, took inventory of how much guests consumed. Twelve turkeys, eight hams, fifteen chickens, four sides of beef. No one knew exactly how much Scotch, bourbon, and gin was drunk. Chroniclers have settled for "uncounted gallons." The food and drink cost about $1,500.

DiMaggio was uncomfortable at large social gatherings. Sometime between the little orchestra's offering of "Sorrento" and George Stinson's tragic aria, Joe and Dorothy retreated to his car. He refused to tell the press where he and Dorothy would honeymoon. They wanted privacy, he said. A friend reports that they drove to Mexico. They were en route while their wedding reception was still in progress.

The wedding and the party made front pages across the country. Some stories pointed out that most of the crowd was Italian-American, as if to suggest that Joe appealed primarily to those whose last names ended with vowels. But patronizing

DiMaggio was a declining game and other journalists played the story straight. The greatest of ballplayers had married a movie starlet. This was more fun to read than the news from Europe.

Dorothy remarked once, in the manner of so many young wives in sundering marriages, "I had the baby to bring us closer together." She would find, like other young wives, that a child created new problems, while the old ones went unresolved.

As far as anyone knows, Joe had not thought through the changes that marriage would demand of him. His life-style was both peripatetic and self-indulgent and as the years would demonstrate, it was not a style he was able to change or deeply wanted to change for Dorothy Arnold or Marilyn Monroe.

He spent winters in the handsome San Francisco house that he had purchased in 1938. There his mother and his sisters met his daily needs: food, laundry, housekeeping. During the base-ball season, he lived a hotel life, cushioned by fawning friends. That was true in 1939, when he married Dorothy, and the mix of a San Francisco base and a hotel existence held until 1984, when he moved to south Florida, where the climate would be easier on his arthritis. His interests were baseball, later golf, and the camaraderie of men who also were interested in base-ball and golf. He has not been a ranging sort of man.

Joe may have expected Dorothy to become simply one more of the admiring and supportive DiMaggio women. She would be decorative, pack suitcases for his trips, perform in bed, cook, and root. All that he excluded from his expectations were Dorothy's own needs.

He wanted to live in San Francisco. She preferred Los Angeles or New York. He wanted a hausfrau, but picked a woman who had rejected domestic life for show business. He wanted a pliant pinup. Instead, he found someone with strong ideas of her own. The marriage never had a chance.

At Dorothy's urging, Joe did break with hotel life briefly and, trying to settle into Manhattan, he rented penthouse apartments, once on West End Avenue, a comfortable but less-than-lavish canyon in Manhattan, and once at 241 Central Park West.

But according to Dorothy, their years were strained almost from the last spasm of the honeymoon. She could not survive, she said, as just one more of the DiMaggio women—handmaidens to the star—in the stone house on Beach Street. She insisted that they move to New York. But New York exposed Joe to the temptations of an endless run of nights out with the boys. Single or married, set in a hotel or an apartment, Joe found evenings with Georgie Solotaire, Toots Shor, and the rest irresistibly attractive. "We had a home," Dorothy said. "I wanted to make it a nice home. But he was never there."

When she confronted him, he turned dour or sullen. Perhaps a child, Dorothy fancied . . .

A theory voiced by various mahatmas of the game holds that a ballplayer can enjoy a happy marriage only if he finds himself "a baseball wife." A suitable synonym might be cheerleader. A nastier word would be servant.

Beneath the headlines and apart from the public glory, a ballplayer is an itinerant worker. He has to pack his suitcases each February and leave home to start the sweaty ritual of spring training. Although this sounds pleasant, particularly to those who spend February trudging through the drifts of winter, it is something less than a vacation in the sun. It is the beginning of a seven-month stretch when the ballplayer has to work at his game almost every day. During that period, he will sleep with his luggage as often as he sleeps with his wife.

As spring training opens, the ballplayer sprints and jogs, performs push-ups and sit-ups, shags fly balls, and takes batting practice, finding out once again what a curveball looks like. After ten days or so, the exhibition games begin and the ballplayer bounces around Florida, riding buses to minor league fields, where he rounds himself toward real playing shape before small crowds. Next, in DiMaggio's time, the players boarded Pullman cars on about April 1 for a series of one-day stands that constituted the slow, wearing journey north (and produced enough gate receipts for management to cover the costs of spring training). Chattanooga, Montgomery, Mobile, Knoxville, Lynchburg—the ballplayers saw them all, played in them all, and cursed them all. Mathewson, Cobb, Ruth, Gehrig, DiMaggio all had to learn how to live out of Pullman berths, grabbing quick showers in moldy minor league clubhouses and sleeping above the repeating clatter of train wheels. Life was stag and spartan.

When the season started, the ballplayer was home for a few days, then picked up his laundry, packed his bags, counted his socks, and headed off for the road again. Cleveland. Detroit. Chicago. St. Louis. More Pullman cars, until at length the road itself begins to feel like home. It is, more than one ballplayer has complained, a traveling salesman's life, at better pay.

One is constantly adjusting from hotel to apartment, from a macho, all-male ambience to family life—in short, from place to place. Not much stability there. "The road," the baseball writer Dan Daniel once pronounced wearily, "is for kids."

Beyond the unsettling aspects of too much travel, a ballplayer suffers mood swings with each day's victory and defeat. A pennant race, with its spurts of victory and mysterious slumps, plays hell with a man's self-image and his emotions. Some, like DiMaggio, try to hide the strain. Some let it show. All feel it.

Ballplayers, like other performers, tend to become preoccupied with their own performances, and journalists' questions intensify an athlete's focus on himself.

"What did *you* hit, Joe?" (Curve. He got it up.)

"How did *you* handle that line drive?" (Saw it good, as soon as it left the bat.)

"Do you think *you'll* be able to hit .400?" (No predictions.)

"Tell us what *you* were thinking when . . . *you, you, you.*"

When the game is done and the team is at home and the journalists have retired to the press box, the athlete heads back to a wife who is trying to contend with life beyond the ball field. He leaves his glove in his locker. His ego travels with him.

A model baseball wife lays aside individual ambitions and sublimates them to the service of her husband, the star. She cooks. She sews. She cheers. She listens sympathetically, without prying. She is housekeeper, mother, mistress, cheerleader. She also learns to accept her place.

Baseball men of DiMaggio's vintage love to tell the story of a slugger who went hitless and whose wife greeted him at home: "What happened out there today, honey?"

The ball player snapped: "You take care of the cooking. I'll take care of the hitting."

When a ballplayer travels, a model baseball wife busies herself with chores and bridge games with other baseball wives so that loneliness and depression do not attack her healthy smile. She recognizes that a traveling ball club is a world of young bucks and she is careful not to intrude. Young women, some lusty, some desperate, some both, materialize magically around baseball teams, anxious to surrender their chastity for a few hours with a major leaguer. These ladies were called camp-followers in DiMaggio's playing years, groupies today. It is a rare ballplayer who can consistently resist these roadside flowers.

The model baseball wife accepts her husband's casual philandering as part of the package she acquired when she married into the major leagues. A prominent star of the 1970s still cringes as he recounts how his wife decided to join him on a trip and appeared unannounced in the lobby of an Atlanta hotel. "I'd had too many Jack Daniel's," he says, "but at least I was alone. Some of the other guys weren't. Afterward, they gave it to me good. 'Can't you control your wife?' A lot of stuff like that." Predictably, this baseball marriage disintegrated into a baseball divorce.

DiMaggio's marriage unraveled painfully, placing his name in gossip columns, which he despised. There was not, there never would be, a single, sharp, clean cleavage. He tried. So did she. It didn't work. *Arrivederci.*

Dorothy settled herself in Reno on several occasions. First telephone calls from DiMaggio and from people with the Yankees convinced her to relent. Another time he followed her to Nevada. He talked about a better life, with more attention to her needs. Dorothy stopped short of court.

Divorce was rare among major league baseball players at the time, but troubled marriages were not. Sportswriters, some of whom had troubled marriages themselves, never touched the topic. So DiMaggio was spared questioning on his personal life and, whatever his private concerns, he blotted them out of mind at the ballpark.

The Yankees would stumble in 1940. After four consecutive World Series titles, the team finished third behind Detroit and Cleveland, even though DiMaggio led the American League in batting with .352.

They won easily in 1941, the year of DiMaggio's 56-game hitting streak, and took a memorable World Series from the Brooklyn Dodgers, 4 games to 1. They won the pennant again in 1942, but a young and speedy St. Louis Cardinal club upset them in the Series. By that time, the country was at war and DiMaggio was closer to his period of military service and his first divorce.

"Those little Japanese, they must be crazy," one chronicler reported, trying to sum up the American mood after the attack on Pearl Harbor. "So we mumbled and fumed on Sunday afternoon [December 7, 1941]. The Japs *were* crazy, but they had sunk half our fleet [except the carriers], crippled a great naval base, reduced our Pacific sea power dangerously. They had driven us into panic, then into rage and confusion. We shook that off [sic]. After December 11 [when Germany and Italy declared war], we were in it up to our ears. The carping clamor of the isolationists died out—to be followed almost immediately by a shrill Communist clamor for a second front.

"Russia was in desperate straits. A war tempo came to America. Blackouts, air-raid wardens, civilian defense, censorship, ration books, draft boards. No more new automobiles. Already our planes were streaming onto English airfields. Shiploads of trucks and tanks were unloading on the Persian Gulf for transit to Russia. We were in Iceland, Bermuda, on the shoulder of South America. We were in it, all right, and for keeps."

Although World War II lives in old movies as a period of united national purpose and unshakable resolve, it was, to say the least, an unsettling time. No war had ever begun so badly for the United States, and underneath the blare of jingoism ("Goodbye, Mama; I'm Off to Yokohama"), terrifying doubts existed. The Axis powers were mighty and could prevail. And this, as Winston Churchill most eloquently reminded mankind, would bring about a thousand years of darkness.

With the debris of Pearl Harbor barely settled into the Pacific, Americans worried that the Japanese might strike next at the West Coast. Actual invasion seemed remote, but bombing raids and naval attacks did not. In a small personal footnote to these large national concerns, one Giuseppe DiMaggio, sixty-seven, found himself "officially barred" in February 1942 from the DiMaggio restaurant on Fisherman's Wharf in San Francisco. The restaurant stood in what the War Department classified as a "defense zone"—an area likely to come under attack. Papa Giuseppe had never bothered to take out U.S. citizenship papers. By virtue of his Sicilian birth he was formally an "enemy alien." In a sweeping expression of anger and fear, the U.S. government restricted the movements of aliens from Italy and Germany and shipped thousands of Japanese, including U.S. citizens, out of California to detention camps. At length, in the case of Giuseppe DiMaggio, the government convinced itself that he was not in league with Admiral Yamamoto, relented, and permitted him to visit the family business establishment.

To DiMaggio himself, the war meant first that he would probably have to serve in the army. A peacetime draft had already gobbled up Hank Greenberg, who was single; the army would steal more than four years from Greenberg's estimable baseball career. As a married man, DiMaggio was classified 3-A, which meant at least in theory that he could not be inducted until all the healthy single men had been sworn in. Across the country, men looked at each day's mail with rising nervousness. You never knew when a letter would arrive beginning "Greetings!" and promptly order you to report for induction.

DiMaggio told friends he didn't like the damned uncertainty. He was going to have to go in sooner or later, he figured, so in a sense he'd just as soon settle things and enlist.

Then why not do it?

"Well, there's a little matter of the salary difference between what the army pays a private and what the Yankees pay me."

His marriage was unsettled and his life was unsettled and he began to experience stomach aches. Late in 1942, Dorothy moved to Reno with Joe junior and took a small suite at the Riverside hotel. She then engaged a divorce lawyer named Joseph P. Haller.

"What's happened? What caused this latest breakup?" asked a wire-service reporter who tracked her down.

"The lawyer has instructed me not to comment," Dorothy said.

The reporter called Haller, who said, "My lips are sealed."

Other reporters traced DiMaggio to the Beach Street house in San Francisco.

"I don't know anything about what Dorothy is doing," DiMaggio said.

"But you're married to her."

"Look," DiMaggio said, "it's my business, not yours, where she is and what she's doing. That's all I have to say."

He then flew to Reno to plead with Dorothy to relent. While he was there, Prescott Sullivan, a popular sports columnist for the *San Francisco Examiner,* telephoned, ostensibly to get a baseball story. The Yankees had just announced that they were going to abandon St. Petersburg as a spring-training base. Wartime travel restrictions meant that they would have to look for another site, in the north, close to New York City.

Sullivan had known DiMaggio for years. "I wanted to ask,

Joe, what effect you think the absence of spring training in Florida is likely to have on your play."

"Spring training won't concern me next year," DiMaggio said.

What did this mean? "Are you quitting baseball?" Sullivan asked.

"I'm not saying. Draw your own conclusions."

"Are you going to announce your retirement," Sullivan pressed, "or do you intend to enlist?" Then, crossing a line and detonating DiMaggio into fury, "Are you trying to reconcile with your wife?"

"None of your business," DiMaggio cried. He breathed deeply, fought for control. "Look, I'll be back in town [San Francisco] in a couple of days. Then I'll tell you what I'm going to do." DiMaggio hung up.

One of the Toots Shor's columnists would have protected DiMaggio from his own outburst. Prescott Sullivan chose, as the saying is, to go with what he had. An engaging and self-educated man who had been named for the city of Prescott, Arizona, and who survived into his eighties, Sullivan went for the biggest story he could write. He reported that DiMaggio would not return to the Yankees in 1943, scooping the entire, protective New York press. And he added that DiMaggio, in Reno, "was trying to effect a reconciliation with his estranged wife."

According to Sullivan, DiMaggio reappeared in San Francisco within the week. He telephoned the columnist at the *Examiner* and began, tight but controlled, "I never told you I was going to enlist."

"You implied it," Sullivan said.

At that point, according to Sullivan, DiMaggio snapped and "called me every kind of son of a bitch in the world."

DiMaggio was frazzled and frantic. He himself did not know what he intended to do. His perfect baseball discipline, his bitter negotiating with the Yankees, his careful investments, had, it seemed, brought him only to an edge of chaos.

He smoked heavily, consumed flagons of coffee, and spent his days in reclusive silence. He called Dorothy repeatedly, and at length she agreed to see him once again in Reno "to talk things through for the last time."

When he reached the Riverside hotel, DiMaggio looked drawn and pale. He went through by-now-familiar rituals. This was a tough stretch for him. He was going to have to go into the army and, Christ, that not only meant he'd have to leave the Yankees. He could get killed.

Dorothy said he could probably get "a special deal" in the army working in an athletic program. That would keep him relatively safe.

Joe said he wouldn't ask for a special deal. That was just wrong and he wasn't going to do it. Besides, even if the army decided to use him in sports, he was twenty-nine years old and it looked as if it was going to be a long war. Who the hell knew if he'd still be able to play ball when he finally got a discharge. His career just might be over.

Dorothy told him he was such a great ballplayer that he'd go on for many years. Joe said that without Dorothy and young Joe at his side, he wasn't sure he wanted to. Didn't Dorothy know that she was the most important person in the world to him?

Ice first cracked, then melted in the winter at Reno, Nevada. On January 13, Joe and Dorothy agreed to meet the press together. They stood arm in arm and they were smiling. "We had a few differences," Dorothy said, "misunderstandings of a personal nature. That's all behind us now. We're going to stay together. We're very happy about it all."

"What about the army?" a reporter asked.

"I'm going to try to get into the service," DiMaggio said. "That's definite, as soon as I get a few things straightened out. I don't know what branch I'll try for, but I'll be in somewhere soon."

From New York Ed Barrow said, "I wish Joe Godspeed and good luck. The Yankees are perfectly in accord with anyone who wishes to serve his country. Center field in our club is now open to anybody who can make the grade."

On February 17, 1943, DiMaggio reported to an army reception center at Monterey, California. He was assigned to a special-services unit stationed at the Santa Ana Army Air Field in Southern California. Dorothy moved to Los Angeles "so we can see each other frequently."

But most of the time, Dorothy was alone with her son. DiMaggio said he would change after the war, pay more attention to her and become a real husband. He said those things, but Dorothy simply did not believe that he actually could change. On October 11, 1943, she filed for divorce in Los Angeles. She asked $500 a month in alimony and $150 a month in child support. She estimated that DiMaggio had earned more than $50,000 in 1942 and $12,000 in 1943. Her charge was cruelty.

Joe continued to suffer stomach aches. He did not contest Dorothy's action. Early in 1944 the DiMaggios were divorced, after, as *Time* magazine put it, "four-and-a-half years of marriage, two return trips to Reno, and one child."

They would go separate ways to separate beds and separate lives, a strong man and a willful woman. Among her other marriages and romances, Dorothy continued to let Joe court her. She seemed to enjoy that—courtship from Joe—as intensely as she disliked marriage to him.

After her second marriage foundered, she tried to pick up the threads of her movie career. When that failed—few threads existed—she found herself looking back on the harsh days as Mrs. Joe DiMaggio with a misty fondness. In 1951, when she was thirty-four years old, she remarked to Hedda Hopper, the famous Hollywood gossip columnist, that "just between us"—and twenty million readers—she was thinking of "getting back with Joe."

Then came Marilyn.

Heywood Broun, columnist for the old New York World *and the father of the gifted commentator Heywood Hale Broun, once remarked that he had discovered the greatest anticlimax in the English language. It was a slogan, the elder Broun declared: For God, for country and for Yale.*

One does best to leave an observation like that alone, but certainly a curious, if lesser anticlimax is watching a motion picture being made. We are all familiar with the finished products, the sleek actresses with every curl in place, the smooth leading men who never stumble or stammer.

But a movie set is an arena where egos, union rules, and indeed, the difficulty of the work itself dictate a laborious tempo. Someone muffs a line. Action stops. The scene begins again. An assistant drops a bound script near a microphone. Start once more. Nobody muffs a line this time but a cameraman notices "a hair in the gate." Dirt near the lens. Everybody waits for the camera to be cleaned.

By now hot lights have caused an actor to perspire. Makeup. Fix his forehead. Try again.

DiMaggio disliked the exuberant vulgarity of Hollywood and he found trips to sound stages boredom without relief. The process of making a movie, the lighting, the camera work, the acting, the direction—and reshooting a scene forty times— didn't hold his interest. It was artificial and endlessly repetitive.

At the ballpark, even in practice, every fly ball was different from the one before.

Marilyn went forth and threw herself into her scenes, working over and over with an acting coach and a director, drawing the last dram of her talent and hurling it into the fortieth take of a scene that would flicker on a screen for all of two minutes. To her, this was an expression of creativity and a rack of pain; to DiMaggio it was a hell of a lot less interesting than catching a ball game on television.

He didn't want to watch her make movies, and the few times he appeared, people bothered him for autographs.

There was nothing for him to do on a set except drink coffee, which upset his stomach. He stayed away.

After he married the most famous movie actress of her generation, he never learned quite what it was she did.

Chapter ★ 7

Marilyn's Moments

Roll all the Cinderella stories into one. Summon all the copywriter's extravagant superlatives. Take the drama and pathos from the greatest novels. Stand her beside the loveliest beauties of all time. Do all these things and they won't compare with Marilyn Monroe, whose sudden fame never has been equalled in or out of motion pictures.

Only in America could such a thing happen . . .

—from an official Twentieth Century-Fox biography

Between *The Asphalt Jungle,* the 1950 film in which she became famous as a sexually charged house pet, and her marriage to Joe DiMaggio on January 14, 1954, Marilyn Monroe

196

performed in no fewer than sixteen movies. As success arrived, she began to complain that her acting range was not being properly expanded, but this would be the most productive period of her life.

She played dumb-blonde roles in musicals, speaking in a breathy staccato voice that seems affected now. It projected beguiling sex in the 1950s to a country that had not yet invented the R-rated Hollywood movie. She played troubled blondes in melodramas, and here her image of lust is enduring. Marilyn lying under a white bed sheet in *Niagara* (1953) smacks of nothing so much as inviting, naked sex. She also played a series of poorly defined roles in films that were not very good. "Hollywood," someone remarked at the time, "is the world's greatest collection of creative talent, all engaged in turning out potboilers."

In addition to acting, her days were filled with pursuits that ranged from the trivial to the intense, part of the lifestyle required of rising movie stars. She made smiling, high-heeled appearances to celebrate the openings of supermarkets and bowling alleys. When she was invited, and she was invited more and more frequently with success, she had herself sewn into a skintight gown and, with barely any breathing room, attended a Hollywood premiere. She gave hundreds and hundreds of interviews to the press, sometimes breaking through with an impudent, sexy wit, sometimes offering stock answers, and sometimes changing the details of her life story, on a whim or because the old version bored her. She was forever posing for publicity pictures. Fox announced in one early press release that "Marilyn was discovered while baby-sitting." She then posed holding a bottle for a multichinned infant someone had dumped in her lap. Someone else said she would "look great even in burlap." She posed in a fitted burlap sack (and looked fine).

She held a wood-headed driver and took a lesson from Henry Fonda in a picture that publicized Fox's annual studio golf tournament. She held a vacuum cleaner in the living room of a *Photoplay* magazine's "Dream House," which

would be given away to a lucky subscriber; she supposedly
became engaged to Charlie McCarthy and posed with both
the dummy and the ventriloquist Edgar Bergen. She was
taken to the Chicago White Sox spring-training base near Los
Angeles and there, wearing high heels, a tight top, and brief,
white shorts, she held a bat; then she bent forward and posed
with a pitcher named Joe Dobson and a hard-hitting outfielder named Gus Zernial. She was always smiling, always
posing. She was evolving into one of the hardest-working entertainers on earth.

Stories about her often focus on work difficulties: the
chronic lateness that disturbed whatever company she was in,
including a range of actors from Clark Gable to Sir Laurence
Olivier; a need for retakes that became a legendary annoyance to the people who directed her and were trying to
maintain a shooting schedule. But both these aberrations did
not peak until her later years, when she was drifting toward
mental illness. The earlier Marilyn, 1950–54, was sometimes
difficult, but her dominant force was a drive to work, to suc-
ceed, to accomplish. Or, as she put it, "to *be* somebody."

According to Howard Hawks, who directed her in
Gentlemen Prefer Blondes, Marilyn before fame was a sadly
shy figure in the film community, unschooled in fashion and
the subtleties of makeup. "Until she got famous," Hawks insisted, "she couldn't get a ride home from a Hollywood
party." This is hyperbole. One of the curiosities about Marilyn is that she attracted such hyperbolic, often nasty wit. Billy
Wilder remarked that she had "breasts of granite and a mind
of Swiss cheese. It's full of holes."

The figure that Marilyn offered on-screen, where she was
gowned in purple or Day-Glow orange, as well as virginal
white, was so doggedly and sometimes implausibly sexual that
Hollywood insiders like Hawks and Wilder found her somewhat comic. Added to this were her real-life aspirations,
which were not modest and approached pretension. She said
she kept a photograph of the great Italian actress Eleonora
Duse (1859–1924) on a night table. Once she had the power

and the funds, she never played a scene without the support of a personal acting coach. She went from dumb-blonde movie bits to musings about how she *really* wanted to play a Dostoevsky role. "Play Dostoevsky," went the Hollywood comment. "First she ought to learn how to spell Dostoevsky." She became a setup for the easy one-liner.

Actually, despite Hawks's wisecrack, Marilyn almost never lacked for a ride home from any party she chose to attend. But fame changed her life, simultaneously thrilled and strained her, made her cast about ever more desperately, and, as with DiMaggio, never brought the buoyant happiness she craved. Someone has remarked in a not-so-easy one-liner, "She didn't need success; she needed salvation."

Her salary moved up in quick steps to a top of $1,500 a week, but that was the most Fox was obligated to pay her under a long-term contract. The income, roughly $75,000 a year, was good money in the 1950s, but less than a fortune. (DiMaggio reached $100,000 with the Yankees in 1949.) As more and more of her movies succeeded handsomely at box offices, she would complain that Fox was "using" her. "I know how much they make on my movies," she said. "They're screwing me with that salary and I don't like to be screwed." She worried about money—this approached obsession near the end—and moved about from apartment to apartment. She didn't feel that she could afford a house.

She seemed incapable of setting down roots, and in her wanderings she collected people, shared intimacies with them, then let them go and moved along to another set.

Acting coaches seemed a remedy to her terrors that she was not performing well. (There is a grave but understandable irony here. She protested that her roles were not challenging but she literally trembled in the face of even the least challenging part.) One of her coaches was no less a light than Michael Chekhov, widely respected and a nephew of Anton Chekhov.

Doctors. She developed a distinct fear of doctors and at the same time remained inordinately dependent upon them.

She was forever contracting minor respiratory infections and she suffered so acutely during menstrual periods that she sometimes cried out in pain. This condition was diagnosed as a symptom of endometriosis, a disorder in which endometrial tissue (the lining of the uterus) spreads through the abdomen. Alternately, her painful cramps were attributed to a general pattern of hysteria.

Dentists. Her new "low" smile was marred by a slight overbite, and when Dr. Walter Taylor performed cosmetic work on her teeth, Marilyn befriended him. Coincidentally, Dr. Taylor drifted into alcoholism. Marilyn is said to have remained his steadfast friend until he died of liver rot.

Psychiatrists. Beyond all persons, places, things, Marilyn was fascinated by Marilyn. As soon as she began to make real money, she repaired to a psychoanalytic couch, where she could explore herself before an attentive, if hired, audience. This led in stages not only to her wretched encounter with the Payne Whitney clinic, but also to a final failed relationship with a Hollywood psychiatrist, which was, to put it tactfully, unusual. She saw this therapist, the late Dr. Ralph Greenson, twenty-eight times in the last thirty-four days of her life, according to the bill Greenson submitted to her estate.

Girlfriends. Marilyn liked to sit up and drink—not only champagne as the publicists professed, but good hard shots of vodka—and when she drank she tired the night with talking. Her drinking conversation ranged from fantasy—Clark Gable was her real father—to the general perfidies of men to a surgical procedure that tightened the vagina and would, presumably, make her even more satisfying to those men whose perfidies so wounded her. Marilyn's usual difficulty in sustaining relationships extended to girlfriends, but with a difference. If she wanted a man in bed, or even the pleasure of merely arousing him, she set after him with iron-butterfly resolve. It didn't matter whether the man was the beau or even the husband of a friend. Marilyn shattered her friendship with one lady who had helped her career by cruising naked through the woman's living room when the woman's husband was about. The scene is more overtly sexual than anything in Marilyn's films:

Husband and wife, sitting at leisure, near the close of a day. Enter Marilyn, naked, her face mixing real and manufactured innocence. Blond hair, "granite" breasts, "the greatest ass in Hollywood," and dark curls about the loins on full display. There is probably no need for dialogue to accompany this picture.

Men. Long after the divorce from DiMaggio, Marilyn became an easy mark for anyone who could get close to her. She told one journalist in a New York bar that she was afraid she had "gotten hooked on sex." Indeed, in her later years she went from one-night stand to one-night stand in a pattern more common to agitated men than women. But the younger Marilyn, the newly successful Marilyn, the hardworking pre-DiMaggio Marilyn, was more comfortable with longer affairs, provided, she said, "he doesn't try to rule me." Which meant that she could sleep around when that particular need ruled *her*.

The marriage to Arthur Miller would last the longest and come to reek of pungent bitterness. But her love affair with DiMaggio, Joe the Slugger, ran in all its phases across ten years, and was the great touchstone of two famous lives, although Miller, who did not attend Marilyn's funeral, has gone to certain lengths to put it (and DiMaggio) down.

Spear carriers. These would be publicists, journalists, housemaids, lawyers, accountants, photographers. They came and went. They worked for her, or in her corona, and numbers of them have given interviews (often for pay) and published memoirs. Most have one thing in common. The spear carrier is depicted as absolutely critical to the life and stability of Marilyn Monroe.

An absurdity is that these people merely revolved around an increasingly tortured centerpiece. They do not acknowledge, the memoirs would not ring so urgently if they did, that Marilyn could engage or dismiss them on whim, replace them with other bodies, and proceed. No one, not the maid, Lena

Pepitone, nor the briskly attractive publicist, Pat Newcomb, could support Marilyn for longer than a short span. They were not family. Marilyn was infinitely self-centered, self-created, self-defeating, and in the end, for all the gamey rumors, dead by her own hand because she wanted to die more than she wanted to live.

Not even the great DiMaggio, whose love for her burned enduringly, a lapping ceaseless flame, not even he could save her, and when he faced that, the worst personal defeat in a life of triumphs, he wept the hard, hot tears of a man who does not like to cry.

In a sense, her suicide was a final joke against all the jokers whom she saw arrayed against her.

Laugh at me?

I'll show you how funny I *really* am.

Funny as death.

Like all performers, she was simultaneously living a confusing variety of lives. There was her actual day-to-day existence, with cars to repair, bills to pay, and lovers to meet and welcome or reject. Then there were the sound stages, where she was variously Miss Caswell, Roberta Stevens, Annabel Norris, Rose Loomis, Lois Laurel, and Lorelei Lee; characters without last names called Nell, Peggy, and Joyce; and opposite Charles Laughton, a streetwalker who was given no name at all. A story is told about an agitated actor who was asked by a therapist if he was undergoing an identity crisis.

"Yes," the actor said, "but I'm not sure *which* identity it's happening to."

Surely you can learn about DiMaggio the person by considering his performances on ball fields. Just as surely you can learn about Marilyn from her performances on film. Not everything, of course, but bits about who she thought she was and who others thought she was and you can even learn from the responses of critics. (Her body fascinated them.)

Critics were slow to praise her acting. They tended to write about her appearance and, since critics of the 1950s did not publicly pant in passion, the result was often something of a joke. "The big question—how does Marilyn Monroe look stretched across a broad screen—" Otis L. Guernsey wrote in the *New York Herald Tribune* in 1953, "is easily answered. If you insisted on sitting in the front row, you would probably feel as though you were being smothered in baked Alaska."

Marilyn, who aspired to be Duse, found herself compared to a gooey dessert dish. She didn't like that, any more than she cared for jokes that denigrated her intelligence. She never responded directly—what was there to say?—but she sometimes made the point that it was the public, not the critics, who had brought her success. The public *liked* being smothered in baked Alaska.

After *The Asphalt Jungle,* she became an increasingly commercial property; there would always be parts for her to play. But the kind of complex and demanding roles that she imagined for herself were simply not forthcoming. For years she took all the work she was offered and polished her act as America's Blonde.

"Do you wear underwear?" a reporter asked at an interview.

Marilyn was ready for the question. Reporters were always asking that. Like anyone else, she wore underwear most of the time. She paused, eyed the reporter, and said: "Men seldom jump hurdles for girls who wear girdles."

The word she might have used is *ambivalence.* She wanted to be an artist, she wanted to be Duse, but the hip wiggles and the girdle stuff brought fame. Well, maybe they would take her acting seriously in time. For now she just had to take the roles that came along.

She played a hard, ambitious character in *The Fireball* (1950), a vehicle for Mickey Rooney, cast as an orphan who makes a name for himself in a roller derby. When Rooney contracts polio, Marilyn loses interest in him. Another woman, the *good* woman, nurses Rooney back to health, and when he returns to the roller derby he becomes an unselfish team skater. By that time Marilyn is gone. Inane, much like the roller derby itself.

As Young As You Feel (1951), with a story by Paddy Chayefsky, was more complex and presented a plot with a current focus. A conglomerate buys a small company and tries to force an executive into early retirement. Marilyn played the secretary to the conglomerate boss and drew pleasant, brief, critical attention.

In *Love Nest* (1951) she was the point of a triangle involving William Lundigan and June Haver, a blonde who never threw off showers of sparks. Jack Paar, later famous as the host of the *Tonight* television show, appeared in the picture as that B-movie staple the Best Friend. Paar has since said that he remembers Marilyn carrying large and weighty books onto the set. He adds, the wisecracks would not cease, that he is not certain he actually saw her *reading* them.

Marilyn drew another role as a temptress in *Let's Make It Legal* (1951) opposite smooth, mustachioed Zachary Scott. But it is Claudette Colbert's movie, rather than Marilyn's, and not a very good one.

She was not yet a major star but her career was developing momentum. Fox lent her to RKO, where she appeared in *Clash by Night,* a picture based on a Clifford Odets play set in a fishing community. Marilyn was Peggy, a cannery worker, and performed well alongside such practiced actors as Robert Ryan and Barbara Stanwyck. *Clash by Night* was released late in the spring of 1952, just as the furor about the naked calendar set off Roman candles. This was a period of fervid McCarthyism, with starchy puritanism cantering close behind.

Charlie Chaplin was prevented from returning to the United States essentially because of his political leaning, which bent left. But his case was not helped by an earlier record of paternity suits, including testimony from one of his lovers that he had stood naked in front of a mirror, examined himself, and announced: "I look like Peter Pan." It was a good idea in the early 1950s to keep your clothes on, if at all practical.

One of Marilyn's chroniclers has suggested that it was she herself who spread word about the calendar. According to this journalist, Marilyn sensed that the picture of her nude on velvet would lift, rather than devastate, her career. This creates a Marilyn more shrewdly calculating than she had become and also a young Marilyn possessed of utter recklessness.

Studio contracts during the 1950s included a so-called moral-turpitude clause. *Turpitude* derives from the Latin *turpis,* meaning depraved or vile, and actors had to promise to conduct themselves according to accepted public morality, or court dismissal and possibly disgrace. Posing naked for calendar art approached the vague border of turpitude.

Marilyn knew that the calendar was potentially dangerous. She didn't chatter about it any more than she chattered about the possibility that she was illegitimate. There is, perhaps, an innocence to the portrait, but it is a long way from the innocence of *September Morn.* She is stretched out naked with one leg extended and the other bent at the knee, with her head thrown back and her mouth open and her eyes looking toward the camera. The viewer takes in her face, the firm breasts, and her belly. She does suggest innocence, but at the same time she seems to be writhing, as though in passion.

The picture is hardly hard-core pornography, but it is distinctly sexual, perfect for public display on the walls of barbershops of the time. The country reacted not with prim revulsion but with a frenzy of delight and even a certain amusement. So this was all there was of Marilyn Monroe.

After that happened she made no effort to deny what was, she realized, readily verifiable.

"Tom Kelley took it," she kept saying in different ways, "and his wife was there the whole time."

"While Kelley was working," a reporter asked, "what did you have on?"

Foolish question, excellent straight line.

Marilyn answered with two words. "The radio."

*   *   *

Marilyn drew praise for her work in *Clash by Night,* both as a "gorgeous example of bathing beauty art" (the *New York Post*) and—for the first time—as "a forceful actress" (the *New York World-Telegram*).

Two of Marilyn's films were released within seven days in July 1952, as Fox channeled calendar enthusiasm toward box offices. *We're Not Married* is an undemanding spoof in which six couples, including Marilyn and David Wayne, Ginger Rogers, and Fred Allen, learn that their marriage licenses are invalid. It was a slick quickie, which gave the *Herald Tribune*'s Otis Guernsey, the baked Alaska man, a chance to write that Marilyn "looks as though she had been carved out of cake by Michelangelo." In movie after movie, good film or indifferent, she continued to overwhelm reviewers with her physical appearance.

She then undertook a difficult, rather ominous part opposite Richard Widmark in *Don't Bother to Knock* (1952). As Nell, she played a disturbed young woman who meets Widmark while on a baby-sitting job. Layers of her neurosis unroll. She has episodes of violence. She becomes convinced that Widmark is her fiancé, although the real fiancé is dead. During one shrill scene, she holds a straight razor and threatens suicide. Calmed by Widmark, she is led off toward a mental hospital.

This was far from a basic Marilyn role, and the most important movie reviewer of the day felt that she wasn't up to it. "It requires a good deal to play a person who is strangely jangled in the head," wrote Bosley Crowther in *The New York Times.* "Unfortunately all the equipment that Miss Monroe has to handle this job are a childishly blank expression and a provokingly feeble, hollow voice. With these she makes a game endeavor to pull something out of the role, but it looks as though she and her director were not certain what."

After DiMaggio established himself as a national figure with the Yankees in 1936, he had, in a sense, crossed to the apparent safety of acclaim. Except for such minor setbacks as his first all-star game, the consistent brilliance of his play became a wonder of the nation. The difficulties with his contract and the questions about his relationship with Gould were stumbling blocks, not minefields. His public life became a tale of triumph, punctuated by ovations and raves.

Marilyn had a more difficult time of it. First, she wanted to become a movie star. After she was properly coached and dressed and undressed, it was only a matter of sufficient exposure before she became one. But then she wanted to be not just a star, but an actress, a real actress, a great actress, and this drove her and pushed her all her life. Indeed, it became a form of torture in later years. No matter how hard she worked, how many retakes she shot, some critic would always suggest that Mme. Duse had played in a different league.

Marilyn rebounded from the sour notices that tolled for *Don't Bother to Knock* with a relatively easy effort as yet another sexy secretary, to Cary Grant's research chemist, in *Monkey Business* (1952). Grant is experimenting with another old Hollywood staple, a potion to restore youth, and when it works on him he runs off from his wife (Ginger Rogers) and rushes about with Marilyn, swimming and roller-skating, a grown-up teenager in love. The formula, of course, wears off, and husband and wife end up together. Paul Beckley wrote in the *Herald Tribune:* "Not having seen Miss Monroe before, I now know what that's all about. She disproves the old stage rule about not turning one's back to the audience."

O. Henry's Full House (1952), a series of bits from the short stories, had her up against Charles Laughton, who was cast as a dandified bum. Laughton wants to get arrested so he can spend the winter in the warmth of a city jail. He decides to accost a woman, expecting her to call for the police. But the girl he accosts in front of an Oriental rug shop (Marilyn) is delighted to be accosted. She is a hooker. Presently, Laughton, not Marilyn, rushes off. He then goes to church, swears to reform, and this being O. Henry, is picked up for vagrancy and sentenced to ninety days. Archer Winsten in the *New*

York Post called Marilyn "a streetwalker of stunning propor-
tions."

Niagara (1953), where she worked opposite Joseph Cotten, was a small breakthrough, a hard role in a convoluted
story, which she brought off well. She is married to Cotten
and wants to leave him; he is older and somewhat depressed.
Cotten rouses himself, kills Marilyn's young lover, and disap-
pears. Marilyn collapses, is taken to a hospital and sedated.
When she regains her senses, she flees. Cotten reappears, and
in a stark and intense scene chokes her to death in a carillon
tower.

Cotten tries to escape by boat, taking along a young
woman (dark-haired Jean Peters) as a hostage. He relents and
lets her climb out to a small rock island. The boat carries
Cotten over the falls, and in a spectacular finish, a helicopter
rescues a very wet Jean Peters.

Marilyn's character, Rose, was young, restless, sexually
charged, and a borderline hysteric. Marilyn played that part
to a turn. She was the girl a man wants because she looks so
glorious in bed and the girl he knows he shouldn't touch because she is hellish trouble. Watching *Niagara* one remembers
the standing adage "Never sleep with a woman who has more
problems than you do." Knowing that and watching, a man
still wants to sleep with Marilyn, providing his hormonal balance is normal. Both major New York critics came close to
the same conclusion, if somewhat primly.

"Miss Monroe," Guernsey wrote, "plays the kind of wife
whose dress, in the words of the script, is 'cut so low you can
see her knees.' The dress is red, the actress has very nice
knees and she gives the kind of performance that makes the
audience hate her while admiring her, which is proper for the
story."

"Seen from any angle," wrote A. H. Weiler in the *Times,*
"Niagara Falls and Miss Monroe leave little to be desired by
any reasonably attentive audience. Perhaps Miss Monroe is
not the perfect actress at this point. But neither the director
nor the gentlemen who handled the cameras appeared to be

very concerned about this. They have caught every possible curve both in the intimacy of the boudoir and in tight dresses. She can be seductive—even when she walks."

She leaped next into a couple of vastly successful 1953 comedies, *Gentlemen Prefer Blondes,* and *How to Marry A Millionaire,* where she sang ("Diamonds Are a Girl's Best Friend") and played her gorgeous-vapid-blonde routine in a rainbow of skintight costumes.

In one scene from *Blondes,* she is seated alone in the dining salon of the *Ile de France.*

Headwaiter: "What can I do for you, miss?"

Marilyn, eyes wide, mouth open, breathily: "Put a gentleman at my table."

A wealthy lady displays antiques she has inherited. "These are heirlooms. They've been in my family forever."

Marilyn, wide-eyed: "You'd never know it. They look just like new."

In *Blondes,* Marilyn's running mate was tall, busty, black-haired Jane Russell. "Miss Russell," Guernsey wrote, "walks through the show with a long-legged stride and Miss Monroe limits herself down to a lazy amble, but somehow they always seem to come out about even."

How to Marry a Millionaire matched her with Betty Grable, whom she was replacing as Hollywood's choice blonde, and an auburn-haired, sharp-tongued Lauren Bacall. The plot has Marilyn so myopic that when she puts aside her spectacles, she bumps into furniture and has difficulty telling one man from another; the story is both intricate and somewhat silly. Both comedies drew pleasant reviews for Marilyn. One critic wrote that "she would glow in the dark." Another noted that the years were beginning to pass but pointed out, "Her shape does not seem to be deteriorating."

It wasn't. She was approaching thirty and looked both more beautiful and more womanly than she had five years before. She played in a Western, *River of No Return,* with Robert Mitchum, and a musical that didn't work, *There's No Business Like Show Business* (1954), opposite Donald O'Connor, whose boyish face and manner were pallid against the sexy, lusty female star.

Thirty was coming into view. Soon it would be her thirtieth year to heaven, and now questions and crises began to press her, as they press most of us when yet one more decade winds down. For everyone, thirty suggests, at the very least, the end of youth. For a ballplayer, who survives by the quickness of his bat, and for an actress, who lives by the firmness of bust and buttock, thirty comes, threatening as a wet October wind, the onset of middle age.

Marilyn wanted to be married. She said she was certain of that. She sometimes remarked that she was ready to marry "the next available man who comes along and can take care of me." But she knew who she was: Marilyn Monroe. By her definition an "available" man would have wealth and status. Marilyn Monroe was not about to marry a bellhop.

She talked about "straightening out" her career. She was coming to enjoy real literature, she had a fine, unfocused intelligence, and she particularly relished those great contentious Russian rivals, Dostoevsky and Tolstoy. This was a woman who could stride naked through the living room of friends, and a little after, retreat into a bedroom to join Anna Karenina.

By contrast to the great characters, whose lives Marilyn *read,* the characters she *played* seemed somewhat silly. They were commercial, she understood, but silly still. And on top of that she was so chronically, profoundly, endlessly uncertain of her talent that even playing silly roles electrified her with alarm. She was a handful for everybody, directors, fellow actors, herself.

Ben Hecht, the prolific screenwriter, once began a collaboration on her life story—it never was completed—and later provided certain insights. "Her critical taste," Hecht said, "exceeded her creative abilities. That happens to lots of people out here. Writers worship Shakespeare and turn out scripts for *Dr. Kildare.* Actors who admire John Gielgud end up as bit players. But these people usually come to terms with their lives. They say, I do the best I can. They say, I could act or write better, but my bosses won't let me. They say all kinds of things. Then they say, What the hell, my work may not be for the ages, but I've got a nice house and I'm going to be able to send my kids to Harvard."

The family, even a fractured family, can serve as a kind of fortress. However long a day, however demeaning that day's work, the family stands as a symbol of safe retreat. *I do all this to send the kids to Harvard.* But Marilyn had no family, or felt she didn't. Her mother was institutionalized. Her "Aunt" Ana Lower died in 1948. And, after divorcing Jim Dougherty, she did not have the best of fortune in romances.

Listing Marilyn's lovers is both a popular fantasy and a fool's game. Bedding America's blonde was an unassailable macho badge; she could not have slept with every man who boasted of having had her without dying earlier than she did, and of exhaustion. The names that bob up range from Chico Marx to Albert Einstein. (Marilyn met Chico during the filming of *Love Happy* in 1950. She professed admiration for Einstein; in all probability they never met.)

But the record of her serious affairs is clear and faintly depressing. Marilyn met the mustachioed actor John Carroll at a party in a Santa Monica beach house late in the 1940s. Carroll was everybody's road-company Gable, a B-movie leading man who found most of his work in quickie Westerns churned out at Republic studios. They flirted enthusiastically, undeterred by the presence of Carroll's wife, Lucille Ryman, a principal talent scout at MGM.

Within months Marilyn moved into the Carrolls' rambling apartment at a building called El Palacio on Fountain Avenue, a few blocks below the glitter of Sunset Strip. This remarkable arrangement continued for some time, and when the Carrolls moved to a new ranch house in the San Fernando Valley, Marilyn moved with them.

Lucille Ryman had to put in long hours at Metro, which led Marilyn to conclude that she didn't really love her husband. No woman who loved a man, Marilyn said, would be off working all the time. Carroll, Marilyn decided, must "be in love with me because he's so good to me."

In the end, Lucille Ryman says, she offered her husband a divorce. Carroll declined and Marilyn moved out. This trio plot offers more possibilities for dramatics than most of the movies Marilyn was making.

Fred Karger was a voice coach at Columbia Pictures who also conducted a society dance band, like Meyer Davis and Lester Lanin, that was often booked for functions in the old-money community of Pasadena. Karger was assigned to work on Marilyn's singing in 1948—her voice was breathy and sexy but she had no microphone technique—and presently, as John Carroll did before him, Karger was inviting Marilyn to move in.

Karger lived in a bungalow on Harper Avenue with his mother, Anne, his widowed sister, Mary, and a number of ambient children and grandchildren. By most accounts, Marilyn found a small apartment nearby, but spent most of her free time with Fred Karger and his family. He bought her dinners in restaurants at Malibu, took her dancing at Sunset Strip nightclubs, and brought her along with the society dance band when he was working.

Marilyn fell in love with Freddy Karger but Karger, who was going through a divorce, was not certain that he wanted to marry again and, if he did, was even less certain that Marilyn was the right girl.

Marilyn later talked about the affair with a touch of rue. Freddy was ten years older than she was, she said, and knew more and used to remind her that he did and tell her that she had an awful lot to learn. He was honest, though. He didn't promise marriage or anything like that. They had good times, but the good times weren't leading anywhere, and after a while what could she do? She just moved on.

For his part Karger said that her towering ambition bothered him. Above all things Marilyn wanted to be a star. He was looking for a homebody, Karger said, and he let Marilyn go. (A few years later Karger married a woman who would not turn out to be a homebody. This was the former Mrs. Ronald Reagan, Jane Wyman.)

Marilyn moved next into a classic starlet relationship with a man much older and more powerful than she. That affair spurred her career, agitated her psyche, and in the end left her tasting ashes.

Johnny Hyde was an urbane and driving executive at the William Morris Agency, then, as now, a mighty fortress in Hollywood, and he had represented a range of stars from the swaggering Al Jolson to beautiful, hard-drinking Rita Hayworth. When he met Marilyn, probably at a club in Palm Springs, Hyde was long since a millionaire and, so it seemed, securely married. Marilyn said Hyde told her that she was going to be a very big star. She was feeling shaky that evening. She said she didn't believe him.

Marilyn captivated Hyde. Her sexy little walk-on with Groucho Marx in *Love Happy* convinced him of her potential; she could become even more popular than the late Jean Harlow. That was his professional opinion. Personally—Hyde was fifty-one when they met—he became infatuated with this beautiful, poignant, lost young blonde.

Hyde was descended from a family of Russian acrobats— the name was originally Haidabura. He stood only about five feet three and, even before he began chasing about with Marilyn, suffered from a heart condition. He had a strong-jawed, weathered face and the look of a man used to control, but he was so short that you cannot fairly call him imposing. With a weakening heart, he had come to a point in his life when good sense, and his physicians, urged him to slow his pace. But after meeting Marilyn, Hyde rushed her about from party to party, from premiere to premiere, as if to show that he wasn't really in his fifties and that his heart wasn't really giving out.

Hyde separated from and subsequently divorced his wife, Molly Cravens, once a starlet at Republic, and bought a sprawling house on North Palm Drive in Beverly Hills. It became standard Hollywood gossip that Marilyn was Johnny

Hyde's mistress and that Johnny Hyde was the sorcerer behind Marilyn's blossoming career.

Hyde loved her passionately and pleaded with her to marry him. Marilyn declined. "I love you, Johnny," she said, "but I'm not *in love* with you." Hyde persisted with increasing intensity.

She could "learn to be in love" with him.

No, Marilyn said, things didn't work that way.

If she married him, Hyde said, and his heart were to give out, she would inherit a huge estate. She would be set for life.

That would be nice, Marilyn said, *really* nice, but it wouldn't be right, marrying someone you weren't in love with.

Well, Hyde said, he certainly didn't want her to leave him.

"I won't leave you," Marilyn said.

"Stay with me," Hyde said, "and I'll make a good provision for you in my will. Not that I expect anything to happen."

"I don't even want to talk about that, Johnny."

"But if anything does happen, you'll be taken care of. Just don't leave me."

Marilyn never left Johnny Hyde. They ran together, played together, slept together, and he worked out her long-term contract with Twentieth Century-Fox. She was grateful to him, she said; he was so nice to her. She would stay with him as long as he wanted. But for all his fortune and his overwhelming passion for her, she could not bring herself to marry him, now or ever.

After an affair that lasted longer than two years, Johnny Hyde died of a heart attack on Monday, December 19, 1950. Marilyn's career was about to rocket to the stars. When Hyde's will was read, she found he had left her nothing.

She wept at his funeral, calling his name over and over again.

His survivors ordered her out of her dead lover's house.

Shortly after that Marilyn tried to gulp enough Nembutal capsules to kill herself. This was when terror of death dried her mouth so that she could not swallow. Someone found her semiconscious, her mouth crammed with what looked like purple paste. It was the residue of the pills she had not been able to get down her throat.

Marilyn was back at work shooting a mediocre movie a few days later.

Distance, to be sure, may lend enchantment, but it can also impose a clinical coldness on the beats of life. From the vantage point of three decades, we see a troubled and troubling lady, successively involved with a third-rate Gable who was married, a slick ballroom maestro who would not be pinned down, and a driving, undersize agent with a large libido and terminal heart disease. That is not exactly a pantheon of lovers.

One feels a sense of pathos and detects a certain seediness: the young actress throwing herself at people and into situations in ways that are not quite savory. That viewpoint is true, I suppose, as far as it goes, but it misses two significant aspects: glamour and irony.

Marilyn was becoming ever more glamorous as she learned about fashions and styles. This was no plain-Jane waif who had to offer her body to get a man. This was one of the most physically desirable women on earth. That she settled for Carroll, Karger, and Hyde tends to diminish the glitter of her walk. But that glitter was so vivid and so palpable that she soon would capture a country.

The irony can be stated briefly. Marilyn became the most popular subject for American male sexual fantasies. And even as that was happening, her own sex life was variously mechanical (Hyde) and frustrating (Karger).

It was out of this background in the spring of 1952 that Marilyn met Joe. After that she began to make a small joke to friends. "Joe brings a great bat into the bedroom."

Chapter ⋆ 8

The Thorns of Glory

*T*he season in which Joe DiMaggio seized glory by the throat fell within a year wracked by bombardment, nightmares, wrenching death. Indeed, to some the world was at an end.

In 1941 Virginia Woolf stuffed rocks into the pockets of her dress as she stood beside the swift-running River Ouse in Sussex. Then she leaped in and drowned herself, rather like Ophelia; the body was not recovered for three weeks. She left behind a note that read: "I have a feeling that I shall go mad and cannot go on any longer in these terrible times."

That spring a single German air attack on London took 1,436 lives. When summer came the Nazis moved east, and on October 3, Hitler boasted to the Reichstag: "Russia is defeated and will never rise again." With December 7 came Pearl Harbor. In giddy, almost manic counterpoint, the

cloistered world of baseball experienced one of its most rousing seasons in the sun.

At Fenway Park in Boston, lean, excitable Ted Williams
was in an absolute prime of youth and sinew. The Brooklyn
Dodgers, a team of comic ineptitude for a generation, rose
up, the wretched of the earth, and won the National League
pennant. The Yankees thundered over all their rivals in the
American League and cruised home by fully 17 games. The
most extraordinary episode of this remarkable season, played,
so to speak, under the spectral shadow of war, was the work
of a center fielder from San Francisco. DiMaggio hit safely in
56 consecutive games.

On May 15 DiMaggio singled against left-handed Edgar
Smith of the Chicago White Sox. He hit safely for all the rest
of May, when President Roosevelt was declaring "a state of
unlimited national emergency." He hit safely every game in
June, when Nazi paratroopers were capturing the antiquities
and battlements of Crete. He wasn't stopped until the night of
July 17, by which time Hitler's soldiers were fanning out
toward Moscow, Leningrad, and the great gate of Kiev. Di-
Maggio was quietly upset when his streak came to its end. "I
wish," he said, "it could have gone on forever." Then he
went out and hit safely in his next 17 games.

A batting streak develops along different lines from most
other baseball accomplishments. When a home-run hitter
moves out smartly, everybody notices; soon newspapers print
boxes comparing his pace with Babe Ruth, 1927, and Roger
Maris, 1961. When a pitcher begins to strike out whole teams,
the effect is dramatic, and activists in the grandstand begin to
clap encouragement whenever he gets two strikes on a rival
batter. A hitting streak is more subtle, at least in its early
stages. It grows at a slow pace, predestined by the schedule. It
can only advance one game at a time. For a considerable
period nobody pays attention. That is so today when media
coverage of major sporting events approaches hysteria, and it

was so in 1941 when the media approach was often downright lethargic.

A small, ebullient outfielder from Brooklyn called Wee Willie Keeler hit safely in 44 straight games in 1897 while playing for the Baltimore Orioles. The record lay in the books largely unnoticed. Keeler was known to have pocketed a pistol in his baggy flannel uniform one July 4 and punctuated a game by firing blank cartridges into the air. He was famous for a single sentence. When asked to explain his batting success, he offered a now-familiar quotation that has eluded Bartlett's, perhaps for reasons of grammar. "I hit 'em where they ain't."

In 1978, Pete Rose matched Keeler by hitting safely in 44 consecutive games for the Cincinnati Reds. Near the end so many reporters were covering Rose that they had to spend hours interviewing each other. Rose delighted them with his poise and availability, but when the season ended the Cincinnati management declined to meet his contract request and this staunch native son of the Queen City had to go and play for Philadelphia. Batting streaks had better be their own rewards.

The New York newspapers of 1941 were slow to pick up on DiMaggio's hitting. He batted safely in 18 games before the *Times* mentioned that he had been getting at least a hit a day. The papers focused on the Yankees' slow start and wondered, after the team's third-place finish in 1940, whether "The Bronx dynasty is at an end." Even when DiMaggio was stopped, few bells or whistles sounded. On July 18, 1941, an eight-column headline in the *Herald Tribune* sports section read:

REDS SHADE GIANT, 5–4; DIMAGGIO'S STREAK STOPPED AT 56 AS YANKEES DEFEAT INDIANS, 4–3.

As the headline indicates, the lead story was the Giants' defeat. DiMaggio being stopped after his phenomenal run was the number-two story, the so-called off lead. Why? New York newspapers followed a rigid policy of topping their sports pages with an account of whichever local team played at home. Because the Giants played Cincinnati in the Polo Grounds, they led the paper. DiMaggio and the Yankees, working at Municipal Stadium beside Lake Erie in Cleveland, were placed no better than second best, according to the prevailing formula.

This restrained, and, in retrospect, flawed coverage, plus the background rhythm of Nazi soldiers trampling across the plains of Europe, made the American response to DiMaggio's streak remarkable. Without much coaching, the public recognized that something extraordinary was taking place in baseball, and put aside global concerns to root DiMaggio onward. Ever larger crowds came out to see him hit. Ever more conversations in New York, St. Louis, or San Francisco began: "Did Joe get hold of one today?" For much of that early summer, the answer was yes.

DiMaggio hitting in 56 games in the 1980s would draw three hundred journalists to the doors of the Yankee clubhouse, where many would have to interview each other and offer their readers secondhand quotes. DiMaggio in 1941 attracted only the reporters regularly assigned to the Yankees, plus an occasional columnist and, to be sure, baseball writers assigned to the visiting team who had the good sense to go with an exciting and ongoing story.

Thus, DiMaggio, the hero of sunlit afternoons in 1941, was not the creation of the press. He was the creation of his own formidable accomplishments. The distinction is roughly that which separates the synthetic and the real, a plastic bat and a fine piece of flame-treated ash, bone-polished to a restrained and handsome luster.

After DiMaggio hit safely in his eighteenth game, John Drebinger of *The New York Times* mentioned, near the bottom of his dispatch of June 1, that a streak was in progress. On June 2, DiMaggio hit a single and a double against Bob Feller, Cleveland's great fastball pitcher. Nineteen. That night Lou Gehrig died.

People were saddened rather than shocked. "When I first came up," DiMaggio told a reporter, "Lou was one of the first veterans to come over and speak to me. After he got sick, he'd come out to the games every day and you could see he was having trouble walking. I'd never known anyone as strong as Gehrig and then to see him like that . . ." DiMaggio's voice dropped. "I could hardly bear to look."

The Yankees were rained out in Detroit while Gehrig's ravaged body rode to a cemetery in Westchester County, but in baseball, a country of the young, life resumed quickly. The next afternoon DiMaggio tripled against a splendid left-hander named Hal Newhouser, and then the Yankees drew a day off to ride Pullman cars to St. Louis. The Browns had not been able to finish anywhere better than fifth since 1929 but the St. Louis writers were considerably sharper than the journeyman ballplayers they had to cover. They asked Manager Joe McCarthy why he thought the Yankees were still bogged in fourth place.

"The boys," McCarthy announced, "are just waiting for Joe to show them how to do it."

That was a curious and demanding remark. DiMaggio had batted safely in 21 consecutive games, which put him within 8 of the all-time Yankee record. He was *already* showing the boys how to do it. But, as though the quote were a spur, DiMaggio now proceeded to destroy the Browns' pitching. He slammed 3 hits in a Saturday game and 4 more, including 2 home runs, in a Sunday doubleheader. The Yankees swept the series; they had begun to roll.

Phil Rizzuto, the wiry young Brooklynite who supplanted Frank Crosetti at shortstop, would vividly recall the streaking DiMaggio. "I was just a rookie," Rizzuto says, "and I had a lot of adjusting to do. Like I didn't have any real money and I was driving a terrible old car until one day Ed Barrow called me in and said, 'That kind of car doesn't look right in the Yankee players' lot. Either get a new one, or ride the subway.'

"Anyway, the way Joe was swinging during his streak, he

hit the ball well almost every time he came up. Very seldom did he hit the ball on the handle or near the end of the bat. And he knew it. He had to know it. One day Joe told me that even when the third basemen played him deep, and they all did, he could still handcuff them with a smash." The short-striding swing was never quicker than in the summer of 1941.

Slowly at first, but with gathering momentum, the streak began to attract notice around the country. It became an item halfway between mere trivia and the doomsday book that was each evening's news from the world's battlefields. "People ask me if I was aware of my streak," DiMaggio says. "How could I not be aware of it when I liked to listen to the radio?" Indeed, numbers of broadcasters began their reports along these lines: "Before we get to the stories from Europe, here's some *good* news. Joe DiMaggio hit safely again today."

DiMaggio did hit safely against the White Sox, the Tigers, the Browns, the Philadelphia Athletics. The school year ended and children gathered in siege groups to get his autograph in hotels where the Yankees stayed, the Del Prado on the South Side of Chicago, the Chase across from Forest Park in St. Louis, and the Book-Cadillac in downtown Detroit. "I became an expert," DiMaggio says, "in back doors, any way out that beat the crowds."

Was he nervous? "The streak certainly didn't affect my fielding," he said later, "and I knew how to relax in the dugout. Just kind of close off my mind and rest. I wouldn't say I was nervous, but I did know what was going on." Michael "Pete" Sheehy, the Yankees' late clubhouse man, insisted that DiMaggio did show at least the symptoms of tension. "Before the games," Sheehy said, "Joe was always gulping coffee. Maybe as much as ten cups. And he would smoke up a storm. A pack easy."

He was playing hell with the lining of his stomach but he continued to show the world a controlled, withdrawn, and somewhat glacial image. That was one part of his machismo; capturing Marilyn would be another. Meanwhile, his belly ached and, pokerfaced, he kept pounding out his hits. "It was just amazing," Rizzuto says.

The Yankees actually streaked around his streak and then, on June 29, when his cannonball run had reached the total of 40 consecutive games, a mysterious stranger appeared and stole his bat. DiMaggio used a Louisville Slugger, model D-29, which weighed thirty-six ounces, somewhat heavier than the bats common in the major leagues today. Ballplayers grow attached to a specific model bat; bats come in a great variety of weight and length, thickness, taper, handle, and knob. Some, like DiMaggio, even become attached to a particular individual bat. There are slight variations from sample to sample, but, more than that, the particular bat becomes a totem. Even Little Leaguers talk about "my favorite bat." The alleged phallic relationship is not necessarily valid.

DiMaggio regularly rubbed his favorite D-29 with a soup bone. That smoothed the surface and made the wood less likely to chip. He applied a mixture of olive oil and resin to the handle and then ran a low flame over the mixture. When that was done, he applied sandpaper. This subtly affected the weight and balance and gave him a grip that was sticky and rough—in short, secure. "I felt I needed a good grip," he once explained to a reporter, "because I had slippery hands." Put differently, his palms sweated under the pressure of daily performance. "You'd be surprised," he went on, "how a bat you've been using for a long time gets to fit your hand like a glove." Although an element of totemism may have been working here, other fine hitters confirm what DiMaggio said. A particular bat has a particular feel. A man gets used to it.

On June 29 the Yankees swept a doubleheader from the Senators, who usually contested with the Browns and the Athletics for last place. DiMaggio lined a double in the sixth inning of the first game. His streak had reached 41.

Between games the Yankees retired to the visitors' clubhouse at Griffith Stadium. The team bats stayed in a rack beside the dugout. Someone—the name apparently is lost to history—jumped out of the grandstand, lifted DiMaggio's

D-29, and fled, without being apprehended or even noticed by ushers or the ballpark police. The thief then went home, to Newark, New Jersey, with DiMaggio's favorite bat as a purloined door prize.

Just before the second game began, DiMaggio realized that his bat was missing. He searched the rack. He went through a large sack of spare bats, starting to show agitation. He turned to Tommy Henrich, the young right fielder, who also used a D-29. "You got my bat, Tom?"

"No, this is mine, Joe. It's got my name on it."

DiMaggio felt a swelling sense of panic. "It's my bat but you can borrow it," Henrich said. "It's a real good one."

DiMaggio did not respond. His eyes became vacant and he looked stricken. Using other bats, he made out three times. "Joe," Henrich persisted in the seventh inning, "you ought to try my bat. It's got, you know, a real good feel."

"Okay," DiMaggio said. "Let me have your bat." He then lined a single against an obscure strapping right-hander named Arnold "Red" Anderson. Forty-two games. His teammate's bat had done the job.

This is surely the raw material of fiction, ranging from children's stories to Bernard Malamud's thickly woven novel *The Natural*. Malamud endows his hero, Roy Hobbs, with a mystical bat called Wonderboy, carved from a tree that was split by a fork of lightning. The bat becomes the Excalibur of Hobbs's story. In batteries of juvenile work, young ballplayers lose or break a favorite bat just before a crucial game. They then come through in a climactic scene, demonstrating for generations of children that the power and the glory lie within the individual, not the totem. This was certainly true of the DiMaggio adventure. The way he was hitting, one of the Yankees said, he could have broken Keeler's record swinging *The Saturday Evening Post*.

Fiction is relevant to DiMaggio's streak. The stolen bat incident may have influenced Malamud, who is said to have followed baseball closely in his younger years. Aside from that, at least two fictional stories have sprung to prominence around the day DiMaggio passed Keeler.

DiMaggio broke the record on June 30 against the Boston Red Sox, using Henrich's D-29. His own favorite bat was still missing. With one out in the fifth inning, he drove a high inside fastball over the head of Ted Williams and into an empty section of the Yankee Stadium grandstand. The pitcher was Heber "Dick" Newsome, a rookie right-hander from Ahoskie, North Carolina. The count was two balls, one strike. The crowd—it was a Tuesday afternoon—numbered only 8,700, which is why the left-field stands were unoccupied. The Yankees did not rush to greet DiMaggio at home plate. Players exercised more restraint forty-five years ago than do today's bouncing, hugging, high-fiving major leaguers. But the team did move to the top dugout step applauding, and Lefty Gomez told DiMaggio: "You not only broke Keeler's record, you even used his formula. You sure as hell hit that last one where they ain't." DiMaggio permitted himself a small grin.

That is what happened. One widely circulated story holds that Dominic DiMaggio, playing center field for Boston, almost stopped his brother's streak with "a supersensational spear of a drive." Dom was playing center, but he caught nothing at all Joe hit that day. Another flight of creative fancy has DiMaggio's missing bat coming back to the Stadium that morning, which, quite simply, is not so. Fantasy materializes like so much ectoplasm around high baseball deeds. In the 1940s careful reporters dismissed it as Hollywood stuff; today some would attribute the fluff to the embellishment that is part of the new journalism.

The bat did appear a few days later. The fan who stole it bragged to friends, not all of whom agreed that stealing a ballplayer's favorite bat was a good idea. At length, someone who knew the thief contacted DiMaggio to strike a deal.

"The guy doesn't want any trouble," the man said.

"I won't give him any," DiMaggio said. "I just want my bat back." An underground railroad was organized and third and fourth parties bore the treasured Louisville Slugger back to the Stadium. The thief remained anonymous and unpunished. DiMaggio proceeded to hit even harder than he had. Across the final 11 games of the streak he batted .523, which is phenomenal under any circumstances and particularly so with every opposing pitcher concentrating above all things on stopping him.

He might have kept the streak alive longer if he had been willing to bunt, but he was DiMaggio, and DiMaggio didn't bunt. Bunting was for mortals and the St. Louis Browns. On July 17 the Yankees played at Cleveland before 67,468 fans, the largest crowd ever to have seen a major league game at night.

Cleveland's third baseman, Ken Keltner, was big and quick, as good a "glove" as anyone around. He played DiMaggio so deeply that a reasonable bunt would have been a hit. Batting against a workaday left-handed pitcher named Al Smith, DiMaggio whipped a smash over third base in the first inning. Keltner would not be handcuffed. He lunged and gloved the ball and threw DiMaggio out from foul territory.

In the seventh inning, DiMaggio hit another hard drive that Keltner subdued. Then, in the ninth inning, facing the right-handed Jim Bagby, Jr., he again scorned the bunt and grounded sharply to shortstop. The ball took an erratic bounce—fate and a pebble seemed to be intervening—but Lou Boudreau, the Cleveland shortstop, had fast hands. He trapped the bad hop near his right shoulder and started a double play. The streak had joined Wee Willie Keeler. It was history.

"Joe was so calm afterward it was remarkable," Phil Rizzuto says. "I remember there were some reporters and some questions and he answered them in a very level voice. You just couldn't have told from the way Joe acted that his streak had just been ended."

Except . . . DiMaggio forgot to pick up his wallet from a trunk locker where the players stored valuables during games. That was the single sign that he was upset. He started walking toward the Hotel Cleveland with Gomez and Rizzuto when he suddenly realized his loss.

"Kid," he said to Rizzuto, "lend me twenty dollars."

Rizzuto obliged. He says he was happy to be lending money to the star.

A few blocks later, DiMaggio and Gomez wheeled into a bar. Rizzuto tried to follow. "Kid," DiMaggio remarked, "I said lend me twenty dollars. I didn't say drink with me."

According to Rizzuto, who tells the story in a muted, bittersweet way, that twenty dollars has never been returned.

Baseball historians tend to fall in love with numbers. Numbers are a constant amid changes of season, faces, and places and changes in the historians themselves. They point out that in his 56 games on Mount Olympus, DiMaggio delivered 91 hits, including 15 home runs, against a cast of forty-seven different major league pitchers. When the streak began, the Yankees lay in fourth place, 6½ games behind Cleveland. When it ended, the Yankees led the league, standing 6 games ahead of the Indians and moving irresistibly toward the pennant they would secure soon after Labor Day.

The numbers provide a frame, a dry but precise definition of what has become the least assailable of modern baseball records. But what strikes me, these many years away from the black rumblings and the dimming glories of 1941, is the element of style. DiMaggio conducted himself as a remote and quietly headstrong young god.

When Pete Rose broke Ty Cobb's hallowed record for major league base hits he hugged his teenaged son and briefly wept. When Roger Maris was surpassing Babe Ruth's mark of 60 home runs in a season, wild mood swings swept through his usually stoic personality. At one point chunks of hair fell from his head.

DiMaggio was a contained and dry-eyed record breaker. Around the ballparks he stayed within himself, a large, subdued, and somewhat forbidding figure. He sustained the public impression that he wanted to sustain: a man always under control. Although his fires to achieve never burned more fiercely, he kept them within and drank his coffee and smoked his cigarettes.

When it was done, the man wanted a drink. And perhaps a little something more. Some of DiMaggio's old teammates say that when he was frustrated on the field he needed nothing more than the favors of a pretty woman. Whatever, time and DiMaggio's sense of privacy draw a curtain on how he spent the Cleveland night four decades ago when two journeyman pitchers, a gifted third baseman, and his own unwillingness to bunt brought his record batting streak to an end.

The next day he showed up ready to play and began another streak.

The late Johnny Murphy, a fine relief pitcher sometimes called "Grandma" for his finicky ways, recalled having a beer with Gomez and George Selkirk that July. "We all decided," Murphy said, "that the other players ought to do something for Joe to show him how much we admired what he'd done."

Murphy was designated to select a gift. His wife suggested a silver cigarette humidor, "but for goodness sake don't go to one of those places that sell perfectly awful things wholesale to ballplayers. Go to Tiffany's and do it right."

Tiffany craftsmen fashioned a humidor that bore a good likeness of DiMaggio swinging his favorite D-29. The phrases 56 GAMES and 96 HITS bordered the figure. Inside the lid an inscription read:

PRESENTED TO JOE DIMAGGIO BY HIS FELLOW PLAYERS OF THE NEW YORK YANKEES TO EXPRESS THEIR ADMIRATION FOR THE WORLD'S RECORD CONSECUTIVE HITTING STREAK IN 1941.

When the gift was ready, the Yankee players booked a sixth-floor suite at the Shoreham hotel in Washington for a surprise presentation on August 29. DiMaggio walked in, escorted by Gomez. His face lit as his teammates cheered. He accepted the humidor and made a halting speech of thanks. Years later he told Al Silverman, a journalist and editor who wrote a book about the batting streak: "I don't remember exactly what I said but the words didn't seem to say exactly what was in my heart. The Yankee club was my home. Every man in that room was more than my teammate. He was my friend and brother."

This was as touching and vulnerable a statement as Di-Maggio has ever permitted himself to utter, tender and open and loving. It is, perhaps, anticlimactic to point out that Di-Maggio charged Silverman $500 for the interview.

The World Series of 1941 matched the Yankees against a loud and aggressive team of Brooklyn Dodgers, managed by Leo Durocher, who had been traded by the Yankees after arguing salary with Ed Barrow in 1929 in what turned out to be an inappropriate manner. Durocher wanted a $2,000 raise and when Barrow said that there would be no raise at all, Durocher answered quietly: "Fuck you."

"I hope I didn't hear you correctly, young man," Barrow said, "because if I did, you will not be a Yankee next year."

"Fuck you," Durocher repeated, more distinctly. He was dispatched to the Cincinnati Reds.

Time hardly mellowed bald, brash Leo Ernest Durocher, and the 1941 Dodgers became an extension of his street-fighter ways. Their pitchers threw at the chins of rival batters. Their dugout rang with caustic, threatening taunts. They were rough-hewn plebeians to a Yankee team that had learned to shop at Tiffany's.

The ball clubs split the first two games and the Series moved into Ebbets Field, an epicenter of plebeian exuberance. The Dodgers were winning Game Three when a line drive to the left thigh drove their starting pitcher, Fat Freddie Fitzsimmons, from the mound. (The baseball bounced thirty feet into the air and the Dodger shortstop, Pee Wee Reese,

caught it.) But the Yankees broke through against Hugh
Casey, the Dodger relief pitcher, and won, 2–1.

In a consensus that reached from Sea Gate to Richmond
Hill, Dodger fans agreed that the line drive was a revolting
development and that tomorrow would assuredly be better.
But for Brooklyn tomorrow was worse. The Dodgers carried
a 4–3 lead into the ninth inning of the fourth game when
Casey, back at work, struck out Tommy Henrich on a sharp-
breaking 3-and-2 pitch. That would have been the final out,
but the ball eluded Mickey Owen, the Dodger catcher.
Henrich reached first base safely. A deluge followed and the
Yankees won, 7–4.

When DiMaggio came to bat in the sixth inning of the fifth
game he heard shouts from the Dodger dugout: "Stick it [the
baseball] in his ear." Whitlow Wyatt then threw two pitches
close to DiMaggio's prominent nose, after which DiMaggio
flied out to center field.

Jogging from the basepath to the dugout, DiMaggio cir-
cled toward Wyatt and yelled: "What did you want to do that
for?"

Wyatt, a quietly rugged character from north Georgia,
snapped back: "Why are you in the game if you can't take
it?"

Nobody in the American League talked to DiMaggio like
that, nor did American League pitchers throw successive fastballs at his face. DiMaggio and Wyatt moved toward each
other and DiMaggio remembers thinking that he wanted the
pitcher to throw the first punch. He intended to slip it and
counter with his own right fist. Peacemakers ran between the
two men before anyone punched anybody else, but the incident survives as the one occasion when DiMaggio lost both
his temper and his composure on a playing field. That was all
he lost. The Yankees won the game, 3–1, and the World Series and the *Brooklyn Eagle* ran a headline that would echo
through years in Brooklyn as a lachrymose chorus: WAIT TILL
NEXT YEAR.

Whitlow Wyatt visited the Yankee dressing room to offer sporting congratulations and wished DiMaggio a pleasant winter. In response, he drew a nod.

That October 23 Dorothy Arnold DiMaggio struggled through a painful labor and gave birth to Joseph Paul DiMaggio, Junior. Soon afterward the Baseball Writers Association designated DiMaggio as the Most Valuable Player in the American League for the second time in three seasons. The Yankees had a world championship; DiMaggio had an MVP award and he was a father. But he felt more drained than elated.

On December 7, DiMaggio and George Solotaire visited the Polo Grounds to watch a professional football game between the New York Giants and the Brooklyn Dodgers. The day was overcast and raw rather than cold, and a large crowd thronged the old green horseshoe of a park. Led by a gifted quarterback named Clarence "Ace" Parker, the Dodgers won, 21–7, beating the Giants into what Rud Rennie of the *Herald Tribune* called "bloody-nosed submission." At least three of the Giants' football players had to be hospitalized that night.

These are no more than footnotes to a day which would live in infamy. At 2:22 P.M. in Washington, Stephen Early, President Roosevelt's press secretary, announced that Japanese planes had attacked Pearl Harbor. The news went crackling over twenty million radios, eliciting spasms of shock and defiance and disbelief and terror.

There was no war announcement at the Polo Grounds, but as the game ground on the public-address system came alive with orders to certain military officers: "Call your base immediately." DiMaggio remembers a buzzing in the stands. Nearby a fan held a heavy portable radio. "We asked him what was happening," DiMaggio says, "and he told us. It took the edge off that football game, all right."

It would be a full decade before DiMaggio retired from baseball, a span of war and peace and yet another war in

Korea, but his adventures on the ball fields were never again quite so glittering as they had been in the nightmare year of Pearl Harbor. "Most gay," as a poet writes in another context, "but not so gay as it was."

Without his realizing it, DiMaggio's baseball life had crested in the summer of 1941 when he was twenty-seven years old. He never ceased to be a star and almost always he was *the* star. Age improved his physical appearance. Lines warmed the long and bony face and his black hair shaded toward a handsome executive gray. His name grew and his salary grew—even as his talents shrank. To the end he was able to play brilliantly in spurts, but with time he lost the strength and stamina and health to perform as he once had across the long, demanding reach of a full season.

The young DiMaggio comes down to us as a player of infinite skills who was not as sympathetic as he might have been because of hints of arrogance and his inclination toward rude and brooding silences. The older DiMaggio, contending with increasing complexities in his baseball world, a most demanding life, injuries, and time's merciless advance, emerged as a more satisfying hero. He kept his discipline with one or two exceptions, and he learned how to be friendly when he wanted to be. He might even have become open, an amiable good fellow, like Babe Ruth in the generation before him. But then came Marilyn, a love that obsessed and then tortured him and brought back the brooding anger of his youth.

In 1942, DiMaggio suffered the strains of his rocky marriage to Dorothy Arnold and felt more concern than most about his future in a country now at war. His batting average fell 52 points to .305, and while the Yankees won yet another pennant—that made six in seven DiMaggio seasons—a swift young St. Louis Cardinal team upset them in the World Series, 4 games to 2. That winter he enlisted in the army air force. Seven months later Dorothy sued him for divorce.

Although DiMaggio maintains he never asked for special treatment, the air force cast him as a celebrity soldier. His tours of duty took him no closer to a battlefield than California, Hawaii, and New Jersey. He found G.I.-issue uniforms "a little skimpy," and hired a tailor to make alterations. Custom-tailored olive drabs. He lent his name to a sports column that appeared in service publications. And, to be sure, he played baseball.

First he played center field for a team at the Santa Ana Army Air Base, where, he said, "our pitching was so bad I once had to spend forty-five minutes chasing base hits around the outfield." Later he was promoted to staff sergeant and transferred to Hawaii, where he starred for the Seventh Air Force team, a Pacific powerhouse packed with drafted major leaguers and managed by a lieutenant named Long Tom Winsett, who had come to Brooklyn with rave notices in 1936 and flopped ingloriously across three seasons. DiMaggio batted .401 in 90 games.

It was a sort of service hitch that seemed like a vacation to millions of relatively anonymous combat troops, but DiMaggio, aware that he was losing earning years in baseball, apparently could not enjoy himself. He developed stomach pains and checked into an army hospital, where he was diagnosed as having ulcers. He played no more air force baseball and drew a discharge on September 14, 1945, never having been shot at, nor ever having fired a shot at anybody else.

He liked to tell a story from the days after his discharge when he visited New York and took his son to a late-season game at Yankee Stadium. The war had so wrenched the established order in the American League that the St. Louis Browns had won a pennant in 1944. The caliber of baseball, including the caliber of Yankee baseball, slipped into mediocrity, and fans at Yankee Stadium were excited by the appearance, even in street clothes, of DiMaggio, the symbol of quality play. As he moved toward his seat, they shouted: "Hiya, Joe. Great to see ya, Joe. Welcome back, Joe."

Joe DiMaggio, Jr., who was four, smiled and looked up at his father. "They know me, Daddy," he said.

The heirs of Jacob Ruppert had recently sold the Yankees for $2.8 million to a swaggering troika of adventurers. The new president was Leland "Larry" MacPhail, whose past exploits included an attempt to kidnap Kaiser Wilhelm after World War I—he failed—and the rescue of the Dodgers from ineptitude in Brooklyn during the late 1930s. Another partner, Dan Topping, was the descendant of copper barons and a social dilettante, whose four wives included Sonja Henie, the button-nosed, blond figure skater who glided successfully from the Winter Olympics to a Hollywood career. The third man was Del Webb, a large, cold-eyed, bespectacled dealer in real estate, construction, and capital gains, who supposedly built "much of Las Vegas." The old and settled Yankee order was dead.

Soon MacPhail, the chief executive, was supervising a remodeling of the Stadium that included, for the first time in memory, the installation of cocktail lounges in a ballpark. Before the group was through with their maneuvering they would sell the land on which the Stadium was built, sell the Stadium itself, then lease back both in a huge and unprecedented transaction that netted many millions. Money was the name of their game and MacPhail, as sound a baseball man as he was a flamboyant character, recognized DiMaggio as a great capital asset. He telephoned DiMaggio, flattered him appropriately, and said that even though things were still unsettled, "I'm ready to pay you forty-three thousand seven hundred and fifty dollars for 1946, the same money you got before you went into service."

DiMaggio had fallen behind in his income-tax payments while he was in the air force. (The restaurant in Fisherman's Wharf and some other investments had continued to make money for him.) He was pleased that the new Yankee management neither pleaded poverty nor tried, as fierce Ed Barrow might have, to use his tax problems to force down his salary. He signed his contract without a howl or a whimper.

MacPhail arranged for the Yankees to start their 1946 training in Panama, and DiMaggio hit harder than he ever had in the spring. *Time* magazine announced in April that "Giuseppe was a changed man. His disposition like his ulcers was better. He still knew that he was the greatest baseball player alive, but he no longer called himself the 'Great Di-Maggio.' He was actually getting to be good company."

Time being *Time,* the reporting here seems to strain for effect. DiMaggio often acted as though he knew he was a great ballplayer but he did not actually go around saying so. If he had been foolish enough to call himself the Great DiMaggio, ballplayers in opposing dugouts would have blistered his ears every time he struck out. The knockabout company of baseball has little tolerance for self-importance.

At another extreme, one idolatrous biographer extols the monastic dedication that DiMaggio brought to his first post-war spring training. This was not true either. In Panama DiMaggio found an exotic dancer who called herself Jade Rhodora. A reporter observed them huddled in a nightclub booth and sought out Miss Rhodora late the next day. "I love Joe," said the dancer. "He's so simple and unaffected." Manager Joe McCarthy was nobody's Cupid. According to a story, which McCarthy would not deny, he fined DiMaggio $50 for breaking curfew.

Despite diversions, DiMaggio hit 14 home runs during spring training. This led MacPhail, his imperial partners, the press, and Yankee fans to anticipate that the 1946 team would steamroller the league in traditional style. Instead they got a sour season.

DiMaggio dropped a routine fly ball in a game against the Browns on May 9. Two plays later he failed to scoop a routine single. Two errors in one inning. Bringing up that inning with DiMaggio today produces no comment and a gelid stare.

MacPhail wanted Yankee baseball to resound with carnival noises. He offered nylon stockings as gifts on Ladies' Day. He booked the team on airlines—he liked the image of the high-flying Yankees—in an era when train travel was both efficient and luxurious. He dispensed great quantities of liquor to the press and was endlessly available to talk about the team, which unfortunately did not get itself untracked. Mac-Phail responded by firing Joe McCarthy in mid-May, ending a stable tenure of McCarthy managing that stretched back fifteen seasons. He suspected that Rud Rennie, one of the *Herald Tribune*'s baseball writers, was recruiting players for the new and unregulated Mexican League, and wrote the *Tribune*, demanding that Rennie be fired. Wilbur Forrest, the paper's executive editor, responded that Stanley Woodward, the sports editor, was on vacation. "If on his return Mr. Woodward needs any assistance in running his section, I'm certain he will get in touch with you." Under MacPhail the Yankees were beginning to resemble the boisterous Brooklyn Dodgers.

Bill Dickey, the new manager, was overwhelmed by pressure and was replaced in September by Johnny Neun, a coach. This was the year, DiMaggio's friends maintained, that he was depressed by his loss of Dorothy Arnold. Whatever, he had his poorest major league season up to that time and batted only .290. The Yankees finished a noncontending third.

After a few drinks one night, MacPhail said angrily, "It looks like DiMaggio came out of service too damn soon." He then attempted to dispose of his star and offered him to the Washington Senators for Mickey Vernon, a first baseman without much power who had led the league in batting.

The Senators turned down DiMaggio and the deal.

That November DiMaggio turned thirty-two, a gateway of old age for many athletes. The postwar euphoria about his return fled and there was talk among sportswriters and baseball men that he was through. Indeed, the rest of his baseball career rang as loudly with medical bulletins as it did with home runs. He would batter ankles and knees, suffer from calcium deposits in the elbow of his throwing arm, and need repeated surgery on bone spurs in his heels. All this on top of stomach ulcers and arthritis. But he was far from finished.

Rather, he was embarking on the final phase of his career, the athlete as indomitable old warrior.

He stormed back in 1947, playing through pain after heel surgery kept him out of spring training. Toward summer he hit safely in 25 out of 27 games, batting .468 across that span. In mid-June the Yankees began a winning streak that reached 19 games and effectively settled the pennant race. They defeated the Dodgers in an exciting 7-game World Series, in which DiMaggio hit 2 home runs but is remembered mostly for having hit an exceptionally long out. That came in the sixth inning of Game Six, when a substitute Dodger left fielder named Al Gionfriddo raced to the wall 410 feet from home plate and outran DiMaggio's mighty drive. "Back goes Gionfriddo," cried Red Barber, a sportscaster who usually practiced understatement. "Back, back, back-back-back." Gionfriddo himself seemed stunned that he had been able to catch the ball. DiMaggio, close to second base, kicked dirt.

Ted Williams had led the American League in batting, homers, and runs batted in, but the Baseball Writers Association voted DiMaggio his third award as Most Valuable Player. Was this sentimentality for a man surmounting physical problems? Was it a choice dictated by the power of the New York press? One astute old Boston ballplayer, who did not want to be quoted by name, said it was neither. "You can't go simply by numbers," he said. "When the Yankees needed a big hit, not a walk, DiMaggio would swing at a bad pitch to help the team. When you had a clutch situation, Joe came through. The other players knew that. It inspired them. Williams was a different kind of animal, the best pure hitter I've ever seen, but he played for himself. He'd take a walk when the Red Sox needed a hit. Whether the baseball writers knew this, I don't know, but they picked the right feller."

MacPhail sold his one-third share of the Yankees, reportedly for $2 million, after the World Series, and George Weiss, an old-line, closed-mouthed Yankee official, took over baseball operations. When the team finished third in 1948, Weiss,

Topping, and Webb dismissed the latest manager, Stanley "Bucky" Harris, and in a move that startled almost everyone, replaced him with Charles Dillon "Casey" Stengel. Although Stengel was well known for a rough-hewn wit, his credentials as a winner looked uncertain. Previously he had managed for nine seasons in the National League without bringing a team home any better than fifth. While running the Boston Braves he was struck by a taxi and suffered a broken leg. Dave Egan, a caustic Boston columnist, suggested that the cab driver was the man who did the most for Boston baseball that season.

Further, Stengel was fifty-nine years old, which led someone to describe him as a proven failure. Subsequently, Stengel managed the Yankees to five consecutive World Series championships.

Publicly DiMaggio insists that he admired Stengel. Others are not so sure. It was Stengel who switched DiMaggio from center field to first base one day in 1950. Later he dropped DiMaggio from fourth, the coveted "clean-up spot," to fifth in the Yankee batting order. Stengel believed in shuttling players in and out of games without regard for major league egos. This worked brilliantly but infuriated some of his players. He also offered daily monologues that became classics of dugout serio-comedy. These drew attention away from DiMaggio and toward the manager. From the day Stengel was hired, the old DiMaggio Yankees began to evolve into the new Stengel Yankees. "Whatever Joe says now," one former ballplayer reports, "he wasn't happy about that then."

In 1949, more heel surgery caused DiMaggio to miss 65 games. Was his great career over? The press swarmed to cover the operation at Johns Hopkins hospital in Baltimore and so many reporters asked so many questions that DiMaggio snapped: "You guys are driving me batty!"

As DiMaggio was being wheeled toward the surgical theater, a photographer appeared in the hospital corridor. A flashbulb popped. DiMaggio erupted into profanity. Although this does not happen often, the photographer relented and agreed to destroy the negative.

During his long convalescence, DiMaggio suffered bouts of depression. In an article he signed for *Life* magazine, he described himself as "almost a mental case." He said the only people he could bear to see were Toots Shor and George Solotaire. When a ballclub paycheck came, he told himself, "You've certainly done a swell job of earning this money!" For two months, "I sat in my hotel room most of the time. At night I had trouble going to sleep. If my playing career was over, what was I going to do? Lying awake, sometimes until 5 in the morning, I figured out at least a half dozen careers. I must have been really upset because right now I can't remember any of them."

When he finally was able to return for a series against the Red Sox in June, he simply exploded, a nova, dazzling to observe. He hit 4 home runs in 3 games and batted in 9 runs. Bad legs or no, he took out Boston's Vern Stephens with a hard slide that broke up a double play. His performance held the country in thrall. Robert Ruark, the late columnist and novelist, proclaimed DiMaggio "the first real sports colossus since the Ruth era." Arthur Daley of *The New York Times* called him "superman in a baseball suit."

The old salary wars were done. The Yankee management paid him $70,000 for 1948 and jumped him to $100,000 the next season. But he would not stride softly into baseball twilight. Again in 1949, the Yankees won a World Series from the Dodgers. The next year, when DiMaggio hit 32 home runs, they swept the young Philadelphia Phillies. But in 1951 the team struggled toward a pennant and DiMaggio had a very difficult time.

He was surely the most famous ballplayer on earth but his old skills were vanished. He would bat only .263. On a few occasions Stengel wanted to bench him, but benching DiMaggio in the Bronx was akin to excommunicating the pope in Rome. The late Milton Gross, an experienced Yankee hand, wrote a careful column in July describing the Yankees at an "emotional crossroads."

The situation, Gross wrote, "revolves around DiMaggio,

Casey Stengel's handling of the fast-slipping outfielder, Di-Maggio's reaction to the managerial hand and Joe's increasing moodiness and introversion." The trigger was an incident in Boston. Noticing that DiMaggio was limping in center field, Stengel removed him from a game.

Gross quoted another Yankee who said "Joe was steaming in the dressing room," and proceeded to a chilling account of an athlete near the end.

"Joe rarely spoke to Casey and Casey rarely spoke to him, but this was no departure from DiMag's relationship with his previous managers. The silence between the two men, therefore, is not new, but the new attitude felt by DiMag's teammates is.

"DiMag now talks to virtually no one with the ball club. He never initiates a conversation. On trains, in cabs and even in the clubhouse, Joe has pulled himself into a shell, which is so much worse than this strange, moody man has ever worn before. Instead of mellowing in the twilight of his career, Joe sits by himself or walks silent and unseeing by the men with whom he has performed and traveled for so many years."

Injuries were not undermining DiMaggio now. Quite simply, he was being conquered by time. His speed was gone. His bat had slowed. His throwing arm was flawed.

Lift a glass to the old days and usher in the new. That is a wise recipe for surviving change.

The Jolter declined it, fought to resist the irresistible, and became nothing so much as a cat who walked by himself. Except, every so often for a show girl . . .

Truman Capote, who was twenty-six, published "The Grass Harp," which Lewis Gannett, in the *Herald Tribune,* praised as "astonishing." That was literary talk in the autumn of 1951. Baseball chatter bubbled about the National League pennant race, in which the Giants under Leo Durocher came from 13½ games behind and tied a great Brooklyn Dodger team for the pennant. The playoff between the Dodgers and the Giants ended on a damp cool day at the Polo Grounds when Bobby Thomson hit his famous home run.

"The Giants win the pennant," cried the broadcaster Russ Hodges, again and again and again. So great a roar rose up throughout New York City that someone wondered if World War III had come.

After that the World Series—the Yankees defeated the Giants 4 games to 2—seemed anticlimactic to almost everyone but the Yankees. This was when *Life* published the Dodgers' scouting report on the Yankees, which made it plain that DiMaggio was finished.

He went hitless in the first 3 games, then, in one heroic final spurt, he came back with 6 hits as the Yankees won the final 3. In his last turn, his 199th at-bat in 51 World Series games, DiMaggio bade farewell with a flourish. He lined a long double to right center field.

Mickey Mantle had broken into the Yankee outfield playing right field at the age of nineteen. In the fifth inning of Game Two, Mantle ran toward center in pursuit of a fly ball. Suddenly he heard DiMaggio shout, "I got it." Mantle stopped short, lost his footing, and crumpled. He had torn ligaments in a knee. At first he lay still, feeling numbness rather than pain, and "scared silly." DiMaggio caught the fly ball, which was hit, in a remarkable confluence of storied center fielders, by the Giants' great rookie Willie Mays.

"The ground in right center here [at Yankee Stadium]," DiMaggio said later, "is as hard as cement. They ought to do something about that. It's a shame the kid got hurt."

Years afterward, in a drinking club outside of Dallas, Mantle told the story from another viewpoint. It seemed to Mantle that "DiMaggio didn't call for the ball until he was sure he could look good making the catch. That's why I had to stop so short. If he'd shouted earlier I might have been okay." Mantle looked into a glass of bourbon and said, "Damn."

DiMaggio wanted to retire. Both shoulders ached. A knee throbbed. He would reach his thirty-seventh birthday in November. Dodger scout Andy High reported, "His reflexes are very slow." His time as a ballplayer was past.

The Yankees wanted him to continue. In baseball dotage, he was still a drawing card. DiMaggio told Dan Topping that he would defer his decision, then left for a barnstorming trip of Japan that had been organized by his old San Francisco hero, Lefty O'Doul.

He felt tired. Not even the enthusiasm of Japanese crowds could keep him going. He quit O'Doul's tour early and at 2 P.M. on December 11, 1951, he announced in a crowded and emotional press conference that he was retiring.

He had insisted on making the formal announcement in New York "because that's where I worked." He spoke with dignity and said he felt "I have reached a stage where I can no longer produce for my ball club, my manager, my teammates, and my fans the sort of baseball their loyalty to me deserves."

The questions were gentle. DiMaggio was somber and then wet-eyed. Casey Stengel, perhaps secretly relieved to be rid of a fading star, told a reporter, "I just gave the big guy's glove away and it's going to the Hall of Fame. He was the greatest player I ever managed."

The press saluted him and filled columns with tributes and mournful farewells. To Jimmy Cannon, Arthur Daley, and Red Smith, DiMaggio was and would remain "the best base-ball player I ever saw."

There would, however, develop a revisionist view. The following spring, *Life* ran an article entitled "They Don't Play Baseball Any More." In it, the author said that DiMaggio was perhaps the greatest natural ballplayer in history but he "made a name for himself without even scratching the surface of his talents. He was perhaps the outstanding example of how modern baseball players neglect to train and keep themselves in condition. He hated physical exertion and as far as I know he never took a lick of exercise from October until March. Naturally he went to spring training with his muscles weakened and soft; naturally he got hurt a lot." The by-line above these heretical and combative words commanded attention. It read TY COBB.

Chapter ★ 9

Joe and Marilyn

The pathway for old ballplayers runs a brambled route. Irony becomes the order of the day. In W. C. Heinz's phrase, once they heard the cheers. Now they have heard so many cheers that they grow deaf to adulation.

A name bannered in headlines. *My name for the world to see.* That lure is common to baseball and show business. But after five hundred headlines and two thousand box scores, most mentions become no more consequential than Tuesday's weather forecast.

The press, all those writers who couldn't play the game, evolves from a complex, somewhat threatening group into a chronic minor annoyance. If the old ballplayer's mood is good, he may answer a few questions without either strain or passion. He has heard them all, or questions like them, before.

Now the old ballplayer steps out through a clubhouse door marked with a clubman's sign that he no longer notices: PLAYERS ONLY! Before him swarm idolaters. The old ballplayer perceives not worshipers but a horde of adolescents, screaming demands and brandishing pens pointed toward his vitals. "Christ," he mutters, and waits for ballpark police to clear a path.

He rides downtown and takes a drink. "What I need most," the old ballplayer says to a friend, "is private time."

If the friend is young or shrill or both, he may object. "Isn't this what you wanted," he says, "as much as you wanted base hits? The fame, the press, the fans? Isn't that what you dreamed of long ago?"

The old ballplayer has difficulty with that one. His body aches from the hard ball game he has played and, in truth, he has lived through so many hard games played before so many multitudes that he is no longer certain what he dreamed in childhood. "Aw," he says, "what do you know when you're a kid?"

Suddenly, with retirement, the crowds are gone and there are no more hard baseball games to play. The old ballplayer is left with memories and, in DiMaggio's case, a healthy income from investments. But aside from paying attention to his wallet, what is he going to do with the next thirty years? Where has everybody gone?

A difficult time, a vexing time. Some old ballplayers say it creates a clammy sense of death. The retired ballplayer wonders if his high deeds really will be remembered.

Often he falls prey to a phenomenon that John Lardner noted in Charles Lindbergh, a man who shared DiMaggio's reserve and his ardor for personal privacy. Lindbergh, Lardner commented, "loathed publicity, but never more than when he wasn't getting any."

*　　*　　*

When DiMaggio began dating Marilyn Monroe in 1952, he was jumping into an arena as public as Yankee Stadium. "Marilyn stops at my house after a day at the studio," wrote Louella Parsons, co-champion with Hedda Hopper of the Hollywood gossip press, "and she sometimes talks about her beau, Joe DiMaggio. I think he's the right man for her. This would be one Hollywood marriage that worked."

Sidney Skolsky, a small, intense character who wrote "Hollywood Tintypes" for the *New York Post,* was probably the first journalist to ask movie stars what they wore to bed. (Marilyn told him Chanel No. 5.) Skolsky was a bit more guarded in his view than Parsons, fearing that a married Marilyn might be less accessible to him.

Earl Wilson of the *Post* wrote numerous columns on Marilyn and her underwear. Did she wear a brassiere? What about underpants? Wilson was the master of such issues. (For the record, Marilyn usually wore both a brassiere and underpants. However, she declined to wear a girdle.) Wilson moved in the Toots Shor group and got along with DiMaggio, although he was not as close to him as Jimmy Cannon was. In his column Wilson rooted for both Joe and Marilyn.

These people and a score like them practiced high-ego journalism. They featured facts, often gathered by anonymous legmen, and then portentously scattered their opinions. What they offered as fact tended to be shaky. Their opinions were precious as pyrite, which is fool's gold.

But they were omnipresent in Hollywood. If you were going to court a movie star in the 1950s—and Joe DiMaggio, retired ballplayer, would court Marilyn with patience and ardor—your courtship was certain to be chronicled in the gossip press, within the limits of what could be printed at the time.

Although Marilyn told Ben Hecht that she had made love to DiMaggio on their first date, a virginal version of that particular evening appeared. In this one, Marilyn kept her distance and gave DiMaggio nothing more than a cool goodnight. Sure enough, someone wrote a syndicated story that "on his first date with Marilyn Monroe, the great Joe DiMaggio struck out!" Before their romance was very old, people were reporting that they were secretly married. DiMaggio, under tight control, said that the stories were not true and that if any announcement was to be made in that area, Marilyn would be the one to make it. Marilyn said, she actually said, "We're just good friends."

Simply to dismiss gossip is elitist and, worse than that, blockheaded. No less a figure than Robert Frost once turned to me during an afternoon of rich and mostly abstract talk at his cabin in Ripton, Vermont, and asked me if I liked gossip. He bore in with a look that said he expected to hear the truth.

"Yes," I answered, wondering about his response.

"So do I," Frost said, "but most people have a hard time admitting it."

The gossip press following Joe and Marilyn during the early 1950s quenched a national thirst and kept their names constantly before the public. This generally pleased Marilyn and delighted her bosses at Twentieth Century-Fox. DiMaggio's comment on the furor sounded like a remark at Toots Shor's bar. "Never mind the publicity, honey," he told Marilyn. "Just get the dough."

"Will Mr. America marry Miss America," somebody asked in print, "and if they split, who gets custody of the Wheaties?" Columnists took sides, made predictions, and the public followed where it was led. Wouldn't it be thrilling if the former colossus of baseball married the most beautiful blonde in the world? There was a rising general expectation that they would marry, that they should marry, that they owed their marriage to the country. Ten million shopgirls and schoolboys bet dreams, wet and dry, that Joe and Marilyn would be wed.

Personally, the lovers found that the gossip strained their courtship and historically it hasn't done much for the cause of truth. So many journalists printed so much material that the right stuff and invented nonsense began to merge.

A recent biographer of Marilyn reported that on the day she and Joe married, January 14, 1954, she telephoned a friend in Los Angeles from the San Francisco City Hall and "whispered, 'I have sucked my last cock.'"

Marilyn had her moments, so the biographer does not dismiss the story. But I remember having heard it thirty years ago. At that time Marilyn was said to have spoken the line after signing her first good contract at Fox.

A fair number of Joe-and-Marilyn tales are similarly doctored or simply invented. There persists, for example, the yarn that she had never heard of DiMaggio.

Matchmaker David March then says, "He's the most famous ballplayer since Babe Ruth."

Marilyn: "Who's Babe Ruth?"

Actually, she knew perfectly well who DiMaggio was and she had heard Babe Ruth's name. She was, however, reluctant to date DiMaggio because she thought a ballplayer would be coarse, unsophisticated, and "maybe wearing a pink tie."

DiMaggio, looking at that newspaper photograph of Marilyn wearing white shorts and holding a bat, is supposed to have said, "Who's the blonde?" But newspaper pictures come with captions. The one here read: "White Sox pitcher Joe Dobson checks over film starlet Marilyn Monroe as outfielder Gus Zernial does the catching." Each knew who the other was before they met. (How do such wrongheaded stories come to be? "Making up gossip," someone has said, "is the most creative work in Hollywood.")

What was the attraction? Each seems to have been roused by the fame of the other, almost as much as they had been roused by their own fame. Marilyn said they were sexually compatible. DiMaggio, it turned out, did not wear pink ties but elegant and carefully tailored clothing. He moved with an aura of gloss and dignity. ("DiMaggio," Mickey Mantle once said, "looks like a senator.")

What went so wrong so quickly? He was neat. She was sloppy. He was repressed. She was hyperactive. Each was willful. Each had a temper. Each was a star. Stars in collision.

Marilyn liked older men, *successful* older men. DiMaggio

liked younger women, *blond* younger women. But when it
came time to play house, reality came crashing all about
them, shattering dreams into so much shrapnel.

He felt San Francisco was his home. She insisted on living
in Los Angeles. He liked days on a golf course and evenings
spent in jock chatter with men friends. At home he was ad-
dicted to watching television. She wanted him constantly to
generate excitement. He was overweening and possessive.
She loved to wear tight, skimpy clothing. Married or single,
she flirted with half the Western world.

She would claim, in testimony echoing the complaints of
Dorothy Arnold, that he was cold and indifferent to her
needs. The old Sicilian kept his code of public silence, but
comments slipped out to friends. They do not want to be
quoted by name; if they are, they will lose DiMaggio's friendship. But one has said, "He married someone who talked
about having six kids. Then, when they were married, it
turned out she didn't mean six kids. She wanted to have six
goddamn Oscars."

Arthur Miller told a reporter that nothing existed to sustain their love affair. No common interests, no intellectual
bond. He then mentioned, as a few others have, physical violence.

What went wrong? Perhaps a better question is what could
have gone right.

"If marriage was only bed," Marilyn said sorrowfully some
time afterward, "we could have made it."

John Crosby, the *Herald Tribune*'s radio-and-television
columnist, lunched with Marilyn in 1952 and sketched a portrait of her as she appeared to a sophisticated, literate journalist. "She is at the moment," Crosby wrote, "the nation's
No. 1 sex thrill. Next to Adlai and Ike, she's the hottest topic
of conversation in Hollywood.

"During lunch she smiled. When Marilyn smiles, she
smiles all over. Her lips part, her eyes narrow, her eyebrows
shoot up and the whole vastly publicized body moves around

a little bit. I suppose that would be a definition of a lot of other smiles, but Marilyn does it more expertly than anyone else. . . .

"She does worry. Some of the Hollywood hatchet girls— and the place abounds in them—have given her the full treatment at parties. That has cut deep. And the critics who have had a field day with her, have wounded her to the marrow. 'They are so cruel, the critics. Sometimes I think they just take out their frustrations on other people.'

"She speaks in a low murmur, the sound coming from the back of her throat. Both her inflections and the structure of her sentences are more European than American. 'Ever since I can remember, I've wanted to be a movie star. I love the movies. When I was a little girl, it seemed the only time I was alive was when I was at the movies. The movies were much more real to me than life.'"

She told Crosby that she could do more than wiggle her fanny. She could play Gretchen in *Faust* or Therese in *The Cradle Song*. Crosby was impressed; he concluded archly, "Somehow I never bothered to ask her what, if anything, she wore under her dress."

Jimmy Cannon, who worked variously for the *New York Post* and the Hearst newspapers, provided the most vivid contemporary pictures of DiMaggio. Indeed, it was said that Cannon was the world's greatest writer on two topics: Joe DiMaggio and Joe Louis.

"There are spectacular men," Cannon wrote, "whose presence creates a climate of gladness. People seem to be neighbors in their presence. All those who are near them come closer together and share the intimacy of small town people living on an old street a long while. It is that way with Joe DiMaggio.

"The memory of sports buffs is brief. They are cruel in their neglect. But DiMaggio's fame is secure and moving around with him [after his retirement] it is as if he were still the greatest ball player in his generation.

"There seem to be no strangers in his life. They don't

maul him with the rude fervor of kids molesting popular entertainers. They are thrilled to shake his hand or shout his name. . . .

"He came into the restaurant, tall and long-boned, graceful in a slouching way, elegantly sombre in his discreetly cut blue suit. They began to whisper and the sound escorted him to the table, the heads turning in unintentional salutes. And these were Broadway people, accustomed to celebrities . . .

"We were sitting at a table near the door. People had to pass it to leave and they stopped to remind DiMaggio that they missed him on a ball field. It was as if this were not a public restaurant at all, but that they were guests leaving a party DiMaggio had given.

"'You look like you could play today,' a man said.

"'I'd run to first and fall down,' said Joe DiMaggio."

They were both news, automatically news, as themselves and even more so as a couple. She was a shade hotter and still rising, which may have caused him stress or at least discomfort. It must have startled the most famous baseball man on earth to find himself married to someone yet more famous. While they courted, her naked calendar pose became an object of cult frenzy. Soon a nude Marilyn was being marketed as an ashtray design, on highball glasses, and on cocktail trays. If she objected, she never sued.

They kept some dates within her apartment. Whenever they went out together, the tireless press set about compiling its daily chronicle. This led first to the outburst from Dorothy, the claim that Joe was subjecting Joe junior to a loose, amoral side of life. When she moved to court, she sought to have DiMaggio's visitations ended, or curtailed, and asked for an increase in child support.

DiMaggio told reporters that her accusation was "ridiculous," and claimed through lawyers that Dorothy was spending some of the boy's support money on herself. Such volleys can grow into broadsides. The ex-wife claims that the husband is a rotten father who runs in a kinky crowd and drinks heavily. Protect the child from these pernicious influences, plaintiff petitions the court. The husband responds that he is a good man and a loving, attentive parent. Since a legal charge is sometimes best answered with a countercharge, the father's lawyers argue by rote that the mother is profligate with child-support money. Each parent's name is damaged. The child, at ground zero, gets the fallout.

Having launched the first strike, Dorothy proceeded to dissemble. Joe junior was attending a private school, Black Rock Military Academy in Los Angeles, and yes, his father helped with the tuition. She was between marriages and times were not the best. A year before, she testified, she had told Joe that she was going to have to sell a mink jacket he had once bought her. DiMaggio responded by giving her an extra $2,000.

On October 16, 1952, nine days after Stengel's Yankees won another World Series from the Brooklyn Dodgers, Judge Elmer Doyle found for DiMaggio in a Los Angeles court. Doyle went further and lectured Dorothy. He told her that she had "made a mistake" when she divorced DiMaggio eight years earlier.

But for Dorothy that caravan had passed. DiMaggio was no longer pining for her. He wanted to marry Marilyn.

Although DiMaggio has been heard to grumble about a broker when a particular stock turned downward, those are just the mutterings of a competitor. He retired from the Yankees in splendid financial shape. Like Babe Ruth, he never managed a major league team, but unlike Ruth he never really wanted to. He measured the stress of the job, worrying about the bats and egos of two dozen ballplayers, considered his ulcer, and decided to avoid that area of combat.

The Yankees had a radio job for him. He could mine further gold through personal appearances. Soon V. H. Monette and Company, of Smithfield, Virginia, a corporation supplying military commissaries and post exchanges, would hire him as executive vice-president for at least $100,000 a year. ("It's more or less a goodwill job," DiMaggio told Jimmy Cannon.)

When Marilyn met him, he was a man of means who owned a fine home in San Francisco, a boat, a Cadillac, part of a restaurant, and a substantial investment portfolio.

She said she liked his sense of dignity and substance and, she remarked to a friend, "Actually he's kind of shy, just like me." She wanted to please him—the push and pull of sex was strong—and he, for his part, showered her with advice. It was at first a kind of Toots Shor's barroom counsel, simplistic but nonetheless sincere. She had to watch out for the phonies. Hollywood was full of phonies. The phonies would just use her. Stay away from them. Don't tell the reporters too much. You had to be careful with the press. Get all the dough you can get as quick as you can and put some away. There Di-Maggio was echoing Iago, although he probably didn't know who Iago was.

She listened. She was appreciative not simply for the advice but for attention from such a famous, substantial, well-groomed man.

As they became more comfortable, he suggested that she dress more conservatively. He didn't understand, or couldn't accept, that showing off her body was her business, and her nature, just as lining base hits had once been his. Still, anxious to please, she wore relatively concealing clothing when they were together.

That was, of course, a storm signal. He had not exactly fallen in love with a nun. She may have perceived warnings, but sheer physical appeal kept them together. She was nervous about marriage. He was confident they could make it together. He moved some clothes into her apartment on Doheny Drive.

They began rituals of introduction to family and friends. She met George Solotaire and liked him. She met his sister Marie and his great buddy Reno Barsochinni, whom Marilyn found somewhat aloof. He met her latest drama coach, Natasha Lytess, who described him as a bore. (DiMaggio dismissed Natasha, her intellectuality and her theatricality, as more Hollywood phoniness. Tolerance never was his long suit.)

Allan "Whitey" Snyder, that feisty, macho makeup man, invited them fishing. DiMaggio, who had hated deep-sea fishing in his boyhood, now enjoyed it as a sport. He, Marilyn, and the Snyders spent several pleasant weekend days on the glinting waters beyond the hills of Malibu.

But there were simply not that many more people. They both had more acquaintances than friends. And the friends they did have came from different worlds.

After *How to Marry a Millionaire,* Fox cast Marilyn as a saloon singer in a frontier movie called *River of No Return,* which was shot under Otto Preminger's direction in Banff. (A river run on a raft gave Marilyn a chance to wear tight, wet jeans for the cameras.)

DiMaggio trailed her to Alberta, and when the press materialized, he said, yes, he was visiting his girl and what the hell was wrong with that. Besides, he'd heard there were good trout streams in the Canadian Rockies. DiMaggio's wilderness companion was Broadway George Solotaire, who suffered serious disorientation wandering that far from a subway. "But he went," someone says, "because he was Joe's friend and Joe needed a guy to help him pack."

Preminger's manner was autocratic—he sometimes referred to actors as "cattle"—and though much of his approach was posturing for effect, he took practical pride in completing pictures under budget. Marilyn was feeling her power; she now possessed a glowing career and a famous lover. She insisted on retake after retake, straining Preminger's temper and his shooting schedule.

Several versions describe what happened next. She turned an ankle walking on a pier and collapsed in feigned pain. She would need a cast and time to recover. So much for the shooting schedule and the budget. That would teach Otto Preminger to push around a star.

Robert Mitchum, who played opposite her, recalled that Marilyn had to rush into the river in one scene and he warned her to be careful. She could break a leg. "And," Mitchum says, "she wasn't careful and she damn near broke her leg."

Whatever, Marilyn did get crutches and a cast and care from a platoon of doctors. DiMaggio, with his hard-earned knowledge of injuries, announced that if these doctors couldn't help her, he'd find her one who would. When *River of No Return* was released, Archer Winsten in the *New York Post* described the movie and Marilyn as "incongruous and strangely stimulating."

Fox next sent Marilyn the script for a movie to be called *The Girl in the Pink Tights*. Marilyn sent it back. She wouldn't play in it, she said, because "it's lousy." The studio joke was "That never bothered her before."

She was trying, perhaps unconsciously, to see what temperament would gain her. Further, she felt the strength that comes with the early fervor of passionate love. She didn't have to make another lousy movie. She had Joe.

The studio suspended her. DiMaggio suggested that they fly to Reno and marry there. Another marriage frightened her. They talked and argued and spent time apart. She missed him. She even missed their arguments. She welcomed him back and this time agreed to marry him in San Francisco City Hall. The date would be January 14, 1954.

DiMaggio had made inquiries about a church wedding. Marilyn was willing to be married by a priest. But John J. Mitty, the archbishop of San Francisco, turned them down. The Church refused to recognize his divorce. When they went ahead with a civil service, the archbishop's secretary, Father Leo Maher, told reporters that DiMaggio "is automatically excommunicated from the Roman Catholic Church."

What did that mean?

"He can attend services," Maher said, "but he may no longer take the sacraments [communion and confession]." A reporter checked with St. Peter's and St. Paul's, the DiMaggio family church. "Joe hasn't been attending in recent years anyway," a priest told him. If DiMaggio was concerned about the sulfurous fires of eternal hell, he gave no sign.

Marilyn wore a black satin coat, with ermine collar, over a simple brown suit. DiMaggio wore his customary dark suit, perfectly tailored.

"Marilyn and the fabulous DiMag," reported the New York *Daily Mirror,* "pressed their way through a swarm of newsmen who raced to the entrance of City Hall when word of their marriage plans spread through San Francisco like wildfire. As Joe and Marilyn were pronounced man and wife by Municipal Court Judge Charles Peery, he took her into his arms and kissed her. Newsreel men and photographers asked him to do it again. Joe did a repeat, then another and another. Nothing like his record of batting safely in 56 games, but close."

His best man was Reno Barsochinni. Lefty O'Doul and Jean O'Doul served as witnesses. Nobody from Hollywood was there.

When had they decided to get married?

"It was pretty sudden," DiMaggio said.

Where would they honeymoon?

"We're not saying."

Are you going to have children?

"Oh, yes," Marilyn said. "I want to have *six* children."

"One definitely," DiMaggio said.

He took her arm and they hurried down a corridor, with reporters and photographers in pursuit. But the corridor was a dead end and the couple stood trapped, with the press swarming at them, a wave of combat troops.

"We've got to get out of here," DiMaggio said. "I've had enough of this." They struggled toward a door and DiMaggio decided to pass up his second wedding reception entirely.

He drove 175 miles south to Paso Robles, where they found a room at the Clifton motel. The clerk reported that DiMaggio did ask if the room came with a television set. And, he said, they checked in at 8:00 P.M. and didn't leave the room until 1:00 the following afternoon. Later the motel posted a small placard: JOE AND MARILYN SLEPT HERE.

According to reporters, excitement about the marriage

had Marilyn acting "like an excited school girl." She was, however, growing sensitive about her age and told the newspapermen that she was twenty-six. Actually she was twenty-eight. "Nothing unusual," pronounced an old Hollywood hand. "It's what we call the Zsa Zsa Gabor margin for error."

The couple retreated to a small house near Palm Springs and stayed there for two weeks. Marilyn said they took long walks in the high country. Then they flew to Japan with the O'Douls. DiMaggio was to hold baseball clinics there. This sort of thing was an old drill for him. Talk about the swing, the throw, positioning yourself in the field. He was the star holding court; in public Marilyn seemed comfortable in what was supposed to be a secondary role. She offered him devouring gazes and an occasional touch of her hand. She told reporters that marriage was "my main career."

But with her bleached hair, her wiggling walk, she became something more than a supporting player. At least as many Japanese shouted her name as his. Tokyo reporters wrote about "the honorable buttocks-swinging madam." A crowd swarmed outside the Imperial hotel, where they were staying, and would not disperse until Marilyn appeared on the balcony. She said she found that odd and frightening. "Like I was a dictator or something."

Someone who made the trip with them says, "This was probably the first time Joe saw graphically how big a star she was. The truth is she was a bigger star than he. Did it bother him? He didn't say but he acted a little surly. He gave her orders. 'No shopping today. The crowds will kill us.' She didn't argue but you could tell she didn't like being told what and what not to do."

At a Tokyo cocktail party, an army officer invited Marilyn to entertain U.S. soldiers in Korea. She was thrilled. DiMaggio pointed out that he couldn't go, that he had commitments in Japan. Good. The men could stay on the ball fields. She and Jean O'Doul would go to Korea.

Marilyn flew to Seoul and then moved by helicopter to

army and marine bases. The servicemen suffering through the winds of Korean winter and the boredom of occupation duty gathered in amphitheaters and whooped her name. She wore a clinging dress, cut low at the bust and decorated with plum-colored sequins. Marilyn was never much for understatement. She wiggled and sang "Diamonds Are a Girl's Best Friend." Amplifiers carried her breathy, sexy voice toward thousands of lonely and randy soldiers. They cheered and stomped. Sometimes they broke ranks to get closer to her. "On two occasions," reported Hanson Baldwin, who covered the military for *The New York Times,* "troops rioted wildly and behaved like bobby-soxers in Times Square, not like soldiers proud of their uniforms."

A colonel ordered her to cut that wonderful old Gershwin song "Do It Again" from her routine. The colonel, who might have come from one of the California revivalist churches of Marilyn's youth, said the lyrics were "too suggestive." Marilyn protested, but dropped the song.

The cheering soldiers thrilled her. The trip, she said, "was the best thing that's ever happened to me."

When she was reunited with DiMaggio she described the crowds and then burst out, "Joe. You never heard such cheering."

"Yes I have," DiMaggio said.

The exchange—what a gulf it places between them—is reported by various sources in this brief and pointed way. Actually, DiMaggio went on a little longer. He told her not to take the cheers seriously because he knew from his own life that they could quickly turn to boos.

Marilyn nodded. A touch of her blond glow faded. But she wasn't really paying attention to her husband's answer.

They settled briefly in his San Francisco house. Marilyn insisted she was having a wonderful time learning Italian cooking. In fact, there wasn't much for her to do. Joe's sister Marie ran the household. She'd been running it for years. Di-

Maggio lapsed into his familiar routine, playing golf and spending evening hours with male friends.

He had what he always seemed to have wanted. The country's sexiest blonde as a housewife. She lounged about and read. She didn't play golf and she could hardly spend her nights as the only female in a jock crowd, remembering long home runs hit fifteen years before in ballparks she had never seen.

She settled her dispute with the studio. She would not have to play in *The Girl in the Pink Tights* and she agreed to appear in *There's No Business Like Show Business*. She couldn't shoot a picture in Hollywood while living in San Francisco. She took DiMaggio in tow and they rented an eight-room house on North Palm Drive in Beverly Hills for $750 a month. Her stint as a housewife was done. DiMaggio found himself back in the Hollywood world among all those "phonies" that he despised.

As far as the public could tell, their marriage was developing nicely. She told a reporter, "I like to iron Joe's shirts. I like to look at Joe in a shirt I ironed. But often I don't have time to do the ironing." She had placed a chair in front of the television set in the living room "because Joe loves to watch sports." She said she liked nothing better than serving a steak to her husband as he watched basketball players dribbling into eternity.

"Do you ever argue?" the reporter asked.

"Oh, Joe and I have our quarrels. You can't outlaw human nature. Marriage is something you learn more about while you live with it."

Actually they were grinding down each other. She was endlessly, interminably sloppy. He wanted to live in a neat house. She studied her lines, traipsed off to work, not always on time, and wondered why he didn't visit her on the set. Watching a movie being made, with the delays, the retakes, and the retakes of the retakes, was just a bore. Besides, he didn't want to watch her wiggling half naked in the arms of another man. When they weren't grinding, they were boring one another. When they weren't boring each other they were quarreling. It was a nasty time.

She said she wanted a social life. He said they had to be careful about inviting phonies to their house. She talked to at least two people about her disappointment. He withdrew into his ever longer silence. Meanwhile, sightseeing buses stopped outside, showing tourists the home of Mr. and Mrs. America.

There's No Business Like Show Business, her first film as Mrs. Joe DiMaggio, was advertised as a musical tribute to Irving Berlin. His songs are generally regarded as the best element in an unfortunate movie.

As Vicky, the hat-check girl with theatrical ambitions, she played opposite Donald O'Connor, then a paradigm of boyishness. Marilyn's beauty was becoming more womanly. The pairing didn't work. Her costumes were so wildly overdone that they reminded one admirer of the rainboat skirts and fruit-salad hats that once adorned the hyperkinetic form of Carmen Miranda. Bosley Crowther in *The New York Times* pronounced Marilyn's "wriggling and squirming . . . embarrassing to behold."

Each day she brought to the set the troubles of a collapsing marriage. On several occasions she could not finish her work. DiMaggio liked her wriggling and squirming even less than Bosley Crowther would and she felt fiercely conflicted. She insisted, she would always insist, that she wasn't lewd and that those who thought she was had lewd minds themselves. But she was playing a sexpot, she was selling sex. DiMaggio stayed away from the set.

He didn't care about show business, she complained to friends. The Toots Shor's advice he offered wasn't worth much. She was trying to reshape her career and they just couldn't talk about that. It was beyond him. He retreated into silence, she would later testify, and not speak to her for days at a time.

She bought him books. He wouldn't read them. She tried

to introduce him to poetry. He said he didn't get it. They had few mutual friends for play and evenings of good conversation. Sometimes Natasha Lytess visited to help with her lines, but most nights it was just Joe and Marilyn, alone, apart, and separate (and angry) in the big empty house on North Palm Drive.

When he did talk, she later claimed, his questions were intrusive. He was starting to suspect men she knew of being her lovers. The best evidence is that she had two or possibly three affairs, all brief, all casual, late in her marriage to Joe. She complained of loneliness and, with stardom, she had become defiant. A one-night stand, often as not, seems like an antidote to loneliness. DiMaggio's possessiveness also pushed her toward new beds. She was trying to get control of her own life. No one else, least of all the brooding and commanding man called Joe the Slugger, was going to control her.

Hot arguments took over their lives. She was sometimes away from home with no good explanation. When she returned, he questioned her. She pouted. He grew angrier. She walked away, fearful of his strength. Sometimes he bolted from the house.

According to Marilyn, Joe was "insanely jealous." According to DiMaggio's friends, he had good reason. It is a familiar story in divorce courts.

Charles K. Feldman, a prominent agent and reputedly one of her lovers, sent her the delicious script for *The Seven Year Itch*. In it, she would play a nameless enchantress called "The Girl Upstairs." Her performance as a not-very-bright blonde is a wonder of shimmering seductiveness. It was precisely the kind of role that troubled her husband the most.

The plot casts Tom Ewell as a summer bachelor. Marilyn, a television model, sublets the apartment upstairs. Marilyn accidentally knocks a tomato plant onto Ewell's terrace and he invites her down for a drink. He fantasizes passionate love but when he actually makes a serious move they both fall off a piano bench. "Maybe we better send Rachmaninoff to the showers," he says.

She tells him how she caught her big toe in a faucet while taking a bath. She couldn't work it loose and had to call a plumber, who worked over her while she was naked in the tub. This sends Tom Ewell's fantasies running through arch, funny, sexy twists. He finally asks her to dinner and a movie, *The Creature from the Black Lagoon.* Marilyn empathizes with the creature, which is the sort of thing she might have done in real life. She is wholly bewitching, an original.

On the walk home, in that most famous of Marilyn's scenes, she pauses over a subway grating. Two trains pass. Marilyn's white skirt blows up toward her navel.

Since this was a 1950s film, Ewell ultimately hurries off to his wife in the country without ever having gotten Marilyn into bed, or even topless, if you can believe that in the 1980s. "This is the picture," wrote Phillip Strassberg in the *Daily Mirror,* "that every red-blooded American male has been awaiting." It was also a portrait of her as she could appear when the mood was right: innocence, seductiveness, blond fluff, and at the center, hidden among smiles and wonderment, awaiting only a proper touch, naked, undulating lust.

DiMaggio did not want her to play so sexual a part. She dismissed his objections. He may have known center field, but what the hell did he know about the movies? Nothing, that's what he knew. He didn't care about the movies; she wasn't even sure he cared about her. It was a wonderful role and she was going to play it. It was her career. It was her life, not his.

She flew to New York for location shooting on September 9. The marriage was one week short of being nine months old. She flew without him.

Later, he joined her at the St. Regis hotel in New York. Then he, who never visited a set, decided to show up for the scene in which her skirt blew high over her thin white panties.

Some say he made her change into more concealing underwear. Some say he simply stood in silent fury beside the Broadway columnist Walter Winchell. Everybody agrees that he left before the shooting was done, left the street scene on a rack of pain and horror.

Late that night they quarreled at the hotel. Stories persist of screaming, weeping, scuffling. A death watch settled upon the marriage. They were through.

He flew back to California, and when her New York work was finished, they managed to live together for a few crackling weeks. He wanted her to calm down. He was sorry he had been so rough. He loved her. She stammered in fright. He might get rough again. It was j-j-just too late.

He did care about movies, he told her. He would prove it. He'd come to see her on the set.

She couldn't stand that, the staring, the possessiveness, while she was working. She talked to Darryl Zanuck and, without publicity, Zanuck barred DiMaggio from the Twentieth Century lot. If the greatest center fielder of a generation tried to visit his wife at work, security men would collar him and, if necessary, call the police.

These were two people in pain, and their agony, like their passionate love, was major news. On October 4, Marilyn told somebody in the Fox production department that she was ill and could not appear at the studio. The production people informed Billy Wilder, who was directing *The Seven Year Itch*. Wilder made plans to shoot around her and passed the information to Harry Brand, the chief of publicity. Brand telephoned Marilyn at home. She began to cry. "Joe and I had a fight. We're splitting up." She told Brand she had hired Jerry Giesler, a Hollywood lawyer who became famous when he defended Errol Flynn in a paternity suit. Brand said there would have to be an announcement. He would handle it.

DiMaggio meanwhile telephoned his great friend Reno Barsochinni, the best man of only nine months before. Reno would travel from San Francisco and help organize his things. He would move out on October 6.

Brand typed a terse statement. Joe and Marilyn were breaking up "because of incompatibility resulting from the conflicting demands of their careers." He summoned five publicity assistants, Roy Craft, Frank Neill, Chuck Panama, Mollie Merrick, and Ray Metzler. Craft said, "We then went to our offices and got on five separate telephones and called the entire Hollywood press corps at the same time.

"All hell broke loose. The switchboard was swamped. About every magazine in America called from Los Angeles to New York. They all wanted exclusive interviews or by-lined stories. They all claimed they'd given Marilyn her first break.

"A New York magazine called *Tempo* said that if Marilyn wasn't available, they'd take an interview with her stand-in. The UCLA *Daily Bruin* wanted a by-lined exclusive. The Reno Chamber of Commerce asked if Marilyn could get her divorce there. The phones rang all day. I'd try to go to the bathroom and then the phone would ring again from London or New York. It was incredible."

Reporters pressed Giesler and Brand. Neither would go beyond the typed statement. The reporters called the house and got a secretary. Neither Joe nor Marilyn was accepting calls. In all, a hundred photographers and reporters swarmed about the lawn in front of 508 North Palm Drive, waiting for one of the principals to emerge.

Inside the house, DiMaggio gathered his belongings and moved downstairs. Marilyn stayed upstairs. He would be ready to leave the next day.

Jim Bacon, then with the Associated Press, once had an affair with Marilyn. He dropped notes through the mail slot, asking her to let him in. "Unfortunately," he says, "DiMaggio was on the other end of the mail slot. The notes didn't help."

A reporter named Sid Hughes jostled Sheila Graham, the gossip columnist, who had once been Scott Fitzgerald's lover. She yelped and kicked Hughes in the bottom. Unable to talk to the principals, the press began interviewing themselves.

"Before Marilyn went on that New York trip," Hedda Hopper said, "she drove to my house. Joe waited in a car, then knocked on the door and said it was time to go. I asked him if he didn't think Marilyn looked wonderful and he just said that she looked nice. I told him he had to do better than that and he said he'd try. His attitude told the story. She's on top of the heap. He's a star without a job."

Louella Parsons said that she thought Hal Schaefer might have caused the divorce. Schaefer, Marilyn's most recent voice coach, had been ill, and Marilyn visited him in a hospital several times. "But I'm not gonna write any more about that piano player [Schaefer]. I'm convinced Marilyn was just being kind, and that was it."

Marilyn finally walked out of the house at 11 A.M. She wore a tight black dress and she leaned on the arm of her lawyer. "I have nothing to say," she announced, and began to cry.

DiMaggio had left a few minutes earlier. "Where are you going?" a reporter shouted.

"I'm going home," he said. "San Francisco has always been my home."

The press loitered. Everybody seemed annoyed that Joe and Marilyn hadn't said more. Someone rushed up shouting, "Hey, the news just broke that Liberace's engaged to be married."

One of the Fox press agents shook his head. "This can knock the hell out of us," he said. "It will wipe us off the front pages."

No it wouldn't. Nothing short of war . . .

DiMaggio's exit line—"San Francisco has always been my home"—would have played well in one of those tough love stories Hollywood often did so well. You hear the line. A Cadillac pulls out of the driveway and heads north, moving farther and farther away until it looks like a Chevrolet. Up cacaphonous music. Fade out.

For Joe and Marilyn life would never be neat. Barney Ruditsky was a bespectacled, amiable man who reminded people of a family grocer. Actually Ruditsky had been a detective with New York's Broadway squad until he retired in 1941 on a pension of $166.66 a month. After World War II, he moved to Hollywood and opened a detective agency and then a restaurant called Sherry's on Sunset Strip. He said he wanted to get out of the detective business.

In July 1949, he was standing in front of Sherry's with Mickey Cohen, a famous mobster, and Neddie Herbert, Cohen's bodyguard, when someone fired several blasts from a shotgun. Cohen was injured slightly. Neddie Herbert was killed. Ruditsky quit the restaurant business and opened another detective agency.

DiMaggio hired Ruditsky to follow Marilyn during the last days of their marriage. Ruditsky established that she was spending evenings in the apartment of a friend named Sheilah Stewart. "Something was going on," Ruditsky said. "These weren't just girlish bunking parties. But after a while, one of Joe's guys told me to close the file. They had decided to get a no-nonsense divorce."

On October 27, Marilyn appeared at a courthouse in Santa Monica and, carefully coached by Jerry Giesler, briefly and impersonally described DiMaggio's silences, his coldness, his indifference. There was no hint of violence, nor any suggestion of infidelity. DiMaggio did not contest her statement. She was granted a divorce on the grounds of mental cruelty.

On November 5, Phil Irwin, a detective who worked for Barney Ruditsky, found DiMaggio in a restaurant on Sunset Strip. DiMaggio had been drinking, according to Irwin. He demanded that Irwin accompany him to Sheilah Stewart's apartment.

When they reached the building, DiMaggio said he was going to break down the door.

Irwin pleaded with him to do nothing. He telephoned Ruditsky, describing the situation, and Ruditsky in turn called Frank Sinatra. "Joe's gonna get himself in trouble," Ruditsky said. "Maybe you can come to where we are and help me calm him down."

Sinatra said he would, and brought along a friend. When the men gathered, they could not mollify DiMaggio.

"Joe was so mad he didn't know what he was doing," Ruditsky said. "If he busted in on Marilyn and caught her with a guy, God knows what would have happened. So I figured out a little ruse. The Stewart woman lived on the second floor."

Ruditsky turned to DiMaggio and said, "Joe, *I'll* go in."

Ruditsky then broke into a downstairs apartment occupied by a single woman named Florence Ross Kotz, who screamed in terror. Florence Kotz continued to scream until, as Ruditsky put it, "we all had to head for the hills."

Florence Kotz later accepted $7,500 in an out-of-court settlement. "Private detective work," Ruditsky said, "is a dirty, filthy, rotten business."

Soon afterward Marilyn moved to the safety of New York. She enrolled in the Actors Studio, and married Arthur Miller. But after 1954, she was able to complete only four movies. She wanted always to become more creative, to transform herself into her radiant ideal, a great actress. Actually, she was fighting to retain her sanity or, at the very least, her will to live.

In 1962, she took a role in *Something's Got to Give,* a piece of Hollywood fluff, the fluff she had come to despise, which later, as *Move Over, Darling,* became a Doris Day vehicle.

The script called for a swimming scene and Marilyn appeared in a flesh-colored bikini. George Cukor, the director, said it just didn't look right. A bit of bra strap showed. The bottom disturbed "the beautiful natural line of your buttocks."

He suggested that she play the scene naked, and promised, "Only the cameraman will look."

"Oh, well," Marilyn said, "it's for art." She stripped and, of course, *everybody* looked.

She was drinking too much vodka and taking too many pills. She began missing days at work. Fox had lost huge sums when Elizabeth Taylor missed her schedule in *Cleopatra.* "We dropped a fortune on the brunette," someone said. "We can't afford to drop another on the blonde."

In June, shortly after Marilyn's thirty-sixth birthday, Fox

fired her and threw in a $500,000 law suit. First they stripped her naked. Then they fired her and, having done those things, they added a suit. Hollywood was showing her a face ugly as a skull.

She died after swallowing between forty and fifty Nembutal pills on August 4, 1962. She died at night naked and alone in a locked bedroom with the lights blazing.

Her half sister, Bernice Miracle, of Gainesville, Florida, arrived. So did Joseph Paul DiMaggio. At Mrs. Miracle's request, DiMaggio organized a funeral at the Westwood Village Mortuary.

He invited fewer than thirty others, including her psychiatrist, Ralph Greenson, and her lawyer, Milton "Mickey" Rudin, but he pointedly kept out famous Hollywood people: Frank Sinatra, who had dated Marilyn briefly in her last years, Peter Lawford, and a panoply of famous movie types.

He wept and prayed.

Someone asked how he could have excluded the pantheon of names that were Hollywood.

"Because," said Joe the Slugger, no slouch at a final comment, "they killed her."

Then, with his beloved entombed in a crypt, he set off on the rest of his life alone.

Epilogue

*I*n response to rumors that refused to die, during 1985 the Los Angeles Police Department released a lightly edited report of its investigations into Marilyn's death. According to one story, she killed herself because Attorney General Robert Kennedy was breaking off their affair. According to another, even more perplexing, the Mafia, seeking to strike back at Kennedy, had some hand in her death.

It may be more stimulating to make charges than to deny them, but a rational reading of the evidence suggests only that Marilyn wanted to die more than she wanted to live. The police released records of her last psychiatric treatment. Dr. Ralph Greenson billed her estate for no fewer than twenty-eight visits between July 1, 1962, and the date of her death, August 4. His patient was slipping away.

The police also released her telephone records, deleting a number, or numbers, she called in Washington, D.C. This indicates to some that she was talking frequently to Bobby Kennedy and possibly even to the President. But the suggestion that Kennedy was responsible for her death is simplistic even for Hollywood gossip.

This was a woman who was subject to severe depressions and who came from a family with a history of mental illness. Three marriages were wrecked. She'd just been fired. She was worried about money. To go on, to fight any longer against the savage god, was quite beyond her.

I submitted Dr. Thomas Noguchi's autopsy to Dr. Joseph Wilder, a professor at Mount Sinai Medical School in New York, for a professional review. Dr. Wilder teaches surgery; before that he was a pathologist. He has no connections with Noguchi, or with Marilyn.

"The first thing about the autopsy," he says, "is that no violence was done to her. With a fair-skinned person, bruises show very clearly to a doctor's eye, as clearly as you'd leave tracks in the snow if you had tramped out with ashes on your boots."

Wilder said that the report was complete, even to the weights and measurements of such organs as the lungs and a description of her pubic hair. Her blood, however, was not tested. He regards this as the one oversight in an otherwise complete autopsy. Noguchi's conclusion, he says, meets the classical standards of "probable suicide by barbiturate poisoning."

Three psychiatrists, engaged by a Los Angeles suicide-prevention clinic, came to similar convictions.

She died by her own fair hand.

DiMaggio has become a successful commercial spokesman for a New York bank and a drip-coffee machine, earning, even into his eighth decade, more than he earned playing baseball. He continues to conduct himself with somber dignity, although a group of debunkers has come along. "I saw him," one says, "at a baseball-card show in New Jersey and he was signing autographs for six dollars each. Why does he have to do that? He doesn't need the money."

I prefer to linger with a different memory. An editor of *McCall's* magazine once called and asked if I could get Di-Maggio to talk about Marilyn. The story would be brief and it could be adulatory. The title would be "This Was a Woman!"

The editor guessed it would take fifteen minutes of tape recording. *McCall's* would pay DiMaggio $50,000.

I got word to DiMaggio. The answer was a quick, courteous no. He enjoys making money, but some things are not for sale.

Like the memory of love.